MW01250940

I am deeply touched and extremely grateful to the people who took the time to read, support and endorse *The Digitally Divided Self*. Being my first English book, and basically self-published, I didn't expect to receive many reviews, much less from such leading thinkers and writers – nor such positive responses.

It was also a surprise to find common interests around eastern spirituality with so many people into technology and media. This makes me hopeful for an evolution of the information society - from chasing external stimulation to inner explorations and silence.

Praise for
Digitally Divided Self

"Quartiroli's *The Digitally Divided Self* is a must read for anyone seeking to understand the ever-increasing hegemony of the digital world in the individual psyche. Drawing on diverse fields and traditions, the author analyzes numerous mechanisms by which IT separates us from ourselves. Readers stand to benefit from such an understanding that is a prerequisite for mounting a defense of one's individuality."

— **Len Bracken**, author of several novels and the biography *Guy Debord—Revolutionary*

"With great insight, Ivo Quartiroli captures the subtle as well as the gross impact that media use has on our individual and collective psyches. The challenge before all of us is how to adapt to the new technology in a healthy way that allows us to retain our essential humanity. He offers us a solution born of his experience and confirmed by neuroscience. This is a must read."

— **Hilarie Cash**, PhD, co-founder of reSTART: Internet Addiction Recovery Program

"It is difficult to offer a spiritually based critique of today's network culture without sounding like a nostalgic Luddite crank. Immersed in the tech, but also in various meditative traditions, Ivo Quartiroli is the perfect person to offer integral wisdom-tech with clarity and bite."

—**Erik Davis**, author of *Techgnosis* and *Nomad Codes: Adventures in Modern Esoterica.*

"Aware of the profound and rapid psychological and social metamorphosis we are going through as we 'go digital' without paying attention, Ivo Quartiroli is telling us very precisely what we are gaining and what we are losing of the qualities and privileges that, glued as we are to one screen or another, we take for granted in our emotional, cognitive and spiritual life. This book is a wake-up call. Steve Jobs and Bill Gates should read it."

—**Derrick de Kerckhove**, Professor, Facoltà di sociologia, Università Federico II, Naples, former Director of the McLuhan Program in Culture and Technology.

"*The Digitally Divided Self* alerts us about the insidious dangers of our growing dependence on Information Technology. Ivo Quartiroli warns us that Internet can easily develop into an addiction that undercuts our connections with nature, with other people, and with our deeper inner reality. The spiritual nourishment coming from genuine relationships is then replaced by the empty calories of fake relationships, with the resulting deterioration of our personal and social lives. Using an incisive style, Ivo Quartiroli can be provocative, iconoclastic, at times exaggerated, but never boring. Behind each observation there are pearls of wisdom that are guaranteed to make you think."

—**Federico Faggin**, designer of the microprocessor.

"Global culture is not only the latest step in the human evolutionary journey. It is also, as Ivo Quartiroli shows in *The Digitally Divided Self*, a critical opportunity to apply non-Western techniques of awareness to ensure healthy survival in the 21st century."

—**Michael Heim**, author of *The Metaphysics of Virtual Reality, Virtual Realism*, and *Electric Language.*

"Question the merits of technology in the past and you'd be called a Luddite. But now technologists are leading the way toward a new, more balanced view of our gadget-driven lives. Drawing from his fascinating expertise in computer science and spirituality, Ivo Quartiroli presents a compelling critique of the corrosive impact of the

Net on our humanity. It's a warning we must heed."
— **Maggie Jackson,** author of *Distracted: The Erosion of Attention and the Coming Dark Age.*

"A profoundly premonitory vision of the future of the 21st century, *The Digitally Divided Self* unlocks the great codes of technological society, namely that the very same digital forces that effectively control the shape and direction of the human destiny are also the founding powers of a new revolution of the human spirit."
— **Arthur Kroker,** author of *The Will to Technology* and Canada Research Chair in Technology, Culture and Theory.

"People today, especially young people, live more on the Internet than in the real world. This has subtle and not-so-subtle effects on their thinking and personality. It is high time to review these effects, to see whether they are a smooth highway to a bright interconnected future, or possibly a deviation that could endanger health and wellbeing for the individual as well as for society. Ivo Quartiroli undertakes to produce this review and does so with deep understanding and dedicated humanism. His book should be read by everyone, whether he or she is addicted to the Internet or has second thoughts about it."
— **Ervin Laszlo,** President, the Club of Budapest, and Chancellor, the Giordano Bruno Globalshift University.

"The Mind-Body Split is a pervasive condition/affliction in the developed world, wholly un-recognized; yet fundamental to the great worldwide problems of health, environment, and economic inequity. Ivo Quartiroli's *Digitally Divided Self* masterfully examines the effects of the insulated digital experience on the mind and the body self: exacerbating illusions and the Mind-Body Split; and contrasts it to the processes of self-discovery, growth, and healing: true inter-connectedness with nature, each other, and our selves. If the digital age is to solve our real problems, rather than create them, it will be with the knowledge contained in *The Digitally Divided Self.* Well done!"
— **Frederic Lowen,** son of Alexander Lowen, Executive Director, The Alexander Lowen Foundation

"Ivo Quartiroli here addresses one of the most pressing questions forced upon us by our latest technologies. In disturbing the deepest relations between the user's faculties and the surrounding world, our electric media, all of them without exception, create profound disorientation and subsequent discord, personal and cultural. Few subjects today demand greater scrutiny."
— **Dr. Eric McLuhan,** Author and Lecturer

"The internet is an extension of our central nervous system. When you operate a computer, you are extending yourself, through its interface, potentially all over the world, instantaneously. Extending yourself in such a disembodied, discarnate fashion only further entrenches your separateness, your ego self. In contrast, the introspective freeing from the physical through meditation also has the effect of creating a discarnate, disembodied state. That state is one that is progressively less identified with the ego self. This is the dichotomy that Ivo Quartiroli explores in *The Digitally Divided Self*. This book is well worth investigating."

— **Michael McLuhan**

"We should all be asking the questions Ivo Quartiroli asks in this bold and provocative book. Whatever you think right now about technology, *The Digitally Divided Self* will challenge you to think again."

— **William Powers**, author of the *New York Times* bestseller *Hamlet's BlackBerry*

"It isn't easy to find an informed and critical look at the impact of digital media practices on human lives and minds. Ivo Quartiroli offers an informed critique based in both an understanding of technology and of human consciousness."

— **Howard Rheingold**, author of *The Virtual Community* and *Smart Mobs*.

"Ivo Quartiroli is mining the rich liminal territory between humans and their networks. With the integrity of a scientist and the passion of artist, he forces us to reconsider where we end and technology begins. Or when."

— **Douglas Rushkoff**, Media Theorist and author of *Cyberia*, *Media Virus*, *Life, Inc.* and *Program or Be Programmed*.

"You might find what he writes to be challenging, irritating, even blasphemous and sacrilegious. If so, he has proven his point. The Internet, Ivo suggests, might just be the new opium of the masses. Agree with him or not, no other book to date brings together the multitude of issues related to how the seductions of technology impinge upon and affect the development of the self and soul."

— **Michael Wesch**, Associate Professor of Digital Ethnography, Kansas State University

"*The Digitally Divided Self* is a refreshing look at technology that goes beyond the standard, well-worn critiques. Ivo Quartiroli charts new territory with a series of profound reflections on the intersections of computer science, psychology and spirituality."

— **Micah White**, Senior Editor at *Adbusters* magazine

It is nearly half a century since Marshall McLuhan pointed out that the medium is the message. In the interim, digital technologies have found an irresistible hook on our minds. With the soul's quest for the infinite usurped by the ego's desire for unlimited power, the Internet and social media have stepped in to fill our deepest needs for communication, knowledge and creativity – even intimacy and sexuality. Without being grounded in those human qualities which are established through experience and inner exploration, we are vulnerable to being seduced into outsourcing our minds and our fragile identities.

Intersecting media studies, psychology and spirituality, *The Digitally Divided Self* exposes the nature of the malleable mind and explores the religious and philosophical influences which leave it obsessed with the incessant flow of information.

Ivo Quartiroli has been a software programmer, publisher of Italian technology and spirituality books, and computer science book author. Complementing his professional accomplishments in information processing, his interest in consciousness processing has led him to spiritual explorations. He shares his perspective on the intersection of media studies, psychology and spirituality on his blog indranet.org and writes for Italian magazines about technology and society. He sits on the Italian Club of Budapest's science committee. He can be reached at ivotoshan@yahoo.it

The Digitally Divided Self

Relinquishing our Awareness to the Internet

Ivo Quartiroli

silens

Milano – www.silens.org

COPYRIGHT © 2011 BY IVO QUARTIROLI

ALL RIGHTS RESERVED

No part of this book, whether in physical, electronic or other form, may be
copied, reproduced, distributed, transmitted, publicly performed or
displayed without the prior written consent of the copyright holder.
Nor may derivative works such as translations be produced.

Printed in the United States of America by Createspace

Cover design and page layout by *Moreno Confalone*

Editor: *David Carr* www.MovingWords.us

Copy editor: *Dhiren Bahl* www.WordsWay-Copyediting.com

ISBN-13: 978-88-97233-00-8
ISBN 10: 88-97233-00-7

Publisher's Cataloging-in-Publication data
Quartiroli, Ivo.
    The digitally divided self : relinquishing our awareness to the Internet /
Ivo Quartiroli.
        p. cm.
        ISBN 978-88-97233-00-8
        Includes index and bibliographical references.
1. Computer networks –Social aspects. 2. Internet –Social aspects.
3. Interpersonal relations. 4. Social problems.
5. Information technology –Psychological aspects.
6. Technology and civilization. 7. Spirituality. I. Title.

HM221 .Q37 2011
303.48/33 dc22

silens
Milano – www.silens.org

To Angelo,
Carmen,
Christian,
Jiab,
Leo

CONTENTS

Chapter 12
The Digitally Divided Self 165

Chapter 13
The Process of Knowledge 189

Chapter 14
Upgrading to Heaven 205

LIST OF PERMISSIONS

The author gratefully acknowledges permission to reproduce copyright material from the following journals, books, authors and web sites:

Advaita Press for permission to reprint from Ramesh Balsekar, *A Duet of One* (Advaita Press, 1989), p.15, from Ramesh Balsekar, *Consciousness Speaks* (Advaita Press, 1992), p.16, 28 and from Ram Tzu, *No Way for the Spiritually 'Advanced'* (Advaita Press, 1990), p. 57.

Alan Wallace for permission to reprint from Alan Wallace, *The Taboo of Subjectivity*, (Oxford University Press, 2000), p.41 and *The Attention Revolution*, (Wisdom Publications, 2006), p. 37.

Alliance for Childhood for permission to reprint Alliance for Childhood, *Fool's Gold: A Critical Look at Computers in Childhood*, (Alliance for Childhood, 2000), p.4, 22, 32, 62, 97. ww.allianceforchildhood.org

Anthony Aguirre for permission to reprint his answer for "The Edge Annual Question 2010".

Douglas Rushkoff for permission to reprint from *Digital Nation*, Interview with Clifford Nass, from *Digital Nation*, 1 Dec 2009: and from an interview with Sherry Turkle on *Digital Nation*, 2 Feb 2010, www.pbs.org

Evgeny Morozov for permission to reprint from "Texting Toward Utopia: Does the Internet Spread Democracy?" *Boston Review*, March/April 2009, bostonreview.net and from "Wrong Kind of Buzz Around Google Buzz," *Foreign Policy*, 18 Aug 2010, neteffect.foreign-policy.com

Frederic Lowen for permission to reprint from Alexander Lowen, *Bioenergetics*, (Coward, McCann & Geoghegan, 1975), p. 328.

Gary Small for permission to reprint from Gary Small and Gigi Vorgan, *iBrain: Surviving the Technological Alteration of the Modern Mind*, (William Morrow, 2008), pp. 31-32.

Standpoint Magazine and the author for permission to reprint from Gerald Block, "Out of this World," *Standpoint*, August 2008, standpointmag.com

HarperCollins Publishers for permission to reprint from James Hillman and, Michael Ventura, *We've Had a Hundred Years of Psychotherapy: And the World's Getting Worse*, (Harper Collins, 1993), p. 95.

Iain Boal for permission to reprint a part of an interview with George Lakoff, from James Brook and Iain A. Boal, *Resisting the Virtual Life: The Culture and Politics of Information*, (City Lights, 1995), p.115.

Institute of HeartMath for permission to reprint from "Science of The Heart: Exploring the Role of the Heart in Human Performance," (Institute of HeartMath, 2001), www.heartmath.org

James Harkin for permission to reprint from *Lost in Cyburbia: How Life on the Net Has Created a Life of Its Own*, (Knopf Canada, 2009), p. 23, 26, 84, 121, 135, 169.

Jerry Mander for permission to reprint from Jerry Mander, *Four Arguments for the Elimination of Television*, (William Morrow, 1978), p. 236 and from *In the Absence of the Sacred*, (Sierra Club, 1991), p.3, 66

Jim Brook for permission to reprint from James Brook and Iain. A. Boal, eds., *Resisting the Virtual Life: The Culture and Politics of Information*, (City Lights, 1995), p. XIII.

Joseph Chilton Pearce for permission to reprint from *The Biology of Transcendence* (Inner Traditions, 2002), p. 192 and from "Gathering Sparks," interview by *Parabola* magazine, selected by David Appelbaum and Joseph Kulin (Parabola Books, 2001), p.73

Kevin Kelly for permission to reprint from "Technophilia," *Technium*, 8 Jun 2009, from "Why Technology Can't Fulfill," *Technium*, 26 Jun 2009, from "Expansion of Free Will, "*Technium*, 13 Aug 2009, www.kk.org/thetechnium

Kris de Decker for permission to reprint from "Faster Internet is Impossible", *Low-Tech Magazine*, Feb 2008

Maggie Jackson for permission to reprint from *Distracted: The Erosion of Attention and the Coming Dark Age*, (Prometheus Books, 2008), p. 165, 226.

Mark Slouka for permission to reprint from Mark Slouka, *War of the Worlds*, (Basic Books, 1995), p. 9, 26, 98, 148.

Mauro Magatti for permission to translate and reprint from, *Libertà Immaginaria: Le Illusioni del Capitalismo Tecno-Nichilista*, (Feltrinelli, 2009), p.7, 265.

Michael McLuhan and The Estate Of Corinne McLuhan for permission to reprint from Marshall McLuhan, *Understanding Media: The Extensions of Man*, (McGraw Hill, 1964), p. 4, 41, 45, 46, 47, 60, 68, 156, 194, 210, from *Understanding Me*, (MIT Press, 2005), p.8, 79, 237, 265, and from Marshall McLuhan and Bruce Powers, *The Global Village*, (Oxford University Press, 1989), p. 95, 97.

Osho International Foundation for permission to reprint from Osho, *Meditation: The Art of Ecstasy*, (Rebel Publishing House, 1976), p. 190, from *The Search: Talks on the Ten Bulls of Zen*. (Rebel Publishing House, 1977), p.122, from *The Heartbeat of the Absolute*,(Rebel Publishing House, 1980), p.88, from *Theologia Mystica*, (Rebel Publishing House, 1983), from *The Book of Wisdom: Discourses on Atisha's Seven Points of Mind Training*, (Rebel Publishing House, 1993) , from *The Psychology of the Esoteric*, (Rebel Publishing House, 2008).

Quest Books, the imprint of The Theosophical Publishing House for permission to reprint from Ken Wilber *The Atman Project*, (Theosophical Publishing, 1980), p. 120.

Random House for permission to reprint from Neil Postman, *Technopoly: The Surrender of Culture to Technology* (Vintage Books, 1993), p.8, 15, 25, 55, 63, 111

Red Wheel/Weiser and the author for permission to reprint A.H. Almaas, *Essence: The Diamond Approach to inner Realization* (Red Wheel/Weiser, 1986), p.92, www.redwheelweiser.com

Sarah Dopp, wife of late David Noble, for permission to reprint from Noble, David F., *The Religion of Technology: The Divinity of Man and the Spirit of Invention*, (Alfred A. Knopf, 1997), p. 72, 95

Shambhala Publications and the author for permission to reprint from A.H. Almaas, *Diamond Heart: Book One: Elements of the Real in Man* (Shambhala Publications, published by arrangement with Diamond Books, 1987), p. 127, from A.H. Almaas, *The Pearl beyond Price* (Shambhala Publications, published by arrangement with Diamond Books, 1988), p.191, 245, 258, from A.H. Almaas, *Diamond Heart: Book Three: Being and the Meaning of Life* (Shambhala Publications, published by arrangement with Diamond Books, 1990), p. 1, from A.H. Almaas, *The Point of Existence* (Shambhala Publications, published by arrangement with Diamond Books, 1996), p. 85, 517, from A.H. Almaas, *Spacecruiser Inquiry* (Shambhala Publications, 2002), p. 250, 294, 358. www.shambhala.com

Steve Talbott for permission to reprint from Steve Talbott, "Multitasking Ourselves to Death," *Netfuture: Technology and Human Responsibility*, 30 Jul 1998 and from "Twilight of the Double Helix," *Netfuture: Technology and Human Responsibility*, 12 Mar 2009, www.netfuture.org

Susan Greenfield for permission to reprint from her speech at the Chamber of Lords on August 2009 and from Derbyshire, David, "Social Websites Harm Children's Brains: Chilling Warning to Parents from Top Neuroscientist," *MailOnline*, 24 Feb 2009

Susie Bright and Brenda Laurel for permission to reprint a passage of Brenda Laurel from Susie Bright, *Sexual Reality*, (Cleis Press, 1992), p.66.

www.monkeyrocker.com for permission to reprint parts of the web pages.

The Digitally Divided Self

INTRODUCTION

Like many people nowadays, much of my personal and professional life is related to technology: I use the Internet for keeping the connection with my work projects and friends wherever I am in the world. I published the first book in Italy about the Internet. I run a blog and a Web magazine, do my investments online, shop on the Net, do interviews by email and Skype, and have even indulged in cybersex. Right now I'm in Asia developing this book – which is full of references to Web articles, blogs and material found only on the Internet – with online support: an editor and writing coach in California, copy editor in India, book designer in Italy, and a printing and distribution service with multiple locations in USA. My life is immersed in the digital loop.

I have been involved in IT since I was a student. As I learned meditation and explored spiritual paths, I developed an inner observer and discovered states beyond the mind. Thus, I found myself going back and forth between processing consciousness and information. Slowly my focus has shifted from what we can do with technology to what technology does to us. As a first-hand explorer, I've observed the subtle changes of our massive use of the Net.

Just as a spiritual researcher can go beyond the mind only after having observed and mastered it, it is necessary to enter the digital world to step beyond it. We can't become aware of its effects without being engaged in it. Since digital technology is unavoidable now, we need to master it without becoming lost in it, using its tools with our full awareness.

In this time, the intensification of mental inputs is a phenomenon that must be kept in balance. Our contemporary culture does not acknowledge anything beyond the mind, but in other traditions the mental world is just *one* of the aspects of our wholeness. In the West a sort of Cartesian "pure thinking" has been given priority. Although the mind is the best-known organ of thought, it is not the only cognitive modality. Nervous systems have been discovered both in the heart and in the belly, and the global awareness that can be accessed by spiritual practitioners is pervasive and non-localized. Yet these modalities cannot be represented digitally, so they are relegated to the sidelines.

Our technological society militates against uninterrupted conscious attention. Several authors have documented the effects of IT on attention, literacy and intellectual skills. It also intrudes on the silent time needed to be aware of inner transformations. We don't realize we have become servomechanisms of IT – precisely because IT has weakened the inner skills of self-understanding. Shrinking of the rich range of human qualities to privilege only those which can be represented and operated digitally arises from the nature of the ego-mind and our particular Western history which has engendered – then valued – mental representations of reality. My focus here is to understand why the mind can be lured by the magic of the tools, while forgetting the person who is using them.

We believe we are empowered individually and politically as we post articles on our blogs and participate in social networks. In actuality, we feed the machine with our "user-generated content" which becomes candy for advertisers who then design ads based on what we say on Twitter, Facebook, and even our emails.

Jumping from information to self-understanding is necessary if we are to regain real freedom, a freedom from conditioning of our mind and the manipulation by information – whether self-created or from external sources. We mistake the transmission of gigabytes of data for freedom.

In our advanced technological society there is a reticence to acknowledge the inner, spiritual or metaphysical dimensions of life. What cannot be calculated – which is, thereby, "not objective" – is considered unworthy of investigation. Even more strongly denied is the relationship between technology and the impact on our psyche. Technophiles declare that it's only a tool, as if our psyche could remain untouched by continuous interaction with digital media, and as if we could control its impact on us. We can indeed be in control of digital media – but only after we become fluent in those cognitive modalities which can't be reached by such media.

To be unaffected by digital media, we need a Buddha-like awareness with sustained attention, mindfulness and introspection. Yet these very qualities which are needed to break out of the automated mind are especially difficult to access when we are drowning in information – information that is predominantly ephemeral and transient, and which lacks a broader narrative. Awareness is what gives meaning and depth to information, but for awareness to expand we need to empty our mind. A story will illustrate this. A university professor approached a master to learn about Zen. Tea was served, but when the cup was full, the master did not stop pouring. The cup, like the professor's mind with its concepts and positions, was full. It must first be emptied to understand Zen. So, too, for the digital world.

The world over, people using the Internet click on the same icons, use the same shortcuts in email and chats, connect with people through the same Facebook modalities. This is the globalization of minds. In the process of the digitization of reality, regardless of content, we use predominantly the same limited mental channels and interact with the same tools. We bring the same attitudes, gestures and procedures to working, dating, shopping, communicating with friends, sexual arousal, and scientific research. And most of these activities are impoverished by this phenomenon. Everything is seen as an information system, from the digitization of territory (like Google Earth and augmented realities software) to our biology.

Judeo-Christian culture places nature and the world of matter at man's disposal. Acting on them is a way to garner good deeds and regain the lost perfection of Eden. In this culture that has considered miracles as proof of the existence of God, we have developed technologies that resemble the miraculous and the divine. We are compelled to welcome the advent of new technological tools with the rhetoric of peace, progress, prosperity and mutual understanding.

The telegraph, telephone, radio, TV and other media have been regarded as tools for democracy, world peace, understanding and freedom of expression. The Internet is just the latest in a succession of promising messiahs. Yet we don't have more democracy in the world. In fact, big media and big powers are even stronger, while freedom of expression has ceded to control by corporations and governmental agencies. The Internet, like TV, will be entertaining, dumbing people in their own separate homes where they will be unable to question the system. The Internet might already be the new *soma* for a society experiencing economic and environmental degradation. But with the huge economic interests connected to it, criticizing its effect is akin to cursing God.

Many technological developments appeal to people because they answer psychological and even spiritual needs – like the quests for understanding and connection with others. Already digital technology has taken charge of truth and love – the drives which are distinctly human. Those primordial needs have been addressed, on the mental level, with information. Reflected only at that level, our soul is left empty with craving for the real qualities, and our mind is left restless, craving more information and chasing after satisfaction in vain.

The need to extend our possibilities through technology derives from the need to recover parts of ourself that were lost during the development of our soul – the states of sharp perception, fulfillment, and peace. Information technology (IT) also satisfies our ancient drives for power and control, even giving us several options with a simple click or touch of a finger.

The endless multiplication of information can keep the ego-mind busy – and thus at the center of the show. IT is the most powerful mental "pusher" ever created, feeding the duality of the ego-mind (which is symbolically mirrored by binary technology). More than TV whose attractions are framed between the beginning and ending time of a show, the Internet, video games, and smartphones have no structural pauses or endings. Hooked on a "real-time" stream of information, they take us farther away from both the real and the appropriate time frames.

The computer charms us by reflecting our mind on the Net. Like Narcissus, we mistake the reflected image and enter a closed loop, charmed by our reflection. The Internet, since the beginning, has been considered a technology which could crumble central governments and organizations. Perhaps that forecast was an external projection of what can happen inside us: disturbance of the integration of our psyches.

Meditation helps us recognize that we construct reality and that the mind leads us astray. Meditation is a path back to reality, to truth, to knowing and mastering our minds – instead of mastering the computer as a way to outsource our mind's skills. It is a way to expand our awareness and join the other global "Net" – of awareness that permeates everything.

Though I am Italian, I am publishing this book for the English market because it is a post-digital book which can be better appreciated in countries where digital culture has spread throughout society. In Italy, one politically powerful tycoon owns most of the media, and uses it to demonize the Net. In that setting, being critical of the Net invokes the accusation of aligning with power to castrate freedom of expression, which is the polar opposite of my intention.

I welcome every medium which expands our chances of expressing ourselves, but I am aware that true self-expression can happen only when there's a true self, which can hardly be shaped by screen media.

I am grateful to my spiritual teachers who opened new dimensions for my soul in my journey toward awareness, especially the intensity of Osho and the brilliant clarity of A. H. Almaas. I thank my copy editor Dhiren Bahl (www.WordsWay-Copyediting.com) for his painstaking corrections of my English text and my editor David Carr (www.MovingWords.us) for his clarifications and stylistic improvements. I'm grateful to my friends, too many to list here, for the numerous talks bringing together heart and mind in sharing our passion for truth.

Editor's note

I am not unaware that the reflexive form of the plural pronoun *we* is *ourselves*. But the immediacy of Ivo Quartiroli's writing in our collective lives needs to be absorbed by the reader in a personal way. Rather than employ the second person *you*, which to me always feels slightly accusatory, I have tried to emphasize the importance of each reader's self-reflection on what almost everyone around him or her (to be painfully correct) is likely doing. We are personally participating in a cultural phenomenon to which each of us must be alert. Therefore, I have chosen to follow Quartiroli's choice of *we* with my singular invention *ourself.* We all are active on the stage he describes, but responsibility for awareness lies with the individual.

David Carr

CHAPTER 1

FROM AWARENESS OF TECHNOLOGY TO TECHNOLOGIES OF AWARENESS

Ever since I was a child the mysteries of numbers fascinated me. When I learned about prime numbers at school, I was captivated by those unique, solitary, unpredictable, indivisible odd numbers.

At 12, I desired nothing less than finding their law. A few years later I discovered long series of numbers which were possibly connected to prime numbers. I found the formulas of the first series, but the more complicated ones had many components in individual numbers reaching fifteen digits. Such numbers were beyond the capacity of pocket calculators, so I proceeded manually.

The slow pace of manual calculation allowed me to "feel" numbers, contemplating each one, sensing its relationship to other numbers in the series. At 15, I entered the *Philips Contest for Young Researchers and Inventors*. There were just a couple of months to prepare my presentation – impossible for me to progress through all the calculations. Yet under the puzzled gaze of my schoolmates, this wild boy turned into a would-be mathematician.

The computational effort took me to the university's computer center to ask for help. Grounded in comic books, I thought I could "feed" the computer with the numbers in the series and have the formulas delivered. At that time, computer laboratories in Italy looked like any other academic laboratories, with high-level technicians dressed formally. I tried to explain my problem to a few students, who mostly ignored me. A kind employee told me simply that computers couldn't find the formulas of my series – they could not even add or subtract such big numbers unless they were programmed to. "Oh really? Are computers *that* dumb?" I wondered.

I understood from her that what I needed was a piece of "software" suited to the problem. "Fine," I said, "can you make it for me?" She couldn't, since it had to be designed for the specific problem – and anyway, computer time was very limited, even for students. I returned to manual calculations.

In 1976 computers were as big and unapproachable as the people who worked with them. In time, computers became more user-friendly and much faster – but not less dumb. Concurrently, computer technicians changed from uniforms to casual or messy clothes, though their detached attitude did not noticeably change.

For my research on those series, I was a finalist in the Italian contest – which led to a personal conversation with the president of the Italian CNR (Consiglio Nazionale delle Ricerche, National Research Council). He discouraged me from searching for the law of prime numbers as "a waste of time, something which centuries of mathematicians had already tried to find, but nobody could." I might instead concentrate my energies on developing useful applications in the scientific arena. He introduced me to the reality that research was most welcomed by society when it could be translated into products and money.

What about the fun and enthusiasm I had doing that research? What about the almost mystical states I reached in diving into the mysteries of prime numbers? What about the development of my perseverance in pursuing such a task, even though (or maybe *because*) it was an impossible one? What about my capacity to tolerate frustration when my long calculations had been faulty from the beginning of the series?

I recognize now that some important inner qualities had been shaped as I chased those prime numbers. I had learned that the path is itself the goal.

Latin *putare* means "to prune," "to cut," "to clean." In the etymology of "computer" lies its implicit goal: something to accomplish, to complete, a clear-cut result to reach.

Computing, that increasingly-present activity in our lives, has created what I call the "digitization of reality." Computing wants answers – well-defined results cleansed of "noise" – and it wants them fast.

Descartes, in his *Discourse on the Method* which shaped Western science, sought a state of pure thinking, free from the body and from feelings – for in his opinion they would distort the scientific quest. He would be proud of contemporary technical developments which allow both scientists and ordinary people to interact with a machine through pure thinking. But if he could peek into this century, I feel he would miss the philosophical and spiritual attitude he had even as a scientist – which is left out of the technological race.

In our rush, everything which can possibly be automated and speeded up becomes digital. Everything which can be represented by bits and bytes is sucked into the digitizing mentality.

I too believed this, when it was time for university, so I went into computer science – partly to fulfill my need to write a program to find the law of my series. In time I stopped chasing prime numbers, but by then I was a programming enthusiast.

What did not change was my propensity for impossible tasks. Since I enjoyed playing the guitar, I wrote a program for creating chords and harmonies. Then, wanting to grab the secrets of guitarists like Jimi Hendrix or Carlos Santana, I translated their improvisations into digital form. After all, I figured, musical scales have a mathematical structure, so if I could decode and deconstruct their creations, then my software could produce amazing new melodies which I could then reproduce on my guitar.

There was still no affordable way to generate good quality sound from a computer, so as output (programming in C language for the UNIX operating system), I had a list of notes, their pitch, duration, and their attributes like sliding or bending – a sort of score I could perform on my guitar. Far from masterpieces, they were funny, like the caricature of a living person.

Meanwhile, I was working for the computer labs of the new computer science faculty in Milan, preferring to learn through practice rather than study for exams. There was a pioneering atmosphere in the very early 1980s – and many of the students later becoming entrepreneurs of the dotcom revolution in Italy.

The peak of impossibility lay in my plan to create an artificial intelligence system, written in the Prolog programming language, to explore people's psychological patterns in depth – according to various models, both psychological and spiritual. It never went beyond a very initial idea.

The Limits of Technology

In searching for the law of prime numbers, for the secrets of great guitarists' solos, or for the understanding of the human soul, 25 years ago, I reached what was – and still remains – the limits of computability.

Finding those limits is perhaps the unconscious secret goal of our drive toward technology. Whatever can be made digital is merely a model created by the mind, which the mind itself can reshape or destroy at any moment.

The mind is by nature dualistic, operating within the same binary logic as computers. The dualistic-binary attitude of looking at the world gives both people and computers a powerful discriminating tool – a tool to produce huge amount of data and to act on matter in powerful ways. Through this dualistic mind we can fulfill our highest "mission" – to be masters of nature, as assigned by the scriptures. But matters that are more than mental – artistic creativity, brilliant intuition, feelings of compassion, love, joy, peace, as well as experiencing spiritual states like a no-mind state of deep meditation – cannot be represented in digital form. Though information technology can point to or inform about those states, more often than not it keeps us stuck looping at the informational level, actually distancing us from them.

As we reach the limits of technology, either it can stimulate our search for something further – jumping from information to consciousness-processing as Peter Russell (1995) defined it – or we can become hypnotized by the infinite forms information can be shaped into. Like a fascinating psychedelic vision, the digital realm can amaze us forever, but basically it goes no further than the mental level which originally created the technology.

My impossible tasks, seen in retrospect, were my self-inflicted koans. A koan is a question with no apparent answer given by a Zen master to a student. The very effort to find an answer is what transforms consciousness and eventually stops the mind. Staying in the unknown is not comfortable for the mind, but it is the best way to link the subject of the quest with our inner void. From this, greater awareness can arise. By contrast, much of the Web industry is designed to cut through, to deliver answers quickly – not in itself a bad thing, but which can and does weaken the drive of our inner quest.

Since the impossible tasks didn't pay, I worked on more practical software and wrote about computer science. In 1982, with the UNIX internal architecture still a well-kept secret and without much documentation for the end user, two other students and I wrote a book about UNIX. We printed it with a low-quality dot matrix printer, and I felt like a technical Che Guevara fighting for the liberation of computer knowledge.

What's Not Computable Isn't Real

Writing for computer science magazines in the mid '80s, I alternated technical articles with interviews of philosophers and psychologists about the inner and social implications of the computer revolution, including a column called "Loops" for *Informatica Oggi* magazine, the leading computer Italian science magazine at the time. My heretical column was scrapped by the publisher after only a few months because some readers complained that those subjects had nothing to do with computer science, and that they'd rather read "real" and "useful" information.

Turning the view 180 degrees toward the inner side, from what we can do with technology to what technology does to us wasn't a very popular move. Anything that smells of the philosophical, the inner, or the metaphysical is still seen with suspicion by people into technology, who categorize those perspectives as "things which could even be interesting, but vague and non-scientific." For the most part, challenging technology has become almost taboo in our culture. As Neil Postman (1993) contended: "'The computer shows…' or 'The computer has determined…' is *Technopoly*'s equivalent of the sentence, 'It is God's will' and the effect is roughly the same."

Technology seems "inevitable." It is rarely considered that people who are sensitive to what technology does to us might embrace and use technology – though they do it from 360 degrees instead of looking just at the bright front side.

In advanced technological societies there is a reticence to acknowledge the inner, the spiritual, or the metaphysical dimensions of life. The inner is seen pertinent only to religion, reinforcing the historical division of powers which gave science dominion over matter and religion dominion over the soul. What is non-calculable or non-objective is mostly ignored, as are the implications of technology for our psyche.

Sensitivity to the inner is easily branded new-ageism, fundamentalism, or plain weirdness. *Meditation* is misunderstood as thinking. The *body-mind connection* is something to decode by DNA sequences. Going *beyond* the mind is misunderstood as going below the functionality of mind, dulled rather than perceiving more deeply. *Understanding* is something which we infer only intellectually. The *inner void* is something we become aware of only when the computer hangs and we are left to stare blankly at the screen. *Mind* is seen mainly in terms of cognitive capacities and performance, a set of neurotransmitters which can eventually be "fixed" or "enhanced" by pharmacological molecules.

The Promises of the Early Internet
After publishing my own books, I became a publisher of computer science books. Around 1994, when the Internet was becoming popular in Italy, I welcomed the Net in enthusiastic terms. Like many early enthusiasts, I saw the Net as a way to produce and share information in a more democratic way that could threaten big powers and even nation-states, and having the potential of shaping global consciousness.

Through Apogeo, my former publishing house, I published the

first books in Italy about the Internet, convincing the traditional media that the Net wasn't just about terrorists, pedophiles and dangerous hackers. For many years there was an opposition between the Internet on one side, and TV and print media on the other. Hostility toward the Internet was about competing interests, as well as simple ignorance. Their distorted, inaccurate and false vision of the Internet continues to this day.

At the same time, it was difficult to find a balanced, critical view of the role of the Net in society and in people's minds. Anybody who criticized the Net risked being branded a close-minded conservative, a Luddite, an "old media" supporter wanting to limit the freedom of expression which the Net seemed to expand.

The fact is, though, that after twenty years of the Internet in our lives, most of the promises have not been fulfilled. We don't have more democracy in the world, big media and big powers are even stronger, no global consciousness has arisen – and even though everybody can upload anything onto the Web simply and cheaply, we know less about what is happening in Iraq and Afghanistan than what we knew about the Vietnam war which was heavily broadcast. Yes, there are sites through which information can leak, but the leakage is a drop in the ocean of information daily available – and on sites read by a small percentage of web users.

Even when alternative information is presented, it is likely to be found on less popular websites that are far down in Google's ranking. This merely deludes us into believing we have a tool for spreading information to the world – when in most cases it is more like a neighborly backyard chat. A chat, in fact, that can be traced and controlled. The big media have not disappeared – and their presence on the Net could make them even bigger.

Furthermore, privacy and control issues by governments and companies like Google and Facebook are, to say the least, worrying. What was once a place with no commercial interests is now full of advertisements, with some free services likely to become fee-based.

As soon as my company could afford it, I published a series on media studies, spirituality and Eastern culture, which reflected my personal life-path as a researcher of the truth. I switched from "updating" myself on the latest technical trends to attending workshops in different spiritual traditions and techniques. I went to ashrams in India and studied in psycho-spiritual schools in the US.

From Information Processing to Consciousness Processing
I moved back and forth between information processing and consciousness processing – from the awareness of technology to tech-

The Digitally Divided Self

nologies of awareness. Information and my mind fed each other in a vicious cycle, making it difficult to stop and turn my gaze back toward inner silence. The mechanism of information incites us to stay within the feedback loop.

My subjective inner exploration was important not only for knowing my inner self, but also for clarity and a broader understanding of the outer world. Freeing my mind from conditioning and acquired beliefs proved effective both in my daily life and for a deeper understanding of reality. (Despite common misconceptions, spiritual paths *are* paths toward reality and clarity.) Beyond the conditioned mind we can see reality in a sharper way.

As every meditator quickly learns, many of our choices only seem to be "ours." They are, in most cases, the result of early-life messages – either explicit or unconscious –which structured our minds. Those knots can never be untied if we don't work on them with our attention and full presence.

Uninterrupted conscious attention along with silent time to look into our inner world are exactly what is rendered arduous by the technological society which, to use a term dear to Mauro Magatti (2009), sequesters our attention. The modality of the Internet, regardless of the actual content we are giving attention to, tends to split our attention – among websites, instant messaging, email, social networks, pictures, videos, software tools and more. With the growing speed of computers and the Net, everyone can keep several windows and websites open at once, jumping rapidly from one to the other.

Links themselves – the cement of the Internet – useful as they are, can be distracting. We approach even the best, most interesting and in-depth information with the same divided inner modality. Marshall McLuhan's awakening phrase "the medium is the message" is true also for the Net. Being more than just another medium, the Net can be considered the summation of all media, and its impact on our inner and outer lives is accordingly stronger than any preceding media.

But we can always be masters of our attention, right? True, but the efforts to direct our attention and maintain it becomes harder with the growing presence of the Internet in our lives.

All in the Digital Mincer
The digitization of reality started with number crunching, a process close to computer language. Computers were initially used for scientific and engineering calculations, later extending to reading, writing, studying, working, entertainment, travel planning, con-

necting with friends and family, dating, sexual arousal, shopping and banking. And these activities are happening *only* online for a growing number of people. The "Internet of things" promises to go even further, radio tagging any object on earth with an Internet address, sucking all matter into the Net like a vacuum cleaner. The Net's voracity doesn't stop anywhere – including Body Area Networks that will be monitoring people's physiological parameters.

The Net continually adds to the list of human activities which can be represented digitally – charming us with amazing applications, digitizing traditional needs and desires, and stimulating new ones. The transformation of desires into needs is one of the main activities of technological society, which in this regard shares the attitude with capitalistic society.

But we can just go offline, right? Again, true – but the Internet tends, like a gas, to expand in time and space. It follows us anywhere, through wireless connections and smartphones. With the immediacy of communication through the Net, there is a reciprocal pressure for answers to be fast. If we stay away from the Net for only a couple of days, we could miss an important job message, our friends' updates, a notification from our airline, a juicy invitation from a person we're attracted to, a nasty comment on our blog or social network page which we need to remove, a credit card transaction, the choices in door handles from our architect, library and credit card late notices, or a message from the insurance company.

With most of our colleagues, friends and family online, being offline will feel like living in a remote corner of the planet. Therefore, we are more than willing to transfer our lives to the Net, display them on social networks like Facebook, preserve our private documents in the "cloud," and embrace technologies which promise to amaze and empower us. We can happily disembody into the cloud like a "pure" angel.

Technology Can't be Challenged

When I started, computers were in transition from mainframes to PCs –a milestone in the empowerment of the individual, who could finally manage his own data, in his own time and place, and on his own computer. Floppy disks may have had very limited capacity, but we welcomed this freedom. Today PCs are more powerful than those mainframes, but we willingly give our data and computations back to Web services in the cloud.

Since the advent of computers, there has been concern about how they affect our minds. As computers spread, Sherry Turkle pointed out how they influence construction of the personal self, and Joseph Weizenbaum explored the attitudes of people working with computers. In reality, however, there are not as many people interested in those subjects as there are people chasing after the latest technological gadgets.

There are on the Net itself articles critical of the information society. Some correctly emphasize the loss of concentration through multiple mental stimuli. "Is Google Making Us Stupid?" by Nicholas Carr (2008) created a wave of debates. Other commentators have written about the prominence which the Net gives to the latest news, and how small chunks of information force historical context and broader implications into the shadows.

Some people express concern about Internet addiction to online auctions like eBay, to porn and cybersex, and online gaming and chats. Parents and teachers are legitimately concerned about protecting minors from information inappropriate for their age, from cyberpredators to cyberbullying.

Even though critical voices are present, it is not easy to criticize technology. In 2009, neuroscientist Susan Greenfield spoke before the House of Lords about the risk of changes in children's brains from overuse of social networks. Bloggers and websites counterattacked with the allegation that she had no scientific proof for her "conjecture and opinions."

This looks like a reverse inquisition. As the Church would condemn anything which wasn't compatible with Holy Scripture, now it looks like nothing has value if it is not backed by hard scientific proof and plenty of data. With that premise, there can be no value in any inner, philosophical, or ethical quest. What's not calculable, statistically coherent or scientifically demonstrable is categorized as mere "opinion" and far from truth. Welcome to Technopoly, as Neil Postman defined it.

Saying that "it is not scientific" or "we don't have enough data" are typical defenses that technologically-oriented people use to counteract criticism or expressions of concern. They also take the position that the answer to any problem arising from technology lies in technology itself: more options, more speed, improved functionalities, a newer version.

We know the common slogans. "Technology and tools in themselves are neutral – it's about how you choose to use them." Any tool, however, has wider reverberations in both the social and inner worlds, aside from the way we use it. The mere presence of cars, for instance, reshaped the landscape and changed our connection with it, relocated people, changed the air we breathe, made people more sedentary, revised geopolitical relationships, and built a huge economy based on the powering, production and maintenance of cars and roads. Being without a car is possible but hard to manage, especially in places where public transportation is not in much demand. Yes we have choices in how we use cars: we can kill people with them or transport food to a poor community, but we cannot avoid their effect on our lives. They extend the possibilities of our legs, which grow weak through disuse. And without use, we tend to detach our attention from them. Likewise, TV extends our vision of the world beyond our neighborhood – but the very act of watching isolates us from neighbors and family.

Computers and the Internet are influencing our lives in more and more powerful ways. If cars reshaped the landscape, computers are making it useless. We can do almost anything in front of our screen without going anywhere. And then when we're outdoors, we can experience the landscape filtered by the "augmented reality" tools of our smartphones. Computers and the Internet have also created a huge economy built on the growing desire for both gadgets and information. They influence our bodies, minds, and inner lives even more pervasively than cars.

Whether we are using the Internet for spreading racial hatred or for organizing support groups for people in trouble, we employ software tools within a certain body-mind setting in front of a screen, and we are communicating with people who share similar settings and tools. Inadvertently, we are feeding the huge Internet economy of software, telecommunication data lines, and hardware – equipment that is mostly produced in countries where labor is cheap and the environmental impact of their production is not debated. Countries that we will likely never visit.

Technology Uses Us
The process of digitization of reality translates our needs into the digital-mental arena, and creates new ones. The fairy tale that we are free to choose how we use technology hides the fact that using technology allows technology to use *us*. McLuhan said that, "by continuously embracing technologies, we relate ourselves to them as servomechanisms." We obliterate the awareness of being servomechanisms by believing that technology widens our choices, our freedom, and empowers us. Like car ads that emphasize freedom and power, showing shiny SUVs in mountains or desert – when in reality we spend hours trapped inside them, stuck in traffic.

Always busy clicking here and there, we pay no attention to how our outer and inner states are changed by technology and information. We are numbed to the loss of certain mental capacities and

inner qualities which have been walled off by technology that emphasizes only the Now and the Latest, till we no longer remember
how we were. This is hardly the *here and now* inner state described
by spiritual teachers like Eckhart Tolle, though that state is being
simulated by instant gratification and release from the burden of
the past and the future by following the endless stream of new information.

Technologically-oriented people themselves express legitimate
concerns. On the social and political levels, many are sensitive to
the implications of the digital divide, as well as privacy and the
openness of software architectures – yet most of them ignore the
deeper implications

Feeding the Soul with Bytes
Traveling from information- to consciousness-processing through
meditation and psycho-spiritual understanding, I became aware
that many technological developments are appealing because they
share deep psychological and even spiritual needs with fake ones.
As those primordial needs are translated onto the mental level of
information, the emptied soul craves the real qualities, even as the
restless mind seeks more information which can never fulfill the
authentic needs of the soul. This very restlessness doesn't allow the
subtle inner qualities to penetrate our awareness.

On the psychological level, one of the appeals of the Net is that
it fulfills the human need to be seen, listened to, and recognized as
we are. Far from being narcissistic, recognition is essential to the
development of our personality – and should be acknowledged in
childhood by parents, teachers, and other role models. We can only
recognize and value our innate qualities initially through the eyes
of others.

When parents don't give enough time and attention to their children (perhaps because of hard work or because they are caught in
the technological loop) or when they lack the inner qualities themselves, their children's need for mirroring is unaddressed. Technology, then, offers a second opportunity to show ourself and relate
to others through social networks. What we receive, however, reflects us only on the mental level, which cannot feed our soul with
the essential human qualities we need to recognize in ourself and
embody.

The spiritual teacher A. H. Almaas (1986) has discriminated
many essential human qualities such as Love, Compassion, Joy,
Strength, Passion, Steadfastness, Perseverance, Intuition, Curiosity,
and Inner Peace. Being seen by Facebook friends is not the same as

assimilating the real qualities through connection with a real human being who embodies them. Since we feel an inner lack which can be filled from the outside only in a very temporary and illusory way, we become stuck in needing to be continually recognized. And the mind will try forever.

The use of technology can have direct impact on our neurophysiology as well. Research points to a stunting of the frontal lobe in teenagers who are heavily into computers and video games (Small, 2008). The frontal lobes are fundamental for developing reasoning and judging abilities, and for long-term planning. The instant gratification of computer use can weaken our capacities for broader vision and planning. Poorly-developed frontal lobes are also typical of schizophrenia.

The Immortal Mind
Through technology and the Net we crave divine as well as ordinary powers. So people like Raymond Kurzweil (2005) appeal to us with a future where technological advances will bring us nothing less than immortality – through downloading our mind to the computer. In the history of Western science, he is not the first to apply messianic and religious terms to technology. After all, humanity has already been saved by the technology of Noah's Ark, so there will surely be a "hack" even for mortality.

What Kurzweil and others are suggesting to drive our evolution through computers and biotechnology is a reflection, confined to the biological and mental levels, of the spiritual quest to elevate awareness beyond our mind. But since the quest is activated through mind-created technology, we can only remain on the same plane as the mind, however expanded and sophisticated it becomes through external supports and enhancements.

Kurzweil claims that "eventually, we leap beyond the boundaries of our planet, and every bit of matter in the entire universe becomes intelligent.... This," he concludes, "is the destiny of the universe." Sure, but this is *already* what the universe is, with no need for any contribution of technology. Enlightened spiritual teachers know that the universe is permeated by a brilliant Consciousness which cannot be grasped by ordinary mind, but which can be experienced through advanced states of consciousness as a result of spiritual inquiry.

Since our culture associates human beings mainly with their minds' contents, then immortality means preserving that information. But if we jump to another level of identification, then the project of preserving our mind is seen as nothing more special than keeping our kidneys functioning by machines in a laboratory. Awareness and the essential human qualities are not a Cartesian matter of a purely mental state. They are a part of the soul which we perceive through our capacity of inner observation. I use the term *soul* to designate the overall entity of the body-mind, the psyche, and spiritual states. As Almaas says about those essential qualities:

> Each of the different ways that Essence appears has recognizable properties and characteristics that differentiate it experientially from the other aspects. Because Essence is not a physical substance, we do not actually perceive its presence with our physical senses, but it can be clearly perceived and recognized through the functioning of subtle inner capacities that correspond to physical senses (2002, p. 250).

Those subtle inner capacities require our awareness of our whole body-mind. We can't transfer essential qualities to the Net and bring them with us on the techno-immortal journey.

Inner Prostheses and Amputations through Technology

Many technical advances are being made without asking the basic questions about what drives us into technology and what technology really does to us. The time spent talking about technology is concerned with how it *works*, not with its *ends*. The implicit belief is that any technological development which seems to expand our options is going to have a positive impact.

McLuhan wrote that "any invention or technology is an extension or self-amputation of our physical bodies, and such extension also demands new ratios or new equilibriums among the other organs and extensions of the body." We tend to look only at the extended parts, not at the shifting equilibriums they trigger. We prefer to look at our extensions rather than the amputations, because our mind has developed to be more comfortable looking outside than within.

We project externally on technologies, which in turn mirror our self-images. But the amputations hinder recognition. The more we transfer our own qualities to technology, the less we are aware of what's missing, having weakened the inner tools of self-awareness. We are, like drunks, in denial of our condition.

Translating reality into information is very attractive to the ego-mind. The ego can thus consider the world as a huge information system to be understood, catalogued, and controlled through software – itself an extension of the mind. The mind becomes then a supreme king.

Minds and digital technologies have much in common. Both can simulate almost anything, and both try to incorporate everything into their domains. The mind and the thinking process are the most cherished entities in our culture. But that is not the whole story.

Beyond the Mind

There are states beyond the mind which can be reached through awareness. There exists a condition of "spiritual enlightenment" which can elevate human beings to the divine and to global Consciousness. Spiritual teachers of every age have pointed to such a state, however difficult it is to communicate through words what is beyond mind.

Words, dual in themselves, are the tools at hand to describe the non-dual state of union with the whole, called *spiritual enlightenment*, *satchitananda* (the merging of existence, consciousness and bliss), *being a Buddha*, *God Realization*, and *Ultimate Understanding*." I have a faint echo of this from the glimpses of higher states my own journey has offered.

But the words of spiritual teachers are the map, not the territory – and my experiences could be no more than delusions. Actually, some teachers say that any *experience* is not yet *that*, so a Zen master would probably hit my head with a stick. The truth is that neither I nor anyone has a way to prove the existence of such a state, since every "proof" would stay on the level of the mind itself. All in all, it's a matter of faith. And even science has its own axioms or postulates, truths which are taken for granted.

The word *faith* has been associated with the monotheistic religions, with fundamentalism and in opposition to an open quest for the truth. Much blood has been spilled in the name of faith. Faith has been used, as well, to mean not acknowledging scientific truths. I am not talking about that faith.

Where my faith comes from is a mystery. Maybe I was touched by reading, maybe I felt an echo of something larger than the mind or I recognized higher states of being in my spiritual teachers.

If I would add anything more than plain faith to the existence of spiritual enlightenment, then trouble would ensue. For instance, when instead of saying "God exists," we say "God is goodness," we are already in a dualistic perspective that can easily slip into "Who doesn't believe in God is evil." Also, if the postulate that spiritual enlightenment exists were extended into "I know the only way toward enlightenment," then we would fall into fundamentalism. The mind wants to pull into its purview even what can never be known by it.

Words are products of the conceptual/dual mind, and nobody can avoid the risk of building structures and dogmas when talking about no-mind. But what's important is to keep an open-ended attitude at the root of any inquiry, whether scientific or self-inquiry.

The Fragility of Beliefs and Information Technology
Science cannot conceive anything beyond the ego and the mind – not even in human sciences such as psychology (with the exception of transpersonal psychology). Thus, abandoning our mind's contents seems like total defeat. In the West, nihilism is often knocking at the door, since what the mind creates – by its ephemeral nature – the mind itself can destroy. Without acknowledging a spiritual dimension, one is tempted to say that there's nothing solid – and ultimately that there's no sense in anything.

A culture which has been developed on the foundation of "I think, therefore I am" will cling to thinking and will produce tools to keep the mind busy all the time. But for the spiritually-oriented person there's a plan B. The abandonment of the ego-mind is equivalent to the metamorphosis of a caterpillar into a butterfly.

The ephemeral nature of the mind becomes clear when, in meditation, we try with titanic effort to *observe* our thoughts and sensations, instead of clinging to them as they carry our mind away. We can see then how weak our skills are to concentrate on a single object, how short-lived our thoughts are, and how little control we have over them. The mind has been compared by spiritual teachers to a drunken monkey. Yet we cherish our thinking process as the highest expression of being human.

Technology and information are also quite ephemeral. The chances of preserving their digital contents are dim compared to other media. Papyrus lasted thousands of years, books hundreds of years, CDs (the very best quality) dozens of years, and hard drives only a few years.

The software I wrote when I was at university was backed up on magnetic data tape. I don't know if there's any compatible tape reader still tucked away in some laboratory. Even if there were, most probably the tape would have been demagnetized by now. But even if not, the software will have been rewritten to work with current operating systems.

In recovering data which is just a few years old, there are both hardware and software format problems. Converting our data to ever-changing computer formats is a huge job – which most probably will never be done either by individuals or institutions. Even if it were, who could make sense of that huge amount of data?

Technology is fragile in other aspects too. As shown by *Low-Tech Magazine*, the energy consumption of hi-tech devices is skyrocketing, especially the energy required to manufacture them. "The embodied energy of the memory chip of a computer alone already exceeds the energy consumption of the laptop during its life expectancy of 3 years" (deDecker, 2009). Digital technology then, like many other developments since we started to drill for oil, is a product of cheap energy. With the growing cost of energy and a lurking peak in oil production, we won't see as many hi-tech devices around as we are used to. Also, many hi-tech products depend on rare earth metals, more than 95 percent of which are found in China – which plans to limit exports.

Hi-tech products are also very sensitive to the electromagnetic radiation of solar wind. The current 11-year solar cycle, which started in 2007 and will peak around 2013, should be significantly stronger than the previous one. Solar flares shoot energetic photons toward Earth, upsetting the geomagnetic field and potentially affecting power grids, communications, satellites, GPS signals and even electronic chips.

A strong solar storm in 1859 shorted telegraph wires, causing fires in North America and Europe. If such an electromagnetic storm occurred today, it would take four to ten years to recover electric power lines, according to a report of the National Academy of Science. Given the strong interdependence of every system, the effects could be devastating for the whole of society.

As with meditation techniques, in which we learn to observe and let go of arising thoughts, maybe we should begin to practice letting go of our attachments to the information loop.

CHAPTER 2

"IT'S ONLY A TOOL"

If there were a law stating that "people should stay in front of a screen for most of their waking time, both indoors and out, avoiding real-life meetings as much as possible, shop without touching or seeing the product, find their soulmates through Internet announcements, consume an average of 34 gigabytes of information daily" (University of California, 2009), there would be a revolution. But if it's seen as our "freedom," then it's fine. Technology can do this because it acts on a higher level than laws, rules or impositions. As Neil Postman (1993) wrote, "Technology imperiously commandeers our most important terminology. It redefines 'freedom' 'truth,' 'intelligence,' 'fact,' 'wisdom,' 'memory,' 'history' – all the words we live by" (p. 8). Facebook now has even transformed the meaning of "friend" and "like."

For most of us, technology acts deeply in moving awareness away from the connection with our inner world – powerfully redefining both our inner and outer life. Sustained attention, awareness and introspection—the qualities needed to break out of the automated mind – become especially difficult when we are drowning in information, mostly brief and directed to the latest news.

Joseph Weizenbaum (1976), exploring the character of compulsive programmers as early as 1976, found them disinterested in their bodily needs and detached from the world around them. We are not surprised to meet such figures in countries where advanced technologies are part of everyday life.

Cubans I met traveling there in 2000 were usually lively people, with direct personal contact, sensual, relating to immediate reality. It was striking to see two computer technicians, on the contrary, detached, immersed in their own worlds, neglecting themselves, communicating with few words. I realized how daily contact with a tool – in this case computers and programming (tools which had been available there for only a few years) – can have a stronger impact on social attitude and personality than the collective conditioning of society.

There is probably a mutual feedback between personality and life choices, but without doubt technology also shapes psyches. Even early in history, Taoists observed that the use of instruments carries the risk of becoming mechanical ourself. Today – from Hong Kong to Brazil, from Lithuania to South Africa, from Egypt to New Zealand – wherever people use the Internet, they click on the same icons, use the same shortcuts in email and chats, connect with people through the same Facebook modalities. This is the globalization of mind.

Technology is not Questionable

Mark Slouka, in *War of the Worlds* (1995), conveyed how eerie it is to be permeated by the digital revolution, with no or little reflection about what it really means, "where the only concern heard in the land, by and large, is that some of us may be left behind" (p. 9).

In the history of media, there has never been much reflection about the impact on human psyches. The few who reflected negatively on it were considered against progress and innovation.

The technological person doesn't believe he can be transformed by technology. In fact, he has been persuaded that he is the *master* of technology. He believes that his inner life (actually as unknown to him today as it was before Freud) cannot be modified by any tool. His mind is supposed to rise above all else; tools can at most extend the possibilities of his mind, but can never influence his choices. While this wasn't even true for mechanical tools, it is even less true for information technologies.

The technological person is subject to the Cartesian separation between the world of matter and the world of ideas – and considers the latter superior. Much before Descartes, the Bible assigned us the role of masters of matter and God's terrain. This unconscious belief that our mind is superior to everything else has contributed to the lack of debate about the transformation of our psyches by technology.

Knowing through the Body

Birds build their nests instinctively, and many animals "know" how to hunt or find food, but humans have been dispensed a limited set of instincts, such as sucking and grabbing. Everything else derives from learning – which is very much an embodied process. Despite emphasis on the 3Rs in kindergarten, the factors most likely to lead to later academic success are play and social skills. Research shows that young children learn through their bodies. For example, the child's early understanding of geometric relationships and physics is almost physical.

A study published in *Nature* by researchers at the University of California at Santa Cruz demonstrated that as animals learn motor tasks, connections between brain cells begin to form almost immediately and become permanently consolidated in the brain. We all know that when we learn something involving the body, like riding a bicycle, this knowledge stays with us.

Along the evolutionary trail, we first see muscles appearing, then motor function as consequence of interacting with a certain habitat, and later the associated neurophysiological functions. Motor activity acts on the brain, which in turn acts back on the body to perfect an action. Engels (1985) perceived that the opposability of the thumb and the erect position of human beings came millions of years before the further development of the brain. It was the activity that altered the brain, and not vice versa. This was later confirmed by the fossil record.

The hand especially, with its sophisticated movements, shaped our nervous systems. The "technologies" of body movement and of manual labor shaped and developed our human brain from earliest times. In mutual feedback, our brain shaped our tools with growing complexity -- until we arrived at contemporary tools. These interact almost exclusively with our minds and shape our nervous system.

In a famous experiment by University College London in 2008, researchers used magnetic scanners to read the brain activity of twenty taxi drivers while they navigated their way through a virtual simulation of London's streets. Using functional magnetic resonance imaging (fMRI) scans, they obtained detailed brain images as taxi drivers delivered customers to their destinations.

Different brain regions were activated as they were planning their routes, spotting familiar landmarks, or thinking about their customers. Brain areas were activated and grew by building information needed to find the right way around complicated London streets. Earlier studies found that taxi drivers have a larger hippocampus – an area of the brain important in navigational abilities – than most of us.

Technology "Does" Us
Technologies which interact primarily with our minds have an immediate effect on our neurophysiology. For example, research using

fMRI on 18 to 26 year olds who average 14 hours a week of violent video showed activation of the amygdala. This almond-shaped structure of the brain in the temporal region is considered part of the limbic system in which our instinctual emotional reactions take place, including modulations of our reactions to threats.

Other experiments demonstrated that only five days of searching with Google by computer-naïve subjects were enough to change their neural circuits, activating in particular the dorsolateral prefrontal cortex – which has an important role in our short-term memory and in the integration of sensory and mnemonic information. Whether we use IT interacting with our minds, or mechanical tools interacting mainly with our bodies, both affect our body-mind – even in permanent ways.

The main body movements required for hi-tech tools are in our hands and fingers with the mouse, the keyboard, or a touch screen. Research by the *Proceedings of the National Academy of Sciences* (PNAS, 2009) found that hand gestures activate the same brain region as language (the inferior frontal and posterior temporal areas), something which any gesticulating Italian will easily confirm.

Ritual gestures of the hands have always been connected with the activation of inner states of the mind. The *mudras* of Hinduism are a path of spiritual gestures formed by the hands and fingers. Ancient disciplines such as the tea ceremony or t'ai-chi involve gestures connected to inner development.

The strongest neural connections are between the hand and the brain. Handwriting itself, with its subtle and highly personalized movements, can even give a glimpse of our personality through graphology. What happens when we use technologies which interact almost exclusively with our minds with no or minimal involvement of the body (apart from the obvious cardiovascular and obesity risks in sitting for a long time in front of a screen)?

Is the activation of certain areas of the brain the whole story about the potential of human evolution? Could it be that our cognitive capacities reside as much in every organ and cell of our body – perhaps even beyond our body – as in our brain and nervous system? Consciousness itself cannot be inferred by neuroimaging, much less can we locate wisdom or ethics in the brain.

If London's taxi drivers developed a part of the brain according to their navigational experience, what happens when we rely only on GPS for our navigation? One of my acquaintances drove his car from the south to the north of Italy. When I asked which route he took and whether he passed one town or another I named, he answered that he had not noticed because he just followed GPS indications. Is there a possibility the same brain areas which develop in taxi drivers can atrophy if they are not used? Even more worrying are studies about the development of frontal lobes of kids.

Technology is a Matter of Life and Death

Our attachment to, fascination with, and need for tools has ancient roots. Human beings, unlike other species, do not have a natural specialization which allows them to live in a specific ecological zone. We would have become extinct a long time ago if we did not operate technologically on the environment.

Technology – in the form of fire, hunting tools, or hardware to fix a plow or a tractor – is essential for survival. Mechanical tools involve the whole body, spatial imagination, attention, and concentration to operate them safely. The capacity to remember the characteristics of the territory, the operating modalities, and the location of the numerous tools is needed.

Even the most primitive populations require some tools to extend their power. For instance, humans can survive only in a narrow range of temperatures unless we provide shelter and clothes for ourselves. And very few environments were once without dangerous predators, so we have needed to provide safety – again, through tools.

We can understand why we are so attached to technology and to the power we get from it. It's about survival. We are also hard-wired to attend to new visual stimuli, in order to discern potential threats. Attending to novel stimuli – which nowadays arrive as pixels changing on the screen – has been evolutionarily rewarded with a pleasurable dopamine shot.

Binary and Inner Duality

Technology has continued developing, bringing us to the contemporary digital technologies. The core of every computer and electronic gadget is made up of *0*s and *1*s, binary sequences which represent the world as encoded texts, images and videos. The inner structure of a tool reflects the ways it is used, just as the molecular structure of a material reflects its macro-features like density, texture and resistance.

Splitting, distinguishing, choosing, and repeating are the main modalities of the Boolean logic that is behind binary technology. In the computer programming languages used to develop software, one of the main logical structures is the "if-then-else" construct ("if A, then B; if else than A, then C") that allows statements to operate on choices and dualities.

The dualistic binary modality of functioning is typical of the rational thinking mind – and the computer extends such cognitive modalities. The basic structures of the mind are also born through the first dualistic event, when a child begins to split pleasurable-good-love-warm-care sensations from unpleasurable-bad-fear-alone-hunger ones. The first mental concepts are born by splitting our experiences. The infant does not yet have any concept or way to understand what is happening around him, but he already has the capacity to perceive and sense.

Within the undifferentiated world of the infant, the first primitive dual mental structures form, closely tied to his physiology – as in feeling good or bad. Later, this dualistic attitude will create more sophisticated mental structures, like concepts and ideas with further refined differences.

In Tibetan Buddhism, the nature of the mind is understood as dualistic. Its job is to reinforce our separation from anything and anybody else. "That which possesses a sense of duality – which grasps or rejects something external – that is mind. Fundamentally, it is that which can associate with an 'other' – with any 'something' that is perceived as different from the perceiver. That is the definition of mind" (Trungpa, 1991, p. 23).

Our mind is not just a mechanical logic-oriented dualistic tool' – we can feel emotions too. Though *thinking* and *feeling* are usually seen as different entities, mind, in the Tibetan Buddhist tradition, includes emotions and sensations. Even the most appealing feelings still pertain to the mind. Emotions support the workings of the mind. "Daydreaming and discursive thoughts are not enough," Chogyam Trungpa explains. "Those alone would be too boring. The dualistic trick would wear too thin. So we tend to create waves of emotions which go up and down: passion, aggression, ignorance, pride – all kinds of emotions" (p. 23).

Emotions support the mind to keep at its separating dualistic task. Even the computer has evolved beyond a tool that merely encourages a dry, rational attitude for our minds. Now it feeds our emotions through music, videos, sex, and social connections.

Knowing through the Heart

The mind is the generally acknowledged organ of thoughts, but is not the only cognitive modality. There is another way, through the heart, that doesn't just deal with emotions, but has to do with the search for truth and with a direct way of knowing. The knowing heart has been considered by spiritual traditions as receptive to the intelligence of Universal Consciousness.

This spiritual heart has a connection with the body in energetic terms. The heart chakra, for instance, is located in the chest area. Even if the energetic connection is considered unscientific, it has been discovered that the physical heart has its own nerve cells which also send information to the brain.

With the discovery that the heart has its own dedicated nervous system, the Institute of HeartMath is researching the critical links between emotions, the heart-brain communication, and cognitive functions. In the article "Science of the Heart" (2001), they reported that the heart is the organ that produces the largest electrical field, about 60 times greater than the brain. An electrocardiograph (ECG) can detect it anywhere on the surface of the body. Also, the magnetic field of the heart is more than 5,000 times greater than that of the brain and can be detected several feet away, in any direction, using SQUID-based magnetometers. Perhaps further research will reveal that the neurophysiology of the heart is the physical counterpart of our capacities for subtle knowing.

The heart can be a cognitive tool wider and deeper than the mind. The heart's modalities of knowing don't come through splitting and reasoning, but in an intuitive and receptive way. A mind emptied of its conditionings and beliefs gives space to the heart's cognitive faculties.

If the mind works with an either/or – or 0/1 – binary duality, the cognitive map of the heart works with a both/and logic, connecting what the mind has separated – including ourself as an individual separate from the rest of existence. The state of spiritual enlightenment in some traditions is referred to as non-dual, suggesting the end of the dualities of the mind.

How do we connect with the spiritual heart? Experientially through love, as one would imagine – but the love of a special lover. A. H. Almaas (1988) perceived that one basic quality of the soul is the love of truth for its own sake, love being the expression of truth. Just as the mental quality of objectivity necessitates love of truth – a quality of the heart – there is an interrelationship between the many qualities of the head and the heart.

The genesis of ego is defensiveness – which is a way of coping with and concealing experience that is difficult to tolerate. Thus the basic quality required for inner realization is the polar opposite of this fundamental aspect of ego. Defense and resistance are detrimental to truth, while love is supportive. Love of truth allows defensiveness to disappear and can reveal the sort of experiences that were initially defended against to establish the pattern of resistance.

The primary split that created the ego and, with it, dualistic mind, occurred at a very early age in reaction to intolerable pain, as we split good feelings from bad ones. That first illusion was the first virtual reality "software." It was a necessary, human and unavoidable act that shapes everyone's life. Nonetheless, it is still an illusion that can be exposed and dissolved through the love of truth in order to regain wholeness.

While the mind can give a great deal of support in working toward the truth, at a certain depth it is powerless, since its very existence depends on hiding the truth. For the mind, exposing truth would be committing suicide. Yet the heart loves to reveal the layers of truth which the mind cannot investigate.

Rudolf Steiner (1991) also pointed to the unrecognized cognitive faculties of the heart. He regarded the capacity for love as the third step in higher knowledge, indispensable for rising to the level of intuition. This can be achieved only by refining and spiritualizing the capacity for love to its acme, though this is not accepted as a cognitional force in our materialistic age. A person must be able to evolve sufficiently to make this capacity for love a cognitional force.

The birth of the dual mind is a necessary part of the development of our soul. In order to recognize ourself, we need to differentiate ourself from others and to become individual personalities. In the more advanced stages of spiritual development, the dualistic mind is transcended along with the individual personality. Osho (2008) offers this perspective:

> Existence is undivided; all divisions are just mental. The very way the mind looks at things creates a duality. It is the prison of the mind that divides. [The] mind cannot do otherwise. It is difficult for the mind to conceive of two contradictions as one, of opposite polarities as one. The mind has a compulsion, an obsession to be consistent. It cannot conceive how light and darkness are one.

And Assagioli (1971), the father of psychosynthesis, expressed it this way:

> Often we can't say where actually a person starts and where another ends. In harmonious groups, in an organized collectivity, the limits of the self, of the personalities of their members, tend to flow away, they aren't clearly distinct. We are literally immersed in a psychic atmosphere, in a collective psyche with its various differentiations (p. 18).

Through duality we lose the intimate connection with wholeness, but acquire powerful mental capacities unknown in other species. Discriminating awareness allows us to define a well-separated ego personality, intervene on external matter, and build sophisticated tools.

Our Identity With Tools – from Chimps to Chips

Apart from humans, only a few animals have the physical characteristics and mental capacities for using tools, monkeys foremost
among them. Hand movements are controlled by the F5 area of the
brain. Giacomo Rizzolatti (Umiltà, 2008) of the University of Parma
recorded the cerebral activity of two macaques after they had
learned to grasp food with pliers. He documented the activity in
the F5 area and in F1, which is involved in the manipulation of objects. He discovered the same cerebral activity whether the monkeys
grasped food by hand or with the pliers. The neuronal activity, he
concluded, is transferred from the hands to the tool, as if the tool
were the hand and its extremity the fingers.

Furthermore, Rizzolatti pointed out that the F5 area is rich in
mirror neurons, a type that he had previously discovered, which become excited both when an act is being performed and when another individual is observed performing that act. The discoveries,
according to Dietrich Stout, an archeologist specializing in the use
of tools, tell us that "obviously, the use of instruments by the monkeys implies an incorporation of the instruments in the body
scheme, literally it is an extension of a body" (Umiltà, 2008).

A monkey cannot distinguish between its own hands and the
tool it uses, as if the tool were an actual extension of its body. This
brings to mind what Marshall McLuhan said about the media and
tools as extensions of our bodies and minds, be it a tool for hunting or the "technology" of language, the printing press or our contemporary cognitive extensions.

Tools may be like body extensions on a neural level even for humans, but our discriminating awareness allows the understanding
that the tool is something "out there." In Rizzolatti's experiment,
the factor of consciousness, still elusive to neuroscience, is missing.
Neither the presence nor absence of consciousness nor what it is
about can be identified by experiments.

The monkey does not experience the duality produced by
human self-consciousness, so it may seem closer to a spiritual condition of "union with everything" – beyond dualities. However, this
union occurs on a pre-conscious level, not as the culmination of a
conscious path toward truth.

Our consciousness of ourself is at the same time both joy and
distress, since it entraps us in the dual mind, separating us from
the rest of existence, and splitting our psyche into conflicting parts.
But it also allows us to achieve intellectual tasks unknown to our
hungry macaque. Self-consciousness, and consequently the development of an ego which separates us from existence, is the inter-

mediate phase between the monkey's mind and a spiritually enlightened state.

Like the monkey, every time we use tools, we can lose the awareness of ourself. Even knowing that we are separated from the instrument, our attention tends to be drawn toward the tool, and we
forget ourself. The monkey cannot recognize what is other than
himself. Maybe humans have the same attitude when dealing with
tools – our old friends – with which we merged since ancient times,
thus stimulating the evolution of our nervous system and, thereby,
assuring our survival.

This forgetting of ourself happens more easily with tools which
act on the mind, like TV or the Internet, which absorb us till we
give attention exclusively to external stimuli. This is reminiscent of
the attention we once needed to give our environment in order to
survive.

Much of the appeal of technology rests on its capacity to arouse
a sense of urgency and wonder in us. Magic tricks are effective when
our awareness becomes redirected or highjacked by the magician.
Electronic gadgets are like magic boxes – decreasing our awareness
of their broader meaning and directing our attention to its seductive glimmer, creating a *totalitainment* society.

When we are involved with any gadget, it is difficult to remain
an observer, to be in touch with ourself instead of disappearing into
the tool and the flow of information.

Reconnecting with the Inner Flow

Then comes a paradox. If instead we totally immerse ourself in an
activity which absorbs us, such as dancing or making love, or even
using a tool like a musical instrument, we do forget ourself – but an
inner "witness" develops. This way, the action and the awareness of
the action align. The subject who acts vanishes, but the awareness
remains. What we forget is our small ego when we are merged with
something bigger (love, music), and we reconnect with awareness.
We abandon, however momentarily, the mental third body to reach
the fourth body – the aware observer, according to the Hindu esoteric teachings (in which the second is the emotional body).

Then we do not become lost in the action like the monkey with
the pliers or a human being with screen media. We find instead a
deeper self in the form of awareness through the action.

Such occurrences, Osho (1990) said, are existential, not intellectual – and when they are experienced by doing something totally,
surprisingly, something new will be felt. By totally singing, a new
kind of awareness arises. The singer has disappeared, and only song

The Digitally Divided Self

remains. But the singer is not at all unconscious. Quite the opposite: awareness will be expanded.

Earlier Osho (1976) wrote:

> If you become one hundred percent conscious, you become a witness, a sakshi. If you become a sakshi, you have come to the jumping point from where the jump into awareness becomes possible. In awareness, you lose the witness and only witnessing remains: you lose the doer, you lose the subjectivity, you lose the egocentric consciousness. Then consciousness remains, without the ego (p. 190).

The Western journey, both in the neuroscientific and psychological fields, does not conceive of awareness without an ego which experiences it. Yet even from our egoic condition we can have a glimpse of enlightenment by being totally immersed in our actions. We can become *one* again. While dancing, we become the dance. While making love, we become one with love and with the beloved. While playing music, we become one with the instrument and the music. Mihály Csíkszentmihályi (1991) referred to it as a state of flow.

Totality is a state of joyful expression and of awareness at the same time. Awareness expands and embraces the action, so the actor and the witness become one. Such states can be reached by meditation practices; by activities involving the body-mind like breathing techniques, intense loving; or sometimes by an impending danger which suddenly expands our awareness.

When we are unaware we lose ourself in the object which grasps our attention, like the monkey with the pliers. The witness disappears and we lose our awareness in the external object – whether a tool, another human being, or screen media. We fall into what is called in psychological terms an *object relation* with that tool or the person.

In an object relation we lose the inner witness, and we incorporate the external reality as if it were a part of our own psyche – for example, when we unconsciously consider a friend or a lover as a functional object standing in for the maternal or paternal relationship. Then we relate to the other person not as an individual with his/her distinctive characteristics, but as an object that is part of our inner structure and expectations.

Turkle (1984) explored how computers function as objects for our psychological patterns. We can merge with a technological object and include it in the constellation of our object relations. A computer can become an object which we relate to as a reassuring fusion with mother.

From Spectator to Witness

When we superimpose our expectations, projections and needs on reality, we are not too distant from the monkey which mistakes the pliers for his own hands. When we fit reality into our mental structures, we do not become one with reality in the way the ego is transcended and when we unite with the whole. We regress, instead, to a pre-conscious state, in which we don't differentiate what our projections are from what the reality is.

It may seem we have become one again, but we lose awareness on the way. Instead of becoming a witness of ourself, we become merely a spectator – bringing our attention toward the external, while forgetting our inner world.

The poet and stage director Bertolt Brecht believed that uncritical immersion into the theater of his epoch by spectators expanded the attraction of the Nazi choreography. Brecht created a theatrical technique that drew audience's attention back to themselves. It was a sort of self-remembering technique, as taught in the West by the mystic Gurdjieff. Since Brecht's time, the fascination with media has grown exponentially, so that today many media are distancing us from ourself, leaving our psyche open to manipulation.

Inner Holes and Techno-Fills

With or without technology, the development of a human being involves both growth and loss. This process of evolution of the soul develops the various inner qualities at different rates during the specific developmental stages. The loss – or lack – of various essential qualities of our soul can occur quite early.

Internalizing our object relations is an essential stage for the development of our personality, but they have to be understood and relinquished in the advanced stages of self-understanding. We need to feed our psyche through relating with others from the time we are born, perhaps even earlier. Later, we internalize those object relations and unconsciously project them on other people and tools – from teddy bears to Facebook. When those relationships fail to properly feed our soul with the needed qualities – as usually happens – we are left feeling the emptiness of our inner holes, which we then try to compensate for.

According to Almaas (1987), the stages in the development of a newborn baby begin with a state of unity. At about three months, a "merged" dual-unity arises that is essential for the development of the relationship with the mother. This period supports the development later of the qualities of Strength, Value, Joy, and the Personal Essence. But these can be only partial, due to interference from and conflict with an imperfect holding environment. Traumatic encounters obstruct specific qualities of Essence, depending on the nature of the trauma and developmental timing. When a quality is ultimately blocked, a feeling of emptiness – like a hole deep within us – accompanies our future life.

It is important for a newborn to enjoy the best psychological and physical care. Yet even with the luck of having had the most attentive familial and social conditions, the partial or total disappearance of the original qualities of the soul cannot be avoided. The process of personality formation itself, from the appearance of duality to the shrinking or disappearance of essential qualities, is inevitable.

In developing self-awareness through a psycho-spiritual path, we can rediscover the soul's essential qualities that were lost in the first years of life. We can even reach a state beyond duality, one quite different from the original indistinct, merged, non-dual state of the infant who lacked discrimination and awareness.

The absence of connection with the deepest aspects of our soul and the loss of the essential qualities leave a sense of emptiness – that we must be compensated for, somehow. Every human being, consciously or unconsciously, feels those empty spaces within them that need to become whole again – if not in a genuine manner, then with a substitute, like a pacifier for a baby. The mind itself will compensate through internalizing the object relations as well as through imagination.

The losses of parts of the soul are felt as amputations – which require prostheses to perceive wholeness again. The place of authentic essential qualities is taken by impostor aspects of the ego which simulate those qualities. For instance, the loss of essential Will – which gives the sense of a deep ground, like the support of the universe – might be compensated for by stubbornness and through pressing/stressing ourself. Strength can be replaced by arrogance; and Compassion by superficial sentimentality. This is the best the ego can do with its limited capacities.

Not knowing that every authentic quality can be found again in our depths, the search for compensation typically is directed to external tools. For historical and religious reasons, the need to extend our possibilities through technology originates from the need to recover parts of ourself that were lost along the path of life, a return to the wholeness of our original state.

In addition to extending our physical bodies – as with cars – we project our inner qualities on technology. For example, three basic aspects of the soul are Inner Peace, Intimacy and Personal Will. TV promises to satisfy our need for peace and relaxation through inducing a passive and receptive inner state. But at the same time it leaves us, as shown by several researchers, restless and frustrated once the viewing comes to an end. To appease this restlessness we seek out yet more TV.

Intimacy can be accessed through social networks and dating websites. When our connections expose the lack of deep contact, we feel even more isolated – and the solution is to find more connections through the Net.

The need for inner Will is projected on tireless machines which work incessantly for our good. This mechanization dominates awareness of our own Will, so we seek more automation and power through technologies.

Using the mind, we struggle to compensate for those qualities which were lost in a time even preceding the formation of the conceptual mind itself. As with a car in mud, the harder we try to get out, the deeper we become mired. Trying to gain anything through external tools can only start a vicious cycle, since the goal will never be reached that way.

In our dependence on technology to recover our completeness, we can become servomechanisms of technology. Lewis Mumford (1934) pointed out that since the advent of the clock, we have gone from timekeepers to time-savers to time-servers. And since the invention of the clock, technology has grown far more sophisticated and encompassing.

Pure Thinking Without the Body

For reasons similar to those which gave technology so much power, we have become disconnected from close, felt connection with our bodies. A sort of Cartesian "pure thinking" has taken precedence over other cognitive modalities.

When the first virtual systems appeared in the 1990s, Mark Slouka (1995) wrote that the context provided by the physical world enables us to judge good and bad. Birth, pain, pleasure and death provide the ground for judging what is preferable. By contrast, virtual systems give a reality divorced from the world, offering a view into a universe with no ethical ground.

The digital environment is basically disembodied. The body has a marginal role – or may even be seen as a hindrance. The roots of this attitude are to be found in the Judeo-Christian tradition which exiled the body to a role far from the divine – the very root of all sin. Our market society is recovering the body almost exclusively in hedonistic terms. Knowledge of our body translated into technical terms comes down to: What heart rate do I need to burn fat on the treadmill? What scores on my medical tests assure me I'm healthy? How can I improve my body-mind with certain chemicals? How can I re-engineer myself through genetic technology?

The relationship with the body easily turns digital when we approach it from outside, without felt connections. Bodies today are managed by technologies – from birth through our last breath. Several studies point out that proper brain development requires a baby to be in touch with the mother's breast, receiving stimulation from both the environment and from appropriate human contact. If deprived of these, intelligence and social skills will not develop correctly. Later the ego-mind is left to recapture something which only the heart, body, and awareness can.

The Western culture, in devaluing the body, negated as well the very roots of compassion which is *felt* in the intersection of body, mind, sensations, and ethical values. It is hard to feel compassion and empathy when there is no connection with an embodied reality. We thus remain unconcerned when the media show people being killed. Repeated exposure to virtuality can weaken our capacity for participation. Laing (1959) said, "the person who does not act in reality and only acts in fantasy becomes himself unreal" (p. 85).

Jerry Mander (1978), in his classic *Four Arguments for the Elimination of Television*, quoted an experience of journalist Jane Margold who entered a "mediated" version of a dramatic experience: "This is real; there's a wounded man lying here in front of me, bleeding to death, yet I have no feeling. It seems like a movie" (p. 236).

In negating the role of the body as a bridge to our soul, compassion becomes merely a mental state. Snatched away from our totality, compassion can then fit on Facebook with the hugging of a teddy bear, or writing "Hope you get better."

Tools for Inner Growth
There are tools and technology that have been employed to develop authentic human qualities. Chogyam Trungpa (1999), an adventurous Buddhist teacher who grew up in Tibet, recalls being attracted by Western life, thinking that Westerners must be very wise. When he was a boy he received a watch and took it completely apart to see how it worked. Though he tried to reassemble it, it would not run. When he was later given a clock that chimed, he took that apart as well. He compared the parts of both, laying them out side by side. Seeing the mistakes he had made with the watch, he was able to put both back together and, having cleaned them, they worked better than before. He was quite proud. Having no concept of factories,

he was very impressed with the discipline and patience required, based on all those little screws that somebody had made by hand. When he came to the West he met the makers of the machines that do wondrous things. He found that there was not much wisdom in the West, though there was lots of knowledge.

His attitude toward tools was as much an inner as an outer perception. Can the aspects of technology – like precision, perseverance and patience – be matched both in the manufacturing and internally? Are tools just a way to "get something done" and to extend our power? Or can they be applied for developing our inner qualities? Through tools, do we need to arrive as fast as possible at a result, without our actual presence and full attention? Or can we use them as instruments for training our souls?

Children use tools in a playful way, without needing to arrive anywhere. Often they discard what they build, for it is the activity of building that they enjoy. In Tibetan Buddhism, there is a practice of creating elaborate mandalas of colored sand. Once completed, sometimes after months of patient work, the mandala is swept away.

A very simple tool, like a small knife for carving ornaments out of wood, can be used with different attitudes. We could start with a design and a plan and look forward to finishing it as soon as possible. We might swear when we don't achieve the shape we envisioned, or be proud when we reach our goal. We could also start with no plan, simply feeling the contact with the wood and the tool, let the design flow according to the moment, integrating our "mistakes" into a novel design. We might consciously discover new skills with our hands, observe where the idea to do a certain thing comes from, look at the different feelings that occur during the carving – our joy, flow, frustration, and silence. In this way, we can develop attention, patience, awareness, and the ability to let go of plans and accept the ever-changing flow of life.

Technology in our culture is intended to give us more power, extension, and possibilities. The emphasis is on what we can *do* with certain tools, not on *how* we do it nor how a specific tool connects us with our inner states. The ego takes charge – after all, that is its job.

For the ego, every repetitive task after a while tends to become unconscious, and attention fades. The ego-mind craves novelties and is easily bored. Once automated, we are no longer there with our presence, attention and participation – since the task is outsourced to the machine. The ego wants goals and power.

The artificial intelligence scientist Marvin Minsky, talking about a new project at MIT at the end of 2009, pointed to the fact that his iPhone can download thousands of different applications, instantly allowing it to perform new functions. Why not do the same with the brain? "I would like to be able to download the ability to juggle. There's nothing more boring than learning to juggle" (quoted in Chandler, 2009).

Minsky believed we can separate the ability to juggle from the inner transformation which occurs in learning to juggle. Knowledge, in Descartes's style, is seen as something "pure," removed from our subjective participation and the involvement of our body-mind. If we see knowledge as something which can be represented digitally, then we should be able to download it into our neuro-physiology, as we do with software in a computer. This is what Kurzweil and others are forecasting.

When we don't give importance to our activities as instruments for growth, nor feel "presence" in our actions, then we want to automate everything that can be automated, including activities which could be helpful for the growth of our soul. The concern shifts from how boring or how useful an activity it is, to how it can shape our soul through the presence we give to that task. In Zen monasteries, even the most repetitive tasks – like cleaning rice and sweeping walkways –are used as a path for awareness. But the ego wants goals – and wants to reach them fast.

The use of tools has been advocated even by spiritual paths such as Zen. One of the classic books on Zen illustrates the path of soul realization through mastering archery:

> The archer ceases to be conscious of himself as the one who is engaged in hitting the bull's-eye which confronts him. This state of unconscious[ness] is realized only when, completely empty and rid of the self, he becomes one with the perfecting of his technical skill, though there is in it something of a quite different order which cannot be attained by any progressive study of the art (Herrigel, 1953).

This description sounds puzzling. The archer, who is supposed to have reached a high level of awareness, "ceases to be conscious of himself." He enters a "state of unconscious[ness] ...completely empty and rid of the self" and becomes one with the instrument. This looks more like the monkey who mistook the pliers for his hands.

But there are fundamental differences between *forgetting* ourself in an external tool and *letting go* of our ego while mastering a tool in a sacred way. As with the media, we abandon ourself prematurely; we let go of the presence and the connection with our body and inner happenings. Our mind becomes filled with information, but we lack the one-pointed attention necessary for mastering an inner discipline. The Zen archer goes through a long prac- tice of turning his awareness inside. His mind becomes empty till he can let go of his ego and hit the center in a state of no-mind.

The external target to hit with the arrow is a metaphor for the inner one. The bow and arrow in Zen are tools that act as a bridge to our inner self, not to an external goal. When we reach that cen- ter through Zen, we no longer identify ourself with the tool nor the goal – and not even with our ego. With Zen archery our mind be- comes completely empty – thus we can connect with everything. With IT we fill our mind till it becomes completely cluttered.

The Mind Itself is a Medium

Media can be employed as well for accessing our soul – consider photographs, novels and poems that move our attention from the external to the interior. According to McLuhan (1964), the inven- tion of the photograph may have led to a revolution in the tradi- tional arts. Then, since it was pointless trying to depict things that had already been shown more vividly in photographs, painters took to revealing the inner process of creativity through expressionism and abstract art.

Writers were similarly affected by photos, print media, film, and radio. Poets and novelists turned to explore the inner workings of the mind by which "we achieve insight and make ourselves and our world." Art moved from depiction of physical reality to the explo- ration of mind and soul with the various media competing against each other.

How about the computer and the Internet? Can they also turn into tools for inner exploration"?

The shift from using computers as productive tools to inner pro- cessing has been stimulated by blogs and social networks which allow us to share our inner lives and thoughts. However, the Net militates against the prolonged attention and silence of the painter or novelist. Like heating water into vapor, there needs to be a crit- ical mass of time without external interruptions in order to change inner states.

The unprecedented competition now is between the mind and the computer as extension/amputation of the mind. The computer manages and expands our mental capacities – memory, searching for information, calculating, analyzing data, planning routes, and much more. When "freed" of those tasks, our mind can give more attention to meta-thinking, to the mechanisms of our thoughts and their inner working.

But the computer, as the sum-of-all-media, expands our mind's possibilities toward external information – which promises to take us even farther away from developing the capacity to observe our mind. The computer mirrors our mind and charms us by the reflected image, just like Narcissus who was so hypnotized by his image in the pool that he could no longer hear Echo's love – so he was transformed into a plant standing close to the edge of the pond where he could always see his reflection.

We can acknowledge that the computer is a medium for outsourcing many of the mind's functions. But what's never considered is that the mind itself has the nature of a medium – a medium which incessantly builds reality, which can simulate the soul's qualities which were lost during development.

Mind is born of the amputation of the original completeness of the soul through the loss of merging with existence. The shock of this loss obliterates the recognition of our original nature. The only thing the mind can then do is simulate the lost wholeness by constructing an ego personality. As with Narcissus, we become numbed by our image reflected by the mind, believing that this self-image is who we really are.

One of the recurring themes of spiritual teachings is that our consciousness is asleep, and in order to awaken it, it is necessary to reel in the mind's contents with the introspective capacities acquired through meditation and inner exploration.

Just as dreams protects us from awakening by including external activity of the mind as part of their story, the mind keeps the illusion of awakeness through incessant activity. When the inner noise is not enough, it can create technologies which multiply the flow of information that calls us. All this makes self-observation difficult and prevents our soul from transcending the illusion.

The conceptual mind, born as a defense against the unbearable experience of separation, is nothing more than a medium which hides our genuine soul. So perhaps, perceiving a distant echo of that fact, we try to become free of it again by outsourcing it to a mechanical computer, so we can again look at reality without filters. But the very qualities of the mind which could free us from the illusion – sustained inner concentration, meditation and silence, feeling the body fully – are the first to be sequestered by IT. The ego-mind has many tricks to retain its dominance.

Our mind, which builds the illusory reality (*maya*), was created by the fall from the soul's primordial condition of wholeness. Computers, simulating the mind, then dazzle us as a reflection of a reflection – a double layer of illusion. This further layer has the potential to stimulate the revelation of the primary illusion. The *Ad-*

vaita tradition invokes the metaphor of a thorn used to dig out another thorn that is buried in the foot, but is then thrown away along with the invader.

The state of self-forgetting and the use of the limited set of mental capacities needed for interacting with digital technologies will not bring us in touch again with our depths. We need to balance the overwhelming attention we give to information with some practices to bring back our fullest cognitive skills – which are mindfulness, subtle discrimination, prolonged attention, and the inner silence out of which creativity can arise.

IT Weakens Our Presence

The very Will to look inside becomes weakened by IT – which also weakens the aliveness of the body, the grounding from which Will is expressed. Our presence, our awareness of inner and outer happenings, and our ability to act from our depth become weaker. On a neurophysiological level, the frontal lobes, which give broad vision and the capacity for long-term planning, are being stunted by long exposure to digital technologies.

Mindfulness and the love of truth are the capacities that can lead us to dissolving the mental structures that imprison us in our old conditioning. They can even expose the primary events which separated us from the immensity of the original whole state.

Spiritual paths, in moving us toward self-understanding, give back to the heart and the belly their roles which have been usurped by the mind. It is said that the path toward enlightenment is a path beyond the mind, or toward a "no-mind" state. This is often misunderstood as a passive state where the mind just becomes still, and maybe even dumb. The image of silent meditators under a tree with stony expressions remains a popular image.

The mind, in fact, does not become any less efficient when it reaches spiritual states. As Gurdjieff said, it reverts to its role of servant when the real master returns home and higher consciousness is foremost. In the absence of the master, the servant usurps the role, even keeping the house from collapsing in the face of no clear direction. The passage from the mind to higher consciousness happens through self-observation. The role of spiritual inquiry is not to annihilate the mind, but to integrate it. It is necessary to *have* a mind before overcoming it – possibly even a well-functioning mind.

When the basic skills of the mind are being managed by computers, we might believe we can shift our attention to more creative endeavors. Not burdened by mechanical thoughts, we should be able to devote our mind to higher pursuits like art, philosophy, or spirituality. One of the promises of technology has always been to "free" us from effort and repetitive tasks – starting with mechanical tools which have taken over much of our manual work, and now IT which makes our intellectual tasks easier.

With the basic mental tasks outsourced to computers, we could use our consciousness for self-knowledge and for investigating the internal processes of our mind. We could focus on the mind's mechanisms for deconstructing our conditioning, and getting to know our mind-medium from the inside. This is the goal of every spiritual path for transitioning from intellect to wisdom, from mind to no-mind, from ego to enlightenment.

But IT seems better able to lock us in the loop of information than to stimulate higher capacities for self-understanding. Survival of ego-mind is in fact supported by IT – yet at the same time IT fragments it, leaving it permanently "under construction." The end-less stream of information keeps us on the same level – only the shapes change, as in a kaleidoscope.

Through IT we risk the atrophy of basic mental skills without developing any higher capacities in return. Part of the mind's func-tion is to hide from us its nature as something created, having no real substance. Mind has even engineered computers to hijack our observing capacities so we cannot see the mind as the unreal con-struction that it is.

> First... you use your mind as the ultimate jigsaw. You take Totality and cut it up into a million tiny pieces. Then... having tired of that game you sit down and try to reassemble this jumble of pieces into something comprehensible. Ram Tzu knows... God invented time just so you could do this (Ram Tzu, 1990).

CHAPTER 3

THE ROOTS OF IT

Constrained to Produce

In the West there are layers of deep conviction that keep us bound to the idea that everything good will come from economic and technological development. Despite a few doubting voices, those beliefs have been part of our society for so long that they've become taken for granted, part of the collective unconscious. The forces behind the "will to produce" can be seen as a self-reinforcing loop.

1) *The expectation of a better world* (social welfare, peace, justice, democracy, rights) through production, distribution and consumption of goods and technologies.

2) *The necessity to intervene in the entire world to achieve such goals.* Exploitation of natural resources is essential to grease the machinery of production. Easy access to the earth's resources requires the consent of governments. The consequence is the exportation of economic, political and cultural systems – a phenomenon known as globalization.

3) *All actions are carried out compulsively and in a rush*, a crucial factor which hinders the ability to be aware of the social and environmental consequences that will be wrought in the middle/long run. It also hinders our capacity as individuals to slow down and reflect.

4) *The radiant future envisioned never arrives*, despite what has been achieved up to that point. The only solution is to increase production. There is never "enough."

5) *We are back at point 1.* This mechanism looks much like the vicious cycle typical of drug addiction.

Although this vision of the world is predominant in ideologies such as "democratic market economics," the Western world is entirely permeated by it. The roots of this thinking are more ancient than the political/social divisions that have emerged with the industrial revolution.

While the basic Western ideas seem to belong exclusively to the political system we call capitalism, even its historical antagonist, Marxism, envisages a similar heavenly condition for mankind. Marx thought that by reappropriating the means of production – machines – people would be freed from exploitation, bringing equality, peace, and progress.

The mythological communist cycle is essentially similar to the capitalist one:
1) There's the vision of a better world through access to the instruments of production.
2) The need to act on a worldwide scale (the Communist International, "workers of the world unite").
3) There is compulsion and rush in the race against capitalism.
4) Work is for a bright future that never comes – every communist society has been in a perennial "transition to communism."

IT was Started by the Bible
The deep roots of the idea that technology will bring a better world come from the Judeo-Christian tradition. The Bible says that God created humankind at the very end of creation. The world and everything in it existed before human beings – and it is all fundamentally different from mankind which was created in God's image and likeness. That leaves the rest of the universe as something objective, "out there," devoid of the divine element. Having souls, consciousness, and free will are what make human beings unique and superior.

Alan Wallace in *The Taboo of Subjectivity* (2000) analyzed how Western inquiry and research have been directed only at the "objective" side of creation, rather than at human subjectivity:

> In order for man to comprehend God's creation, he must divest his modes of inquiry of all that is merely human, which, after all, came at the very end of creation. Man must explore the universe in ways that approximate God's own perspective on creation. He must seek to view the world beyond the confines of his own subjectivity, just as God transcends the natural world. In short, he must seek a purely *objective* (divine) God's-eye view and banish all *subjective* (profane) influences from his empirical and analytical research into the objective universe. In this way, the seeds of objectivism were introduced into Mediterranean thought by Jewish, Christian, and Muslim theology (p. 41).

The scriptures say that only human beings were created in God's own image and likeness. However, according to this tradition, humankind will never be able to completely reach the divine in this earthly life, with one exception: Jesus Christ. The Bible also says that nature was created so that human beings could make use of it for their own benefit. Man, therefore, has the right, bestowed on him by a superior authority, to use creation for his goals.

Christianity adds the concepts of sin and free will. Human beings, although born into original sin, are also given free will – therefore, they can decide whether to act for good rather than evil, and thus redeem themselves. These messages have been essential for the technological and social development of the West.

In the ancient Taoist culture, tools were known but intentionally discarded. In classical Greece, the massive development in art and philosophy did not arise with any big technical development. "They could not even devise ways of using horsepower efficiently. Both Plato and Aristotle scorned the 'base mechanic arts,' probably in the belief that nobility of mind was not enhanced by efforts to increase efficiency or productivity" (Postman, 1993, p. 25).

Technology as Returning to the Lost Perfection

David F. Noble (1997) analyzed the events that led to the current relationship man has with technology in the Christian world. He concluded that the dynamism of Western technology has its actual roots and spirit in the Middle Ages. In classic Christianity, manual activities were disregarded, but in the early Middle Ages technology began to be identified with transcendence, linked to the Christian concept of redemption from sin.

As time went on, technology became more clearly identified with the possibility of renewing human perfection after the Fall. Erigena, one of the most important forces in medieval Christian Scholastic philosophy, affirmed that knowledge of the arts, innate in the perfect man, was in time clouded by the Fall. However, its recovery, through study and hard work, could help restore man, at least partially, to his pristine state. Progress in the "useful arts" became the identification mark of the divine image in mankind. Learning the useful arts was preparation for redemption.

Technology as a route to transcendence was particularly strong during the later puritan revolution – which shaped the beginning of capitalism with its colonial aims by linking "faith" and "useful arts" with "the glory of God" and the recovery of control over nature. New scientific ventures of that time widened the fields of human intervention.

Recovering our lost perfection was no longer enough. Science was progressively expanding toward divine knowledge. And action – no longer limited to the original creation –was moving toward a new creation. The Christian project of redemption through practical actions started to slip out of hand, however, as scientists began to consider themselves creators.

Francis Bacon foresaw that mankind one day would create new species and become like gods, because "the footsteps of the Creator [were] imprinted on his creatures" (Noble, 1997, p. 67). Science has carried on the work of giving man dominion over nature, as originally bestowed by the Bible. In so doing, it has also demonstrated that man is created in God's image and likeness through divine acts.

To recapitulate the messages that Christians have received: Human beings should consider themselves special within creation, though basically they are sinners. They have the chance to redeem themselves through good deeds, which include technological creations. To do this, nature is at their disposal.

But there is a problem. Good deeds will not bear fruit during the earthly life of doers. In fact, according to the scriptures, eternal life and happiness belong only to the kingdom of heaven. All we can do in this lifetime is prepare to deserve our future afterlife by our virtuous actions.

However, one could argue, a man has existed who was joined with the divine while in human form: Jesus. The Bible, though, considers Jesus God's only son, and no one else can ever aspire to such a state. All we can do is imitate his example. We cannot meet the divine in this life – at best we can only deserve that in the future.

In scriptural truth, there is another way to reach the divine: salvation at the end of time, after a phase of calamity and destruction: the Apocalypse.

New recap: human beings have a special place in creation, but they were born in sin. Using their free will, they can redeem themselves through their actions, emphasizing creation to this end – but they cannot expect to meet the divine in this lifetime, because that was exclusively for Jesus. They have the chance to enter the kingdom of heaven in the future, presumably after death (if they have behaved well enough), unless they live during apocalyptic times.

In contrast to those religions which contemplate reincarnation, Christianity clearly states that we live only one life on Earth. Therefore, there is no second chance. Redemption from sin must be attained in *this* lifetime. Which demands another ingredient: haste. If we are in a rush to act for "good," our lack of responsibility in preventing the future consequences of our actions is inevitable. And if we stop producing, developing, expanding our interventions in the world, we will feel lost and our lives will lack meaning.

God can give us signals to guide our choices toward redemption. But since we have free will, the act of redemption depends entirely on us. If we behave badly, we will wind up in eternal damnation. However, even if we do good in the world, we won't benefit from it in this lifetime.

Contradictory Messages Short Circuit the Psyche
After receiving such messages, human beings find themselves trapped in a series of double binds – which were defined by Gregory Bateson (1972) as contradictory messages with a highly emotional content, lacking both an exit route and a clear interpretation of the messages themselves. For instance, someone asking for a hug, but then becoming cold and stiff when approached. Bateson conjectured that such double binds could lead to schizophrenia.

Here are the double binds of life in the West:

We were born in the image of God and must imitate the virtuous actions of Jesus, but we are never able to reach his connection with God.

We have to redeem ourself through doing good deeds, but have no certainty of attaining salvation.

We are separate from the world and special, and are to exploit nature for our own aims, but since in reality human beings – both environmentally and spiritually – are not separate from the world, the attempt to relate to nature as a separate entity will necessarily lead to alienation and to digging our own graves through environmental disaster.

We are to work for eternal salvation and a bright future, but it will never come in this lifetime.

Confused and anxious to free ourself from the labyrinths of double binds, we try to resolve them by creating heaven on Earth – by using technology for our salvation. We feel fine when our conscience is clear because we perform virtuous actions, however separate they are from the integrated world. But despite virtuous action, we can never be like Jesus, as we are unsure of achieving salvation. Therefore, technology leads to the search for a pseudo-salvation within this earthly life – such as using biotechnologies to operate on the divine plane of creation and immortality. The same culture that has considered miracles as proof of the existence of God has now developed technologies that resemble the miraculous.

To abandon the drive toward production with its search for

miraculous technologies would also mean abandoning hope of redemption and salvation. We must also then let go of the idea that mankind has a special place in creation, concomitantly releasing the individual identity built on what we have "done" in life. Individual action can lead to redemption on Earth, but without being able to act on nature, human beings would feel lost, crushed by guilt feelings.

Children of a Lesser God
As God has only one son, Jesus, man feels like the unworthy pseudo-son (on top of being born in sin). Redemption, then, as in the personality type Five of the Enneagram (an introduction to which can be found in the Appendix), comes by withdrawing, specializing, and then coming back to show off his abilities – which through technology have become as powerful as the divine's. Technology becomes a way to show God we are as good in producing miracles as Jesus was, and so regain the approval of a God who punishes us for our original sin. If He won't accept us, at least we have made a heavenly Earth by creating the radiant future in this very life.

But of the promise of heaven on Earth and the radiant future, that carrot we have been chasing for so long has become rotten, environmentally and socially. Nature, which was supposed to be at our disposal, does not meekly bend to human whims – and when its delicate balance is disturbed, it turns dangerously against us.

The vision of a happier future is no more than a mirage. Yet we cannot live in the present, because we have never practiced doing so. We work more and more, we consume more and more, but we never feel we have enough – and actually become less and less happy. Even economic development, science, and technology – once our pride – are betraying us, as they turn out to be incapable of addressing environmental and social crises.

Psychological Defenses
Frustrated and pressed between a gloomy future and an unhappy present, the schizoid man reacts with defense mechanisms.

Denying everything and going straight toward a liberating apocalypse
Examples of this are denying that climate change is our responsibility, that natural resources are running out. In the Christian world, Apocalypse is firmly linked to redemption, to salvation for all. Therefore, if the future will be apocalyptic, even if caused by our own doing, it will bring liberation. Otherwise what is the explana-

The Digitally Divided Self

tion for the amazingly little responsibility we take for our future, despite refined models and scientific knowledge which give us the awareness of what is really happening?

Pushing for more growth
Another tentative way out is pressing the development pedal through increasing trade, lowering interest rates, printing money, promoting consumption, avoiding stopping, reflecting and metabolizing the tragic path our culture is leading us along.

Technology as the Ultimate Savior
One of the leading themes of the West is the redemptive image of a bright future. Such a vision, applied to industrial society, has witnessed the birth of different myths to obtain a limitless source of energy, thus freeing all humankind from the pain it was condemned to after the Fall.

The myth of an infinite source of energy we can freely draw from is a projection of heaven on Earth. The myth of our infinite divine nature fails because we don't believe we really are divine, being born in sin and incapable of attaining what only Christ had. In the last few centuries technological visionaries searched for the ultimate energy source – from the coal-driven steam engine to electricity, to oil, then passing beyond nuclear power plants to cold fusion, hydrogen, and finally renewable sources.

Historically, every time a new technology or source of energy was introduced, it was welcomed in transcendent terms, as if it were a way back to a heavenly condition.

Morison, a pioneer of railroad engineering who became the leading bridge-builder of his day, described the technology of his time in evangelic terms:

> No changes have ever equalled those through which the world is passing now [Morison wrote]; "the new epoch differs from all preceding epochs" and will create an entirely "new civilization." This epoch will see the final and "inevitable" destruction of "savagery," "barbarism," "ignorance," and "superstition." And in its wake, "mankind must settle down to a long period of rest," marked by "contentment," "comfort," and "happiness." Moreover, "it will not be the condition of a town nor of a nation but of the whole earth, with nothing to change it unless communication should be opened with another planet (Noble, 1997, p. 95).

The printing press, the telegraph, railways, radio, TV, space technology, telecommunications and the Internet have all been welcomed in cure-all terms.

M. Kaki quoted *Scientific American*, June 1996:

Computer networking offers the soundest basis for world peace that has yet been presented. Peace must be created on the bulwark of understanding. International computer networks will knit together the peoples of the world in bonds of mutual respect: its possibilities are vast, indeed (Kaki, 1996).

But the quote was a joke. The sentence was actually from *Scientific American*, but 50 years earlier, and it was about TV. Substitute "computer networking" for "TV." Something similar happened in the field of education.

Larry Cuban, professor of education at Stanford University, has documented how U.S. education policymakers have careened from one new technology to the next – lantern slides, tape recorders, movies, radios, overhead projectors, reading kits, language laboratories, televisions, computers, multimedia, and now the Internet – sure each time that they have discovered educational gold. Eventually, the glimmer always fades and we find ourselves holding a lump of pyrite – fool's gold (Alliance for Childhood, 2000, p. 97).

The Nature of the Mind

Much of the environmental destruction can be blamed on the political, economic, and technical forces in society – but there's an attitude of the mind behind that. If the world's governments could promote renewable resources as a priority, the state of the planet would certainly improve. But unless we become deeply aware of the roots of our yearning, there will be no resource – however effective, clean and renewable – that will ever satisfy the black hole of "not having enough."

Double bind messages by religions have an important role in the mechanisms that lead us to compulsive production, but they are not the deepest cause of the greed. Ultimately, it's the process of construction of the ego itself that leads us to think that we are something special within creation. Ramesh Balsekar (1992) says:

Intellect is what enables the human being to discriminate and interpret what is cognized, which the animal need not do. So it is this power of the intellect to discriminate and interpret what is cognized that gives the individual being a sense of individuality and makes him consider himself something special in this manifestation. What is more, he goes to the extent of believing that the entire manifestation has been created for his benefit! So, all the time he is thinking, "In what way can I benefit by exploiting nature?" And the extent to which the human being had "benefited" himself, we can all see (p. 16).

Even the roots of the hope for a brighter future come from further away than technology and Christianity. Almaas (1996) illustrates this point:

> The center of the ego-self, the center of its initiative, action and perception, is a psychic structure characterized by a specific pattern and by incessant psychological activity. The pattern, or the particular psychic organization, provides the direction of action, while the activity provides the drive to act. This gives the self a sense of orientation, center and meaning. The psychological activity includes hope – the self is hoping, consciously or unconsciously, to achieve its aim or ideal. This implies that we project on the future the possibility of accomplishing a certain objective... Hope initiates desire (p. 85).

The nature of the mind is more ancient than religion. The will of the ego to achieve unlimited power is a vague hint of the infinite spiritual nature present in every human being. Reaching this inner infinite is the real quest – but it has been appropriated by the ego-mind and implemented by technology as a will to power.

Human beings have the potential to know themselves as divine. Not even the ego can ignore the call of the infinite, so it does what it can in its own limited plane, trying to become something "more."

> [Spiritual] Realization proposes no transformation of the finite by violence, because its nature is to love and not hate limitation. The entire chaos of the Western world springs from this radical separation of creation and redemption, prompting the technological attempt to transform nature by violent alteration (Watts, 1950, p. 188).

Conceptual Debris and Technology as a Holding Agent for the Psyche

The last few centuries of Western philosophy and science have dismantled many of the certainties carefully built over the previous centuries, beginning with Kant who discerned the limits of the mind in understanding the "thing in itself." Then Nietzsche and Heidegger challenged the nature of reality and our capacity to understand it. While Gödel found the limits of any formal system, quantum scientists shook our sense of reality by the roots.

Neuroscience added doubt about the nature of the individual self and the existence of our free will. Now artificial intelligence has begun to deconstruct our thinking processes. In recent decades we have witnessed the end of ideologies, and religions have shown their darker underbellies. We are ethically and ideologically emptied, and economically and environmentally threatened.

No more certainties are left under the sun. To defend against the insecurities this has engendered, we of the twenty-first century react in different ways. One is backward: clinging to old certainties through religious sects and territorial identities, bringing a surge in fundamentalism, parochialism and racism.

Another reaction is giving up. With no certainties and no hope, many people become depressed. Now there's a third way. Postman (1993) wrote: "Amid the conceptual debris, there remained one sure thing to believe in – technology" (p. 55).

The Quest for Immortality

With the certainties of the mind threatened by philosophy, epistemology and science, the technological being starts a quest for immortality, especially as immortality of his mind – which is the entity supposed to be closest to God.

The mind is considered the highest expression of human beings. There is historical precedence for the quest for immortality of the mind. The printing press, for example, was initially considered a tool for immortality, because people could leave a record of their thoughts for future generations. The ultimate upgrade would be to download our minds to the Net, preserving the contents forever.

Bright scientists and powerful entrepreneurs are supporting such a project. Larry Ellison, president of Oracle, one of the most powerful IT companies, sponsors the Immortality Institute, an organization with the mission "To conquer the blight of involuntary death."

Google and NASA are backing the Singularity University, whose chancellor is the immortality proponent Ray Kurzweil. Singularity University brings corporate leaders, students and entrepreneurs together to study the "unprecedented advancement caused by the accelerating development of various technologies, including biotechnology, nanotechnology, artificial intelligence, robotics and genetics."

Ray Kurzweil, futurist, brilliant inventor, and author of *The Singularity is Near: When Humans Transcend Biology* (2005) looks forward to an era when humans, in their evolution, will be linked to machines through electronics and biotechnology. His research and inventions range from music to artificial intelligence, from speech recognition to optics. Kurzweil defines The Singularity as "an era in which our intelligence will become increasingly nonbiological and trillions of times more powerful than it is today – the dawning of a new civilization that will enable us to transcend our biological limitations and amplify our creativity."

Kurzweil and Grossman (2004) forecast the enhancement of our intelligence by merging our brains with nonbiological intelligent nanobots, so our neurons can communicate with nanobots on a local area network. We'll be online all the time, directly from our brains, communicating with other brains through the network.

This quest parallels the search for radical life extension – even immortality. He believes that through biotech we're developing the tools to reprogram our biology at the most fundamental level. When Kurzweil was interviewed by *What is Enlightenment* magazine (now *EnlightenNext*), he stated that we are at the intersection of IT and biology where we understand life, death, disease and aging as information processes.

In his opinion, with our knowledge we can start to reprogram genes which are looked at as software codes. Merging our biological intelligence with nonbiological intelligence will vastly expand human intelligence, so that the thinking process will be a hybrid of the two. The nonbiological portion will be much more powerful, giving birth to new and enhanced forms of intelligence. In Kurzweil's words:

> This also relates to longevity, because the reality of longevity for nonbiological systems is different than for biological systems. Right now, the software of our lives is the information in our brains. I estimate it to be thousands of trillions of bytes, which represents all of our memories and experiences and skills and just the whole state of our brain. So that's software, and it's inextricably tied up with our hardware. When the hardware of our brain crashes, the software dies with it (Hamilton, 2005).

Kurzweil considers our whole live as information files which he calls the "mind file." When the information in our brain becomes independent of the hardware, then we might have reached the stature of immortality. He was asked, "What would you say to the idea that it's unnatural to want immortality? That this quest for life extension goes against the natural cycles of birth and death, and that if we attained immortality, we would have stepped so far outside the natural order that in some sense, we would no longer be human?" He responded that in his view, our species is unique in that we constantly endeavor to transcend the natural boundaries of what we can be. We have not remained confined by our biology to terra firma, nor even by the limitations of our intelligence. The highest purpose of human life is the development of knowledge in all its facets, from art to science and technology (Hamilton, 2005).

Behind Kurzweil's motivation for immortality there's a poignant story. His father Fredric died when he was still a boy. They shared many conversations about music and science and he tried to please his father in many ways, being a bright young inventor. Kurzweil said in a *Rolling Stone* interview (Febuary, 2009) that through his father's DNA and nanobots which could roam in people's brains to look for recollections related to his father, one day he could reconstruct his father's mind and give him a form, like a virtual-reality avatar or a fully functioning robot. He responded to being asked what the first thing he'd say to his father would be, "Remember those conversations we had about creating musical sound by computer, and how they could be ultimately better than analog computers? Well, I actually did work on that."

I was touched by the amount of love he had for his late father. At the same time, I can't avoid seeing Kurzweil as still a kid seeking his father's approval, not accepting his departure, and wanting to reconstruct his mind to continue an interrupted connection. I'm sure, though, that he shared much more than "mind-files" with his father.

Copying, Improving and Creating Minds
Kurzweil is not the first to forecast a messianic world driven by technology – and he won't be the last. If the mind is considered the ultimate in evolution, then we can point it in the direction of being a more efficient, more powerful and an everlasting mind, supported by electronics and genetic engineering.

In a 1969 interview with *Playboy*, McLuhan compared the electronic media to the Second Coming of Christ, in terms of fervor:

> Psychic communal integration made possible at last by the electronic media could create the universality of consciousness foreseen by Dante when he predicted that men would continue as no more than broken fragments until they were unified into an inclusive consciousness. In a Christian sense, this is merely a new interpretation of the mystical body of Christ; and Christ, after all, is the ultimate extension of man (McLuhan, quoted by Harkin, 2009, p. 58).

We find the roots of the drive to download our minds on the Net as far back as 1964 when McLuhan wrote that "having extended or translated our central nervous system into the electromagnetic technology, it is but a further stage to transfer our consciousness to the computer world as well" (p. 60).

Another radical proponent of technologies, Hans Moravec (1999), stated that the mind's contents could be copied on a mechanical device – and perhaps even transplanted like any other organ. He postulated that while the capabilities of a biological brain might be enhanced far beyond its natural lifespan by an optimal physical environment, it is unlikely to function effectively forever, since it evolved to operate only for a human lifetime. Instead, advanced neurological electronics could, in his view, replace it gradually as it begins to fail. Superior electronic equivalents may bring better clarity to our personality and thoughts, though our original body or brain may not remain.

In this rejection of the natural transformational cycle of the human mind, there is denial of the wisdom of ages of evolution in the processes of birth, growth, decay, and death. What our society (including a large part of neuroscience) does not see is that even though the short-term memory of the elderly and the speed of their mental processing no doubt decrease, what is called "presence" of the soul and the awareness matured during life isn't much affected by age-related factors – it actually becomes steadier.

Rather, decreased mental abilities may have even evolved in order to lessen our identification with our mental contents and to naturally slow down the mental activity, thus giving space to the observation of thoughts, as happens during meditation. Yet the transformation of limitations into human qualities might happen only if during our lifetime we exercised our deeper awareness; and if we accepted letting go of our identifications as a growth rather than a loss; and if we could accept the experience of empty space without considering it as a lack of something.

It is true, as Kurzweil says, that human beings don't need to follow only the biological course. As conscious beings we have the ability to overcome the limitations of the biological plane both at the bodily and at the spiritual levels. But while Kurzweil and Moravec see this development as something brought from an external technology, thousands of years of inner meditation "technology" have been effective in changing the direction of the "natural" mechanisms of the mind which identifies with its thoughts. A spiritual path can free the mind without preserving it in a mechanical medium, and can attain immortality within awareness.

In societies less productive than ours, elders are considered wise people much sought-after for guidance, while in our society they are considered useless. If our intellectual development is not matched by a parallel growth of the soul's qualities, decay of the intellect becomes a major problem, since there is nothing to substitute for its qualities as its unavoidable decline progresses.

While it is possible to delay the mind's biological decay with food supplements and a healthy lifestyle, substituting the mind with neuronal electronics prevents the natural process of disidentifying from the body-mind as we age. New research points out that older brains may truly be wiser brains, compensating for slowness with a broader amount of data in the field of awareness.

The technological dream of transcending the body and acquiring an immortal mind is a revival of the separation between the "impure" body and the "divine" mind promoted both by Christianity and Cartesian science. The vision of Hans Moravec – who is perhaps the most visible, yet only a representative of the collective dream – moves toward preserving the identification with the mind beyond a connection with a biological body, cleaving to identity with the mind's contents, while passing indifferently through biological and electronic supports.

What then would be the subjective state of our minds on the Net? According to some artificial intelligence and artificial life specialists, we will be conscious because the Internet itself will become self-aware. "It might already have a degree of consciousness," said Ben Goertzel, chair of the Artificial General Intelligence Research Institute. And Francis Heylighen, who studies consciousness and artificial intelligence at the Free University of Brussels (VUB) concurs: "Adding consciousness is more a matter of fine-tuning and increasing control... than a jump to a wholly different level" (Brooks, 2009).

Consciousness is seen by science as a by-product of a growing complexity of information, something which "emerges," while in fact it is found on an entirely different level.

CHAPTER 4

THE DIGITIZATION OF REALITY

The technological society increasingly permeates more segments of our life. Social connections, finance, work, research, news, dating, entertainment, shopping are some of the activities that have moved massively to the Net. These call out different qualities of our soul that have functioned in vastly different external settings.

Our inner attitude shifts as we work, shop, talk to a friend, or communicating with someone we are intimately attracted to. Different archetypes, muses, and aspects of our psyche activate us as we move from offices and laboratories to homes, nature, shops, and beds.

As different parts of ourself are drawn on, inner qualities, mind, and body can remain integrated. However, when we engage in this variety of activities in front of a screen, our setting is constant – and our mind utilizes a limited set of skills (speed, efficiency, rationality), while our body remains mostly in the background

Regardless of what we are doing online, we use predominantly the same mind channels to interact with the computer, and there is no substantial difference whether we operate on Windows, Mac or Linux. Using the same modality for dating, shopping, communicating with friends, sexual arousal and scientific research impoverishes most of these activities.

Separation of the immortal mind from the mortal body by religions and philosophies formed the basis for representing intelligence and life in digital terms. Despite our neurophysiology telling us that our reason *is* embodied, this separation goes on. Our mind can't function separated from our body. There is no "pure mind." Concepts and reason are as much embodied processes as the digestion of food.

Yet because of the separation, how we interact with the computer is fertile territory for psychological ego defense mechanisms – in particular rationalization, dissociation, and splitting. These defenses are activated when the ego is feeling threatened – and are a protection against the re-emergence of the irrational states experienced during adolescence and difficult stages of adult life (Zanarini, 1985). Digital media can reassure us with their (supposed) predictability – we can feel in charge of a situation with just a click or a touch to the screen

Mathematicians, engineers, logicians, and philosophers have all contributed to understanding the mind in terms of its mechanical operation. George Boole, Charles Babbage, Ada Lovelace, and Bertrand Russell created the bases for representing the thinking process in such mathematical terms that it could be replicated by a machine. Postman (1997) looking at Babbage's realization of mechanically manipulating non-numeric symbols, compared it to the third century Greek discovery that each letter of the alphabet had not only a unique sound, but that they could be grouped together into written words. They could then be used for the classification, storage and retrieval of information.

Measurements and numbers are the essential components of the digitization of reality. The philosopher Comte, the father of positivism, regarded anything which could not be measured as unreal. Measurement of matter could be applied to human beings, establishing an equivalence between people and objects. Without numbers and quantitative values, the "exact" sciences would be lost – but so, then, would the humanistic disciplines like sociology and psychology.

We grade students with numbers (or substitutes for numbers). We calculate intelligence with an IQ index. Most of medical science is about numerical values related to physiological parameters. I recently saw an advertisement for a toothbrush bragging that it "enters 50% deeper between teeth and removes 25% more bacteria." *That* information – numeric – we can trust.

Consciousness, however, cannot be measured – much less any subjective inner state or ethical behavior. Thus human values lie beyond the purview of the information society. Magatti (2009) concluded that in techno-functional systems, the world is seen as a calculable objectivity, and its measurement is equivalent to truth. This way a chronic discrepancy has been created – in that whatever is outside technical modalities, like non-scientific language, can never be elevated to "real" or "truth."

Paradoxically, calculations and mathematical models of reality – considered the ultimate objectivity and understanding of reality – create, instead, space for illusion and unreality. Building models of reality based on the manipulation of data detached from the organic, ethical and spiritual levels, can easily create models which only apparently match what is authentic. One example is the financial bubble which continued inflating, with few people warning about its divergence from the reality of true value.

Rationality itself, efficient in manipulating views and data to stake a logical claim, can deceive us as much as irrationality.

Data is King

The power of data is manifest in the massive data centers that major IT companies have built. Google, Microsoft, Amazon, Yahoo, Facebook, all have hundreds of thousands of servers, working in parallel and managing huge volumes of data on the order of petabytes (a million billion bytes). (Those data centers, which allow us to work more efficiently, coincidentally consume increasing amounts of energy, despite more efficient microprocessors.)

Chris Anderson (2008), in an article for *Wired*, wrote that with the amount of information available for processing nowadays, theory and models are no longer needed to make sense of the world – statistics and mathematical analysis are enough. He points specifically to Google, which does not fret about models. Peter Norvig, Google's research director, said it clearly: "All models are wrong, and increasingly you can succeed without them."

This attitude appeals both to people who perceive the limits of models and even paradigms, as well as to people who just don't care about models and complex thought. Models have been mauled in the last century and certainties have been demolished by both philosophers and quantum scientists, so that we are losing the ground beneath our feet.

The last centuries have seen the melting of our accurately-erected certainties. From Kant, who saw the limits of the mind in understanding the "thing in itself," through Gödel's incompleteness theorems, which demonstrated the inherent limitations in formal systems, to Heisenberg's uncertainty principle, we have been thrown into doubt about the possibility of knowing physical reality. This is what Edgar Morin (1986) meant about there being no certainty base, no founding truth – that the very idea of a foundation is collapsing along with the idea of ultimate analysis, ultimate cause, and primary explanation. The terrain we are left to live in is data. Looking for truth, on the other hand, is both an inner activity for our soul and an outer exploration of external and objective – historical and psychological – material.

Even though we cannot arrive at the ultimate truth through models created by the mind, we can reach ever-more refined approximations of truth. However, Anderson pointed out the impossibility of using the scientific method with such enormous quantities of data available. Hypothesizing, experimenting, and data analysis are now unwieldy. His attitude means that what *works* is being promoted as "true." Yet it is consciousness that gives meaning to information.

In fact, giving data so much importance is its own ideological model, born from the belief that through digital data we can understand, reproduce, and process reality. The way IT companies organize and interpret data is also a model in itself. In Postman's (1993) opinion, though *Technopoly*'s experts are experts only in their specialized fields, they still claim knowledge of all other matters as well. When data is allowed to rule, it can be regarded as a tool for understanding, and then acting upon, any aspect of our human canvas. It becomes a totalitarian model to which reality must be made to fit. So we find our culture in the situation, to use Postman's example, where it is not enough to stand up for desegregating schools, but it must be proven with standard tests that reveal that segregated blacks score worse and feel humiliated.

The Digitization of Territory

Our planet is losing traditional civilizations, animal and plant species, forests and rivers – leaving us humans with a sense of loss and anxiety for the future. Not to mention the mess of our economies.

There is little acknowledgement that the problem is in our attitude – giving ego the predominant role and ignoring the spiritual aspects of life. Our civilization has little capacity to go beyond the constructs of the mind – and our answer to the uncertainties is to push the intellectual aspects even more, creating the world anew from that level.

The Net has expanded its role in the re-creation of reality. When the Web was first introduced, we could only explore data. It allowed us mostly to hunt for information and when obtained, our task was completed.

Communication occurred mostly through email and real-time chats. Within a few years blogs, gaming communities, and social networking sites emerged. People began to spend more time on sites, enriching them with their own writings, pictures, videos, music and thoughts – the way they might personalize a new apartment they move into. Then a more encompassing capacity appeared – to build and inhabit virtual spaces. Second Life and similar virtual worlds went in the direction of building alternative realities from scratch.

When somebody noticed that good old reality still wasn't online, Google, Microsoft and others raided the territory with cameras to digitize, mirror, and present the world in the form of data. Mirror worlds like Google Earth appeared that invite us to roam and fly about digital territory to discover layers of territorial data.

Those layers could bring awareness to an environmentally devastated territory. But from the safety of our screens, we don't necessarily feel the implications for our practical and inner lives. Through Second Life or Google Earth, we are creating on the Net a new earth – a digital earth which we can mold to our wishes – which allows us to deny the loss and avoid responsibility for a devastated world. We trade the reality of our precious earth for other options, designed according to our dreams and inhabited as if we could live independently of the material world.

Augmenting Reality

Plain old reality looks quite boring for information-hungry people, as if it should be "augmented" to match online experience – which has become the only experience available for many people. Instead of deepening our inner view of reality and our sensitivity toward it, we turn toward the multiplication of data available through "augmented reality" (AR) technologies.

AR defines the connection between the physical world and technology. It extrapolates more information from the territory – like tourist information about a place on which our smartphone's camera points, details about a piece of art in a museum, atmospheric data or traffic conditions when our device gets information from sensors and cameras in the territory. Even our biological state can potentially be available to the Net through sensors connected to our bodies.

The possible applications of AR range widely from mechanics to medicine, from physics to biology, from architecture to tourism – and, of course, to military applications, the arena where many of the innovations begin.

At the extreme, Internet and mobile technologies are acting on the territory at a fundamental level. Even more than digitizing it and distancing us from it through mirror worlds and AR, they are making territory useless. We can operate on our bank account from the screen, shop, communicate with friends, search for a soul mate, and work at jobs which have been translated into digital form (writing, designing, accounting, marketing). And new professions are born from the Net itself.

Just as highways have forced most people to buy a car, information highways are forcing almost everyone to buy a computer and hook up to the Internet. AR is advertised as a way to "enrich the experience" of the real territory, superimposing layers of interpretation on it. These interpretations have the potential, then, to become *the* way of looking at reality. In a short time, real territory could be considered dull and unappealing if it's not augmented.

Now radio-frequency identification (RFID) and the "Internet of things" promise to give every product, object, animal or person a radio tag connected to the larger Net by radio waves. This will allow superimposing even more data on everything.

The Mind as the First Virtual Reality Tool
Much before the advent of digital technologies, the processes of digitization and remodeling of reality started with the separation between mind and matter that granted higher status to the mind. Through this attitude, territory which was first remodeled (or even devastated) physically – a process which gained momentum with industrialization – can now be rebuilt and simulated through the abstracting capacity of digital technologies. The human mind itself is a tool for the creation of alternative realities – even on the neurophysiological level with the simple activity of seeing. What enters our eyes is filtered by many layers, starting with the photons that hit the retina.

The creation of alternative realities is an expression of Enneatype Five (see Appendix for an introduction to this map of psychospiritual structures). Fives can construct realities and inhabit them – until their investment in them becomes more important than ordinary reality, even replacing it entirely. In a virtual world we can have as many sunsets a day as we like, a body shaped to our wishes, no pollution and virgin landscapes. A world where we seem able to construct new certainties.

In the July/August 2007 issue of the MIT magazine *Technology Review*, there was an extensive report about the possible convergence of virtual and mirror worlds. The author, Wade Roush, a long-time user of Second Life, wrote, "And if the world we create together is less lonely and less unpredictable than the one we have now, we'll have made a good start." This clearly affirms his attitude toward a lonely, threatening and unpredictable world which can be rectified by withdrawing from it.

The same article quotes Michael Wilson, CEO of Makena Technologies, which developed the virtual world There:

> What if we could model a Europe where the sea level is 10 feet higher than it is today, or walk around the Alaskan north and see the glaciers and the Bering Strait the way they were 10 years ago? Then perceptions around global warming might change (Roush, 2007).

I'm sure that Michael Wilson has good intentions, but I doubt that clicking a computer simulation of the effects of global warming would trigger a change in our attitude about nature being at our disposal to remodel according to our wishes. Our care of nature will begin only when we feel part of it, rather than something special in creation by virtue of our "superior" mind.

In our culture, which sees matter and spirit as separate entities, there's a general misunderstanding that giving attention to the soul would distance us from the tangible. A spiritual path is, instead, a process of contact with what is real – "what is" – which includes matter and our physical body. From a spiritual perspective, direct contact with physicality and taking care of the planet are integrated in a wider awareness that begins with awareness of ourself, of what we really are, and what we truly need. We can, then, join with reality again through our spiritual ground. With spiritual awareness we perceive what is real – while with only our mind, we can stray from both our roots in matter and our wings in spirit.

Solutions to environmental problems are almost always seen as technological. Insofar as technology is employed in the care of the planet, it is seen as a messianic savior – which is a childish magical omnipotence projected onto technology.

The Digitization of Biology
The scientific vision of reality as collection of data has been extended to the whole of biology. Norbert Wiener, whose cybernetics theories have influenced much of today's IT, wrote in *The Human Use of Human Beings* (1950):

> Given that the individuality of a body is written in our genes, there is no absolute distinction between the types of transmission which we can use for sending a telegram from country to country and the types of transmission which at least are theoretically possible for transmitting a living organism such as a human being (quoted in Harkin, 2009, p. 27).

Sixty years later, Craig Venter, the scientist creating synthetic biological organisms, said, "Life is basically the result of an information process, a software process", and, "I think the fact that these cells are software-driven machines and that software is DNA and that truly the secret of life is writing software, is pretty miraculous" (CBS, *60 Minutes*, 2010). Medicine and biology were already on the way to seeing the human body mostly in mechanical terms, but once genetic codes could be sequenced, the marriage between data and biology could be fully celebrated.

Biology, in the form of data, is no longer limited to understanding what life is. Genetic engineering can bring the "imperfect" body back to its original perfection. As gods, we shall create new forms of life. Venter's announcement in 2010 about the creation of the first synthetic form of life moves us in that direction.

While many Christians oppose genetic engineering, the roots of a vision like Venter's sprout from the same culture which considered miracles a sign of the divine. Yes, the same culture which dismisses the possibility of meeting the divine in this embodied life. No surprise that, having only one life available, we desire to create heaven on Earth and achieve a lost perfection through our deeds.

The digitization of the biological system has been accelerated with the DNA sequencing of the Human Genome Project. This work required an incredible amount of number crunching. Initially it sequenced less than two percent of the total length of the human genome. The rest was considered junk DNA since it did not serve to code protein.

Then a few scientists started to doubt the uselessness of the main part. Since some very primitive organisms contain hundreds of times the DNA of a human, most probably a small amount of human DNA was not the whole story of our biology. Scientists realized that ribonucleic acid (RNA), the "junk," is essential to regulating protein production and genetic expression. Genes do not control our lives: they can be inhibited or expressed according to the "junk DNA" sequences – and, I suspect, by other factors such as our thoughts. It has been estimated that humans have more than two million proteins, each with a different function – which the Proteomics Project is attempting to catalogue – but merely 25,000+/- genes that can produce only limited numbers of proteins. So we have a new race now to make sense of the 98–99% of unsequenced RNA, classify the proteins, and understand the mechanisms of gene activation and protein production. It is starting to be accepted that genes don't determine nearly as much as was supposed. And there is no end in sight to the illusion of knowing humans through (in this case biological) data.

Sequencing RNA and the classification of proteins will probably require billions of times the computational power needed by the Human Genome Project of 2005. Since proteins interact with each other, I expect scientists to then want to understand their combinations and roles. This will require calculations of other orders of magnitude. I can imagine that other factors will surface once (if ever) the end of those sequencings and calculations are approached – which will require even more computational power. Why not measure the interactions between two people's DNA, or within entire groups? If human biology is to be seen as an information system, then there will be no end to the possibilities of combining elements.

I have nothing against seeing reality through the lens of information. Numbers fascinated me early in life and I am awed by the computational patterns of life in biology and physics. But *the map is not the territory*. Biology and physics can be expressed on an informational level, but this does not mean that is the *only* level at which we can understand their nature. It's like saying that human beings are made of the minerals found in different proportions in their bodies. That's the level of material physical reality. But we won't discover much from that about what it means to be human, even with the most accurate calculation of every element.

We try to allay our anxiety of the unknown by collecting data that we can store, interpret, control and manipulate – but we are deluded that we thereby know the universe. Since our science looks for truth mainly on informational levels, it is not surprising that we consider information the fundamental nature of human beings – as in this era we identify ourself with our genes and DNA, believing they determine our physical, intellectual, emotional and even ethical attributes.

There are many services on the Internet which can bring genome information to the consumer. One such company is 23andme, co-founded by Anne Wojcicki, the wife of Google's co-founder Sergey Brin. Google invested in it.

In 2008 I applied for the 23andme report on my DNA. A test tube came in the mail. I filled it with saliva and returned it. After a few weeks an email informed me that the data was ready. I went to the website with a mix of curiosity and apprehension to learn my characteristics and medical risks.

Among the reports on health, traits, and medical research, I found I have genes which lead to a high probability of ankylosis spondylitis. (Yes, I've had it since I was 16). It's an autoimmune disease which causes inflammation of the joints which sometimes becomes debilitating. Curiously, while some of the data predicted a high probability of contracting it, other data showed only a minor probability. Perhaps this could partly explain the fact that the typical pattern of degeneration stopped at a non-advanced stage, allowing me to lead a normal life, even though I sometimes experience pain and discomfort.

It could be that the genes are activated and deactivated due to undetermined circumstances. Since I never took systemic synthetic medicines for it, I can suppose that natural treatments and awareness practices have had their role in the remission of symptoms – especially the improvement following inquiry into traumatic life events. But those are just my hypotheses.

23andme also tells me that I have a tendency toward obesity. This needs at least "more studies." I have been thin all my life. I have a bit more weight now at the age of 49, but I remain fundamentally slim, with a fast metabolism.

According to the results, I also have the Restless Legs Syndrome gene and a slight tendency toward Tourette Syndrome. The typical Restless Legs Syndrome manifests as an irresistible urge to move the legs when falling asleep. I sometimes move my right leg in a rhythmic manner during daytime while seated, so people ask if I am nervous – but this is not the case. Maybe by allowing my leg to move as much as it needs to during the day, it obviates bothering me at night.

Tourette Syndrome is characterized by uncontrollable and widespread tics. I have a slight tendency toward tics, particularly when I'm tired or the weather changes, but its expressions are very mild. At times I believed that my will and awareness were weak, since I could not control a simple tic. But with time I've learned to accept it, much like other metabolic processes I don't consciously control.

In general, the information is accurate. They warn that in many cases the main risk factors are connected to diet and lifestyle as much as to genes, and that there are still few studies about the relationship between health and genes. It is an important warning, but resembles the "it's not enough" mantra in other fields like technology ("we need higher speed, more memory, more Internet connections") or economics ("underdevelopment and poverty are still present because the market economy is not yet widespread").

Through 23andme we can also explore the gross data of our DNA – which reads like a software code that we're not trained to understand. So we might wish we had software with a user-friendly interface for making changes – and consequently give us more desirable characteristics. I can't imagine the power Google would have

The Digitally Divided Self

if it linked our genetic information with our Web navigation, preferences, documents, and the people we connect with.

Biology seems the new frontier of IT in its unstoppable race toward the digitization of reality. We can certainly read a human being on the plane of information, but it is easy to forget that every plane communicates with and influences all other planes. From the time of Watson and Crick, who considered genes to completely determine human characteristics, the matter has became more complicated. Steve Talbott (2009) has observed that chromosomes are composed of chromatin, which contains DNA, but also a much larger proportion of proteins that give it shape. As geneticists were concentrating on the controlling wizardry of the coded genes, these proteins were largely ignored. But many laboratories are now discovering how the chromatin affects the genes. Meanwhile, the thread of research is leading from chromatin to new and numerous challenges in deciphering components like the "methylome" and "membranome," the "histone code" and "RNAi-interference code." The most overarching is the "epigenome" – all the varied cellular processes that control the genes, which affect whether or not a gene is copied and even alter the sequence of genetic letters.

Talbott suspects that almost everything is involved in the regulation of almost everything else. If the role of single genes is elusive and difficult to ascertain, things get even more complicated when genes work together. Bob Holmes (2009) wrote about the systemic and collaborative relationship between different genes: "Genes rarely act alone. Instead, they operate as part of networks of interacting genes, in which multiple genes affect each trait and each gene affects multiple traits."

So it seems that the theories of "selfish" genes (Dawkins, 1976) – considered for a long time the bible of evolutionary biology – has had its day, just like Reaganism and yuppies. Nor are Darwinian principles of competition and survival any longer the whole story. Collaboration and altruism are being seen as important in the survival of the species.

Holmes suggests that in an area of a biotic zone that has lost its balance (like the mixed native forests of New England when early settlers arrived to farm) and is thereby susceptible to dramatic environmental events, the companion species develop a pattern of protection of the larger ecosystem (like the quick regrowth of white pine that provided habitat for the eventual flourishing again of mixed woodlands).

23andme rightly affirms that diet and exercise can impact our health, but there is no concept of genes being changed from the *in-*

side. Yet there are people who think differently. Epigenetics (*epi*, above, as the control that stands above the genes) is a science which Bruce Lipton (2005) and Dawson Church (2007) – in a strong challenge to the current paradigms of biology – have expanded by their explorations of DNA being affected by thoughts,.

The digitization of biology can lead us back to our ancestors, and the construction of our identity connects us to our family history. Lacking such connections today, sites like geni.com or 23andme.com profit from the need to belong to a historical lineage. Technology allows us to look for people who share our DNA and might be part of our family, as we try to reconnect with our roots – which have been eradicated by technology itself.

Analogical Models of Reality

Esoteric Eastern traditions hold that we are composed of several "bodies" on different planes which interact with and influence each other. The biological body can be transformed through diet, exercise, and the environment – and by other planes as well. For instance, the emotional or mental bodies can change the functioning of the biological body. And shocks to the physical body can conversely affect the emotional and mental bodies.

Studies like 23andme try to answer the ancient question "Who am I?" but purely on an informational level, not as an inner quest. Yet self-knowledge, one of the main drives of human beings, can be approached purely through meditation techniques and psychological investigation, as well as by models and systems.

From Taoist theory of the five elements to Ayurvedic types, from Jungian archetypes to astrology, from the chakra system to the subtle bodies, from the I Ching to the Enneagram, symbolic systems for understanding reality and the human soul connect the individual with the larger macrocosm – to universal energies and archetypes. Those systems operate as bridges between inner awareness and external knowledge.

In my quest for self-knowledge I explored several symbolic systems, finding value in each. Just as the map is not the territory, systems have intrinsic limits to our self-understanding. Nonetheless, as with words, they can bring us far along our path. The symbolical system I love most is astrology, which I've studied since I was 19, when I stayed up all night reading my first book on the subject. I am not speaking of the astrology of the media's daily horoscopes. Astrology is about self-knowledge.

What was a sacred science practiced by Galileo, Descartes, Newton, as well as Jung has been misused and trivialized. But the knowledge is still intact for those who want to reach it. Astrology is neither an exact science nor is it deterministic – just as genetics is not. However, through astrology we can know ourself on different planes and we can connect with eternal symbologies. My astrological natal chart tells me by the synthesis of several factors (planets, aspects, houses, and complex interactions among them) that the planet Mercury characterizes me more than any other, though there are certainly other influences.

Being Mercurial is compatible with Restless Legs Syndrome and the tendency toward Tourette Syndrome, as well as being slim, communicative, and the problems with joints so essential to movement (even if joints are associated more with Saturn) that I experience. Mercury is the planet of quick movement, communication, and the media. I have always been involved with publishing and communicating knowledge. Astrology, through its open symbology, portrays me on more levels than what genes or even psychology can.

I also have high levels of the metal mercury in my body, detected by a mineralogram, which probably has accumulated from dental fillings and contaminated fish. I then can ask myself if my body has accumulated mercury only from mechanical influences, or if it comes of being of the nature of that planet as well, for the symbolic nature of the metal mercury shares common characteristics with the astrological planet.

Acknowledging the similarity of my nature to the astrological symbolism of Mercury helps me accept both the qualities and idiosyncrasies of the planet. If I don't connect with the symbolic and mythological qualities of my nature, but consider only the digital sequence of my genes when I evaluate the risk of contracting a certain disease, I miss the value of the rich personality of the archetype.

Archetypes are not digital, not a binary-dualistic *this* or *that, 0* or *1,* open or closed. The symbolical view of myself leads me to accepting even the "shadow" qualities of the archetype or planet. The symbolism of Saturn, for example, conveys a heavy, slow, earthy nature, connected to solid structures. On the bodily level, such structures are represented by the skeletal system, while at the personality level they are expressed as discipline and steadfastness. On the level of the mind they can give the capacity for prolonged research – or a tendency toward melancholic states. Socially, Saturn is connected to structures of social order and to long-lasting institutions.

Connecting with the symbology of Saturn means accepting the archetype fully. Sadness, which has been pathologized by pharmaceutical companies, was seen in traditional Japan as a gift for developing strong character. "The gods have become diseases," bemoaned Jung. The slowness of Saturn, instead of being considered unproductive, brings awareness to walking through life. With Saturn on my side I can feel like a still samurai, giving roots and substance to my fast-changing mercurial nature.

Our Digital Nervous Systems

We now know that "pure mind" does not exist – not even in the mind. Neurophysiology has demonstrated that our thoughts cannot exist without the connection to our feelings and our bodies (Damasio, 1995). After many centuries of denial of the body, since the 1960s we have been wanting our bodies back. But at the beginning of the new century, we want them back digitally, in the same modality of digitization as everything – the body as "data."

The body has become the new territory of conquest by companies: cosmetic surgeries, neuroenhancers, smart drugs, body building, diets, even sex toys. The orientation is toward a hedonistic relationship with our body – yet only in a mechanical way. This does not connect our body with our soul. As in looking for a "pure mind" with IT, in dealing with the body, we envision what is an unbalanced "pure body." The same split remains, seen the other way around.

The nervous system conveys information through the body, is faster than other bodily systems, and works through electrical signals. And its structure of neurons and synapses resembles a net of Web pages and links. It appears possible to represent the nervous system digitally as an information system – which is how IT industries are interested in connecting with it. These properties make the nervous system the best candidate for digital technologies.

Neuroengineering projects range widely from brain implants to delivering information in and out of the nervous system. Some projects are attempting to create prosthetic devices that simulate the work of specific regions of the brain, such as the hippocampus which has a role in the formation of memories.

Other projects use self-powered microchips, Wireless Identification and Sensing Platforms (WISPs), and Wireless Body Area Networks (WBANs) which, inserted into the human body, will detect physiological parameters or health problems which can then be transmitted over the Net.

Interest in the nervous system goes toward implanting chips (hardware), as well as changing molecular chemistry (software). The era of psychedelic drugs as consciousness-expanding tools has passed. Now drugs are "smart." Neuroenhancers or "smart drugs" – like Adderall and Ritalin – are legal psychostimulants used to in-

crease alertness and concentration. They are basically ampheta-
mines whose effects are similar to cocaine. Prescriptions for Ritalin
widely used to treat attention-deficit hyperactivity disorder (ADHD)
in children – has increased rapidly in the last years, partly driven by
over-diagnosis and partly from a real rise of this social disorder in
media-overstimulated kids.

Apart from medical use, there's a huge demand for neuroenhancers by students and people who want to be more efficient in
coping with the demands of the information society. Modafinil allows reduction in the need for sleep to a couple of hours per night,
with no apparent side effects. The army and astronauts had great interest in the development of such a drug – but now, besides the
therapeutic uses (e.g., for narcolepsy), it is being used as a recre-
ational drug and a support before exams.

While the use of neuroenhancers in a non-therapeutic setting is
illegal, it is probably a matter of time for their use to be liberalized
– as they will be increasingly necessary for the everyday functioning of a mind which is losing its capacity to focus and needs to cope
with growing volumes of information. No doubt somebody will be
concerned about the "neuro divide," since some people will be enhanced while others won't.

Even though the brain, which is part of the nervous system, is
considered the place where thoughts are produced, spiritual teachers – who have seen the nature of the mind from the inside – perceive a different reality.

> Thought is not yours or mine; it is our common inheritance. There
> is no such thing as your mind and my mind. There is only mind –
> the totality of all that has been known, felt, and experienced by man,
> handed from generation to generation. We are all thinking and
> functioning in that "thought sphere," just as we all share the same
> atmosphere for breathing. The thoughts are there to function and
> communicate in this world sanely and intelligently (U.G Krishna-
> murti, 1988, p. 43).

Programming
No digitization of reality could happen without the incredible
amount of programming needed to translate reality into a language
comprehensible by computers. It has been a long road since the
times of Babbage and Lovelace who established the bases of programming.

> Wherever computer centers have become established, that is to say,
> in countless places in the United States, as well as in virtually all
> other industrial regions of the world, bright young men of di-

sheveled appearance, often with sunken glowing eyes, can be seen sitting at computer consoles, their arms tensed and waiting to fire their fingers, already poised to strike, at the buttons and keys on which their attention seems to be as riveted as a gambler's on the rolling dice. When not so transfixed, they often sit at tables strewn with computer printouts over which they pore like possessed students of a cabalistic text. They work until they nearly drop, twenty, thirty hours at a time. Their food, if they arrange it, is brought to them: coffee, Cokes, sandwiches. If possible, they sleep on cots near the computer. But only for a few hours – then back to the console or the printouts. Their rumpled clothes, their unwashed and unshaven faces, and their uncombed hair all testify that they are oblivious to their bodies and to the world in which they move. They exist, at least when so engaged, only through and for the computers. These are computer bums, compulsive programmers. They are an international phenomenon (Weizenbaum, 1976, p. 115)

Weizenbaum compared programmers to gamblers – driven by compulsive behavior, with little spontaneity or pleasure. Psychoanalysts including Freud have found that the main characteristics of the psychic life of the compulsive gambler were megalomania and fantasies of omnipotence. For compulsive programmers, life is only a program running on an enormous computer, with every aspect understood in programming terms. They seek reassurance from the computer (Weizenbaum, 1976) – just as a small child does from its mother.

Science can proceed only by simplifying reality. The first step is abstraction – which means ignoring all the empirical data which does not fit available concepts. According to Weizenbaum, the megalomaniacal fantasies of compulsive programmers are only an extreme version of that – a phenomenon inherent in all self-validating systems of thought.

Weizenbaum warns us about trying to fit the world into a system of thought. There is a risk of considering reality merely a computable sequence of events connected by a cause-effect mechanism and by algorithms.

Programming requires the ability to detach oneself from some aspect of reality in order to see it in objective terms and observe it in its essence. But this detachment is double-edged. It can lead us to a schizoid detachment from reality – and particularly from our very Self – while if the same observational skills are turned inward and integrated with the body and feelings, we might pass beyond our own mental patterns.

Often programmers also are interested in inner states – but they reach for them with technical, pharmaceutical or neurotechnological tools, not as something which can arise from inside.

As a programmer I loved the thrill of unlocking the mysteries of reality, getting to the essence of a procedure, deconstructing and mastering a slice of reality through computational tools. If I could write a program about music, I would feel like the god of music himself able to analyze melodies and harmonies and thus compose any sort of music, deluded into believing I had found the philosopher's stone of music. A programmer can feel like the master of a whole terrain, be it digital pictures, sound, animation, communication between humans, weather forecasting, physics experiments, or the properties of materials.

Thinking that we can understand and reproduce the mechanisms of reality through programming can easily make us arrogant. The "end user" is literally considered the bottom of the caste system, with programmers the chosen few. The end user is then seen as merely a procedure interacting with algorithms, one which has to be boxed within well-defined borders because he, being basically an idiot, could mess things up.

Google's chief executive Eric Schmidt told a crowd of 4,000 developers in May 2009 about his future plans. "I'm one of those people who believes that computer scientists are at the center of the universe. Scalability and power, as evidenced by the internet, is just the beginning. We're at the beginning of this right now."

That computer scientists are at the center of the universe is not just a catchy phrase to seduce his public. Their role in manipulation of data and algorithms for Google is quite clear.

Thinking like Software

The chess master Garry Kasparov (2010) wrote in the *New York Review of Books* that everybody can now have a chess program that will crush most grandmasters. But those programs work on the brute force of calculation, rather than style, patterns, theory or creativity. "Although we still require a strong measure of intuition and logic to play well, humans today are starting to play more like computers." He pointed out that new and innovative ideas in chess software are not needed, since brute-force programs are efficient enough for the goal of winning.

While chess software has become less creative with the strong computing power now available, chess players have adopted this same attitude of merely looking for "what works." There is undoubtedly a mutual feedback between the digital representations of reality and the way we approach those aspects of reality. Musician friends have told me that since the advent of software for composing music, their creative attitude has changed along with the mechanisms of musical software production.

Graphics, video production, architecture, music and countless creative activities are now being aided by software. And algorithms and the programming attitude are extending from computers into real life. Losing weight, talking to an audience, finding the right partner, keeping her/him, having great sex, improving our self-esteem have all become "how-to" problems. With the right instructions and following the right procedures we believe we can master anything in life.

Yet computers still can't do many things which are easy for humans – so we adapt human work to the machine's needs. Amazon Mechanical Turk service describes precisely how it supports creation of the human servomechanism:

> Developers can leverage this service to build human intelligence directly into their applications. While computing technology continues to improve, there are still many things that human beings can do much more effectively than computers, such as identifying objects in a photo or video, performing data de-duplication, transcribing audio recordings or researching data details (http://aws.amazon.com/mturk/).

In the July 2007 edition, *Wired* introduced Luis von Ahn, the creator of the Captcha system. Von Ahn devises games in which human intellectual skills are used to solve problems the computer cannot solve, such as image recognition. He concluded: "As humanity goes online, it's becoming an extremely advanced, large-scale processing unit."

Human history is full of connections between humans and technological instruments. And the use of tools to extend our possibilities has been a big step in human development. But what we are facing now is something new. With Mechanical Turk, all human activities are first converted into digital ones, even those requiring imagination and intuition which lie beyond the ability of computers. Then human brain resources are used to decode actions that the machine is incapable of performing well. It is like a modern assembly line where, in place of physical and manual repetition, we repeat banal mental activity – such as recognizing an image and classifying it, or transcribing a spoken text.

As more and more human activities are being translated into digital form, we need to supply the computer with the broader mind power of the human. We participate in order for the tool itself to expand its possibilities, no longer just to expand our human capacities. It can be said that in the end it's humans who take advantage of the human-computer interaction, and it is still humans who decide what to process and elaborate. This is true in a way, but in the movement to digitize even non-computable aspects that require massive human intervention, humans are becoming servo-mechanisms of technology as they feed the machine.

> Among the many and enormous advantages of efficient automatic machinery is this: it is completely fool-proof. But every gain has to be paid for. The automatic machine is fool-proof; but just because it is fool-proof it is also grace-proof. The man who tends such a machine is impervious to every form of esthetic inspiration, whether of human or of genuinely spiritual origin (Huxley, 1945, p. 171).

Since Huxley's time we have greatly expanded our options, yet grace still has not appeared.

Digitizing All Life Events

Lifelogging is a technology to capture, record, and digitally archive everything which happens in a person's life. Text, pictures, audio, and videos can be recorded by wearable cameras – and eventually even biological data could be recorded by sensors. Archived data could then be searched by that person – or by others.

As with every technology, I ask myself what the deeper need for this is. Apart from the practical reasons to record everything that happens in our lives, I suspect that lifelogging reflects a more spiritual, evolutionary need – translated on the informational level and monopolized by the ego.

Most of the time the depth of reality just slips beneath our awareness. Our experience of presence is total only in special moments, unless we are spiritually advanced. When we can participate fully and deeply in the flow of life, our awareness expands. Freezing streams of life digitally might be a way to become aware of the fullness of the lived moment, though we can't record the multidimensional inner experience. On the technological/mental level, we are only able to translate the quest for full awareness into recording bits and bytes.

When we are fully present, our individual consciousness is not separated from the event: our experience is immediate and unmediated. We are one with the experience and the awareness of it. But if we're not fully present, how could we possibly be aware of it later through some digital support? The awareness of the moment can occur only *in the moment*.

Many arts and technologies have been created to grasp the essence of reality and of the human soul: books, portrait painting, photography, tape recorders, videos. All of them help – up to a certain point – to raise awareness and expand the capacity to know different aspects of ourself. But full awareness is inseparable from the moment it happens and the inner state of the person experiencing it.

CHAPTER 5

INTIMACY AND SEXUALITY

Since Sherry Turkle first described how computer users project their psychological object relations onto the machine (Turkle, 1984; 1995), technology has progressed in the race toward the digitization of reality. Today, through social networks and dating sites where real people live on the other side, we can apparently bring our object relations back into the realm of people. Actually nothing much has changed since we first boxed people inside windows, transforming them into small icons and clickable objects. Once people become objects in our minds, there's but a small step left to becoming insensitive or potentially abusive.

In the process of the digitization of reality technology is being assimilated into more human activities. Social life is moving massively inside social networks, and the search for a partner or romance is happening through dating sites.

Sex is huge on the Internet, one of the main driving forces behind the spread of the medium (as happened earlier with home videos). Some statistics: 35 percent of Internet users are active in some kind of online sexual activity, masturbation, or cybersex – and sexual material accounts for more than one-third of all downloads. Almost half of Internet users are porn-viewers, with 35% of female users visiting porn sites. "Sex" and "porn" are among the top five searches for kids under 18.

A survey of 2,700 Canadian students made by campuskiss.com in 2006 found that 87 percent of the people who responded had sex via the Internet, through chats and webcams. I understand that cybersex can be quite appealing and fun, but such a high percentage – which surprised even the managers of the site – is a sign of the breadth of the change in how sexuality is being expressed.

In the last few decades, Western countries have experienced the growth of porn, and it has accelerated in the last ten years with the Internet. Porn was born as the other side of sexual repression: acting out desires and letting the wild side be free – at least in the imagination. The dichotomy between women as Mother Mary and as Mary Magdalene has not been integrated, so we have displaced the wild sexual aspects to the porn arena.

Porn itself has developed in divergent directions – the extremization of sexual practices, and the easy access through technology and the media. Images that would have shocked me as a young man are now a click away for everybody – and few people are shocked by them anymore.

Eros and the Sexualization of Society

Eros, the ancient Greek God of lust and desire, is an essential energy of the human experience that has been redirected – and often repressed – by religions and societies. Contemporary society is probably more permeated by sexual messages than any in history, and the trend is only on the rise. But Eros is yawning.

There were societies in the past where Eros flourished and was accepted – like the libertines of ancient Rome, though they were circumscribed within a limited segment of society. Sexual messages are now present in every corner of society. Porn on the Internet is pervasive, and advertisers use sexual images to promote any sort of product in magazines and TV. Popular magazines challenge each other on who reveals about more "secret pleasurable spots" and "great tricks to become a sex God/Goddess." At the same time, Eros is missing in our daily life.

Eros is not just about lust – it is everything connected to the senses. Often Eros is presented with Aphrodite, which suggests the merging of beauty and desire. Yet our urban landscape no longer includes this erotic merging that nature can offer with its smells, colors, and sensations for the body. We limit Eros to the erotic pull between people – and we allow even that only in prescribed ways.

The more this erotic desire is stimulated by the media, the more the everyday sensual connection between the genders is filtered by social norms that actually prevent spontaneous eroticism flowing among people – leaving Eros commoditized in the marketplace.

Apart from the lives of couples and discreet places where erotic energy is accepted (as in swingers' clubs), its flow in daily settings is seen by most people with suspicion, or even as threatening. Being overwhelming, Eros can enter society only in surrogate ways. When

Eros is not present in everyday life, it sneaks in in safer forms, like porn and cybersex – where we can avoid the complexities of a real encounter, while releasing the tension in our busy minds.

Real Eros has no function in the market society. Eros is freely available, needs few products. As Wilhelm Reich has explicated, Eros even gives our energy a direction that prevents unhealthy aggression. The aggressiveness of Eros *connects* people, while aggression in war *separates* them. Despite the sexual revolution of a few decades back, we have not yet integrated or accepted Eros in its authentic form, so it remains as revolutionary as ever.

Sex is a beautiful opening of our feelings, connection, and pleasure. At the same time, true sexual exploration can be an uncharted path full of pitfalls. Raw, unmediated Eros is chaotic, overwhelming. Sex challenges our feelings, conditioning, self-images, practical lives, and even our integrity. It can lead to addictive behaviors, disease, condemnation, and conflict with laws – which vary in different countries. Oral or anal sex are still against the law in many places. Women risk death for infidelity, and homosexuality is banned in many countries.

The journey of sexuality, when taken authentically, is as challenging nowadays as it was in ancient times. In ancient sacred sexual disciplines, like tantra, the path of sex was only for courageous souls who were willing to face both the gods and their inner demons.

Eros carries powerful energies, powerful enough to squeeze itself into the virtual – but not without limiting its scope, leaving the mental component prevalent, and the multidimensionality of the erotic experience reduced to the plane of digital data.

As happens during carnivals when our masks allow us to live out different facets of our psyches, Eros can express itself in uninhibited ways on the Net, since there we can sneak beneath the social radar.

Cybersex

Cybersex is so prevalent that some women complain that men only want sex chat. But the data indicate that both sexes are active. The number one female sexual fantasy, according to several magazine polls, is offering a private striptease. Catalyzing a man's excitement is a thrill for her, as well as reassurance of her attractiveness. For men, visual stimulation is a turn-on, as is the hunt for women online – where there are no strings attached.

The appeal of sex chatting is that sex, like music, is a universal language. Sex chats then supersede cultural differences, as they reach toward the roots of our instincts. And in many cultures cybersex can bypass cultural and religious conditioning. Where the rules are strict, cybersex can be regarded as "not real sex" – just a hint of hypocrisy as the inner judge relaxes.

McLuhan defined the distinctions between *hot* and *cool* media. Hot media have an analytical, precise and well-defined message. The messages conveyed by hot media usually don't need much participation. Most of the visual media, especially the high-definition ones, are hot, as are radio, photography, and lectures. Cool media require participation of the audience. Comic books, cartoons, and seminars all require active participation. McLuhan associated hot media with industrial and individualist societies and cool media with oral, village and tribal societies.

"Less is more" is a rule of seduction. When women show only a part of their bodies, it activates the imagination of her audience (like picturing the complete removal of her clothes). Lingerie is a "cool" medium. A club where women dress in sexy clothes is more exciting than a nudist beach.

Low-resolution video is more engaging than high-definition. Though porn producers are worried that high-definition TV will expose small flaws in their actors' bodies, the real threat comes from the better definition itself – inviting less participation on the part of the viewer. 3-D porn will be even less participatory instead of more. From the neurological perspective, Patrik Vuilleumie at the University of Geneva discovered that the amygdala, a region of limbic emotional processing that activates dopamine, norepinephrine and epinephrine, is more active when looking at blurred faces than better defined ones.

Sex by webcam is highly participatory because the resolution is low and the frame rate often slow. Seeing the whole body of a naked woman on a webcam requires even more participation, since her sexual organs are less evident – and often partly covered by her hand if she "participates" with her fingers during cybersex.

"The ear turns man over to universal panic while the eye... leaves some gaps... free from the unremitting acoustic pressure and reverberation" (McLuhan, 1964, p. 156). If *seeing* less invites more participation, *saying* less gives space to project an inner picture of the other person. Women often prefer to communicate with less defined statements and more first-person subjective messages. Men in general are more inclined toward objective, hot-media messages, both verbally and visually. I use "women" and "men" as I'd use "yin" and "yang" – more as an energetic quality than a gender issue.

The voice as a medium requires our full attention and partici-

pation. We can't communicate orally to as many people simultaneously as we can with chat writing. Using the voice in cybersex adds
vulnerability and strengthens connection, somehow exposing ourself even more than just displaying our naked body.

When we see something about reality, there's a very short period to see it with fresh eyes, before the conceptual mind takes over
with its structures and concepts. In a cybersex meeting there's also
an initial period when we know very little about the other. Few
senses are involved – no embodied presence, no voice, maybe not
even pictures of the other.

With fewer elements to base our projections and our preconceptions on, we are lured by the spontaneity of cybersex. And without the controlling inner judge, anonymity invites communication
to flow unobstructed. But this freedom is double-edged. On one
side, there's room to flow freely with our desires and passions –
even kinky ones – but on the other, we are only apparently free by
a limited image of the other – for as our ancient emotional-instinc-
tual limbic system takes over, we activate "pre-conceptual" automatic reactions, which are based on the very earliest conditioning.

The Transformation of Seduction and of Relationship

For most women sex starts in the mind and then enters the body.
The right words can perform miracles on a woman's desire. The
Buddhists were right: there is no difference between thoughts,
emotions and sensations. It's all about mind. Seduction is the art of
stimulating the mind – balancing gentleness and passion – and
knowing the right moment when boundaries can be crossed. Today,
with less patience for delays and long narratives, the slow pace of
seduction is being overridden by the desire for instant gratification.

Seduction will perhaps be replaced by teledildonics that allow
different kinds and degrees of stimulation by programming sex toys
and uploading various strokes and vibrations onto the Internet. It
will be sex driven by the mind – like seduction, except that traditional seduction requires words that touch the soul – and makes
connection with the other person on several levels.

While online seduction becomes faster, real meetings become
shorter. Young peoples' culture of "hooking up" and having no-
strings-attached sex has been reported by Laura Sessions Stepp in
her book *Unhooked* (2007), describing the girls' culture of avoiding
commitment, attachment and feelings.

The attitude of non-attachment typical of the online world fits
with current reality. Swingers clubs and group sex look like the natural outgrowth of the needs for instant gratification and quickly

switching our objects of desire –as we easily do in sex chat rooms.

Cybersex meetings function in the same modality as group sex clubs. A gal or guy can meet a new partner via chat, have cybersex with or without webcams, then switch to another, perhaps engaging in cybersex with more than one partner at a time. Or they might just be a voyeur enjoying other people broadcasting their sexual acts (either alone or as a couple, depending on the site they choose). Many swingers clubs opened during the last decade, though with a different attitude than the sexual revolution of the '60s.

Masturbation and Sex Toys

Many activities which began as social, with time transform into individual ones – especially with the media and technologies. One example is in transportation, where personal cars took over from communal forms of travel. Another is TV: at first it was viewed collectively, then every family had a TV set, until there is now one for every individual. There are obvious commercial benefits, but these co-emerge with psychological phenomena.

The tendency toward individuality also develops in arenas which are naturally to be shared, like sexuality. Masturbation is an increasing activity. Among the reasons is the AIDS crisis, which did not yet exist in the "golden years" of free love. Others include the growing number of single adults, frequency of short-term relationships, and the ease in finding sexual material in the privacy of our houses.

Even though solo sex has always existed, is still not socially accepted in many parts of the world, especially for women. During the so-called sexual revolution of the '60s and '70s, women established a more direct and aware relationship with their bodies, which included the right to masturbate without guilt feelings. And like anything which starts as counterculture or a spontaneous social movement, once it became accepted in the mainstream, it was ripe for the market economy.

The new market sells porn, sex toys for the meek and the extreme, and even technologically complex sex machines (the Rolls Royce of sex toys). These can be creative, fun, safe and liberating, but they mark an anthropological transformation in human sexuality.

Sex Toys

As its function becomes part of technology, sex picks up the digital attitude of "at your fingertips." Pleasure has to be immediate, personalized, with various options and, of course, efficient – a quick and guaranteed orgasm. Waiting for an orgasm would be as annoying as waiting for a website to appear with a slow Internet connection.

Titled "Now You Can Have a Partner that will Always Hit Your Spot, Anytime You Want, for as Long as You Want," the Monkey Rocker™ website is one of the thousands which sell sex toys – or even more complex sex machines. Here is how they introduce their inventions (I hope tongue-in-cheek):

> Obviously, you deserve all the pleasure you can get. But human partners can sometimes let you down. If you find yourself wishing your lover or lovers were more dependable or more available, may we suggest one that will get you off anytime, every time.

Technology is great in giving control, so why deal with the ups and downs of your lover(s)? You can decide when, how, and how long you want your pleasure to last. And if your self-esteem is low because your lovers aren't available, or if you think they are all passionless wimps, now you can get the perfect partner!

> Though it can't hug you back, or cuddle, it's perfectly understandable for you to develop feelings for your Monkey Rocker™... In fact, with no motors to plug in or break down, your Monkey Rocker™ is always ready to play. You and your fantasies are in complete control. Monkey Rocker™ relies entirely on your movement to do all of its thrusting. You set the pace. Quick short strokes, long and deep, or anything in between. It's all about you. No guilt, no risk, no one's getting hurt.

Fast boot, perfect control of the machine, no need to be receptive and open to anybody – you are finally empowered! And you can surrender to the machine with no shame or guilt. You could develop feelings for it... It's perfectly understandable.

> YOU can scream if you like, but Monkey Rocker™ won't make a sound. If you can keep YOUR sound level down, total privacy is yours.

Those annoying moans and screams of your partner – what will the neighbors think? Maybe they'll suspect that I have sex with a – oh my God – with a human being? That's so last century. And with the machine I can scream as much as I want without feeling like a slut.

> And when you're done, you're done. That's it. Your Monkey Rocker™ doesn't have any expectations.

No need to keep any further connection, just like in chat rooms where there's no obligation for any commitment beyond the moment.

Another possible advantage is reducing your performance anxiety. If you're not certain you'll be able to satisfy her, Monkey Rocker™ can. And she'll think better of you that you care enough about her satisfaction to have a backup ready.

You can now outsource the whole of sexual activity to the machine, or you can take care of your partner's satisfaction, having the machine available as a "backup" when needed.

The sex machine stops the voice of the superego – that inner judge and controller which limits our free and authentic expression. At the same time, it promises unlimited pleasure any time we want it. Furthermore, we can avoid the task of facing our vulnerabilities: the fear of not being accepted, the embarrassment of poor performance, or of candidly showing our desire to a partner.

The road to a mature sexuality involves psychological exploration of our fear of rejection, shame about our fantasies, and the full acceptance and expression of our desires and pleasure. These difficulties have to be investigated if we are to integrate our ability to relate in depth and passionately through sex.

Digital sexuality shares the same attributes which give technological gadgets their attraction: control (cybersex and sex toys can be started and stopped at any moment with a simple click); options for expanded choices (sex toys for every kind of sensation, websites devoted to every sexual taste where we can find like-minded people); predictability (while a live person with real complexities is not); independence (technological sex doesn't need to be attached to any particular person); immediacy (going straight to stimulation, pleasure and orgasm, avoiding delays). Additionally, fast sexual release brings attention back to the body and its sensations – which we need in order to balance the overcharged minds of our information society.

Since prolonged working online brings dissociation from the body, a way to reassure ourself that we are still sensing our body by stimulating it through masturbation – which is one way to balance the monopoly of the mind. The jokes about "writing with one hand" attest to the widespread practice.

Orgasm 2.0

There are many reasons for saying that orgasms are good. First, they feel good. Then, when a person has an orgasm with a partner, they trust the partner enough to release control and be driven by an overwhelming energy. Orgasms make us vulnerable – we show their intensity, letting our partner hear our spontaneous moans of pleasure. As a man, it's beautiful to see and feel the excitement of my partner as she has an orgasm.

Orgasms trigger the release of many hormones, among them oxytocin which induces feelings of love and bonding. They are good for health and blood circulation; they can start in the body but expand to involve the soul, or vice versa – a holistic experience that integrates the individual. Take a reading break and compile your own list of benefits in the margin.

However, having "ordinary" orgasms seems not to be enough anymore. G-spot orgasm, trigasm, multiple orgasms and squirting are all musts now for a woman. Men usually have no problem reaching an orgasm, so the frontier for them is to become multi-orgasmic, have a 30-minute orgasm or reach a prostate orgasm.

I have always loved to experiment, being intensely intimate with a partner. A few years ago, before those different kinds of orgasms were defined, we just experimented spontaneously with our sensations in a playful and passionate way, carried along by Eros and Aphrodite. Now we are required to achieve the "other" kinds of orgasm. "Darling, did you squirt while I was playing with your G-spot with that new sex toy, or was it just the air-conditioner draining?"

The profits for *Cosmopolitan*, *Men's Health* and other magazines attest to the demand for "how-to" information. Nevertheless, if we don't let our controlling mind relax and if we don't surrender every goal while having sex, we won't reach deeper states. There are experiences in life – from meditation and falling asleep to sudden insights, from defecating to becoming enlightened – that happen more easily when our personalities don't interfere, when we just let go.

Every woman knows that the harder she tries to have an orgasm, the more difficult it becomes to reach. Of course, orgasms can be sparked mechanically – sex toys are here for that, and they can be a lot of fun. But we don't invite Eros to guide and transport us anymore. We want to be guided by the how-to's, as if sex were a technical matter. However, the best orgasms are still connected to a receptive attitude.

Orgasms have not moved much from the space they've always been relegated to in our psyche by religions – under the control of the superego as prohibitions, inhibitions, and judgments. These are still there – merely disguised as "have-to," "the right kind," "how many."

Why do we give such importance to climax? One obvious reason is that it feels good but, I think there are two other ingredients in the collective conditionings. One is the obsession to finish, to complete – a typical digital and male attitude. The other is, paradoxically, religious. In religions which permit sex only for reproduction, at least the man needs to climax.

Not necessary for reproduction, women's orgasms have been long ignored. It's good that female orgasm has come out of the closet. However, the masculine needs to reach an orgasm and to have a goal have been exported "technically" to women – without being integrated with other dimensions.

Cybervirgins

Sex information is now spread through magazines, TV and, of course, the Internet. Magazines with large circulations include a section of sexual "tips, tricks and secrets." According to those sources it looks like the world is composed of free and multiple sexual meetings. In some parts of the world that really happens, but the planetary diffusion of sexual messages doesn't match the majority of cultures. The reality is that at least two-thirds of the world has a traditional, rather restrictive – if not repressive – culture regarding sex, especially in the Middle East and Asia.

The massive process of worldwide urbanization and the growing number of singles is a phenomenon that began in emerging countries during the last ten or fifteen years. In Shanghai, Delhi, Seoul, Bangkok, Dubai, Manila or Jakarta, the growing class of office employees is formed mainly of women – who are connected to the Internet.

They often live alone or with female roommates and are members of Internet social networks and dating sites. It seems like the same lifestyle as many women in the West, but there's a fundamental difference: they live in a traditional society as far as sexual attitudes are concerned. Even though some countries, like Thailand, are well-known for their hot night life, the great majority of people follow tradition in sexual behaviors and lifestyles.

In sharp contrast to their upbringing, a culture with no filters can sneak through their computer screen with its dating sites, erotic chats, and porn. The ease of getting in touch with men through dating sites is very different from what ordinary reality offers – and allows. Since the culture of a country evolves much more slowly than the speed of technology, the gap with traditional culture becomes wider. Out of that gap emerge the cybervirgins – women who have never had sex with a man, but are sexually active online. They are college students, employed women, even mature women.

It would surprise a Western man to know that a good percentage of unmarried women in their 30s or even 40s are still virgins. This is common in Asia and Muslim countries – which include most of the world's population.

Such cultures limit the chances of a single woman meeting men, especially if she is no longer young – beyond the inner limits set by

The Digitally Divided Self

self-judgment and the fear of social condemnation. Their solution arrives via technology. The Internet opens infinite possibilities of meeting, in contrast with the boring life of home and work. Self-judgments are partially overcome by the protection of the screen and the fact that nobody else will know. The medium helps her to know men and sex. A world of seduction, intimate confessions, desire, eroticism, sexual fantasy, lust, pornography, and cybersex enters her life through the screen.

In the '70s, Nancy Friday published hundreds of interviews about the sexual fantasies of women which revealed vivid, complex, creative, sometimes extreme sexual lives that debunked the cultural myth that women "don't think about sex that much." Now those fantasies can be shared online – but for a cybervirgin the world of sensuality and lust is restricted to the Internet.

Cybervirgins are well aware that there is a big difference from real relationships, even if they have not had any. But after prolonged experience online, subtle mental mechanisms gain strength. The medium itself elicits a peculiar attachment. She can define a boyfriend as a man with whom she has only had online contacts, and who perhaps defines himself the same way with other women.

In some cases she can become addicted to porn or cybersex, or masturbate compulsively with various sexual fantasies. Since women, as Taoism says, have an unlimited source of yin energy and climax a number of times, they can match the unending information loop with a parallel loop of arousal and release. At the opposite end, the extreme nature of some Internet porn creates shock and inhibition instead of liberation, further postponing their acquaintance with real sex.

But most of all, cybervirgins can become attached to the attention given to them in dating sites – to be seen, heard, desired and seduced. An email carries all the emotion of a love letter; a long chat session becomes a romantic evening.

For a man's seduction to be successful, he must flow with her sensitivity – otherwise he'll be deleted from her contacts with a sudden click of her mouse. This gratifies and hooks her. The intimacy makes it possible to share without shame and to open in ways which could hardly happen in reality with a stranger. She, of course, is always looking for Mr. Right who will love her forever. But after a while the process of searching itself can become the end – which is less risky for the heart than a real meeting.

The few real meetings she has had (if any at all) disappointed her. By remaining in the virtual world, she can continue to feed the dream of finding her prince and avoid the risk of heartbreak. Staying virtual also supports her cultural and religious injunctions to give attention to the "higher layers" beyond the body and its feelings – which feeds the world of dreams and the lack of contact with reality.

I have written about the female universe because I have chatted mostly with women. Men enter the online world through different modalities, which are nevertheless complementary – withdrawing from reality, mostly by feeding the ego through seducing women, and with the attitude of no-strings-attached. Real meetings, as much as they are longed for by men, carry the "risk" of chaining them to women who could potentially limit their roaming.

The explorations by cybervirgins can become extreme. A woman I knew online, a virgin in her early 30s living in a country with traditional attitudes about sex, told me that she had an online friend who was her sex slave and with whom she played BDSM (a compound acronym derived from the terms Bondage Discipline Dominance Submission Sadism and Masochism) online. She could order anything and her slave would do it on webcam. It is rather surprising how somebody can go into those practices – virtual, but with a real person on the other end – before having had any real sexual contact. Centuries of cultural conditionings about sex can rupture abruptly on the Internet.

Cybersex can easily slip into addiction. Once we obtain the objects of our desires, that achievement becomes of no value because the ego-mind is interested in what is still not attained. Since the mind – and the Net as its extension – can create infinite objects of desire, we can easily be caught in repetitive compulsions.

Until a few years ago pornography could be accessed only in a limited way in most parts of the world. The impact of porn is particularly strong in countries which were quickly transformed from complete denial to availability in the intimacy of home.

What happens when sex, an experience involving many layers, is mediated by a screen, and only on the mental and visual planes? If this approach to sexuality is the first and the only one for a long time, what type of imprint does it leave on the psyche? What type of relationships will be shaped in the future? Do Internet cyber-meetings smooth the way for more open and deep meetings in reality – or do they increase the distance from the real, bringing unfamiliar inner challenges?

Gender Issues and the Vanishing Male

The Disappearing Male, a Canadian Broadcasting Company (CBC) documentary, showed how the presence of pollutants in the environment is having a strong effect on the male reproductive system, including a rise in testicular cancers and widespread lowering of sperm count in boys – now less than half what they were in decades past.

Bisphenol-A and phthalates are chemicals used in many of our daily products, including plastic, cosmetics and furniture. They act as endocrine disruptors, messing up the hormone balance in the body, especially mimicking estrogen and causing earlier puberty in girls and the feminization of boys.

David Deida has explored in his books the major issues in men's lives – from work to women, sex, intimacy, and love. He says that not only does a man need direction in life, but his embodiment of a direction and goal is what makes him attractive to women (Deida, 2006). The information society, pulling us in several directions, actually weakens our steadfastness and sense of direction, distracting us from a clear path which can only arise from within.

How many interruptions a day do we get from mobiles, email, and the variety of notifications from computers and smartphones? At any time with a call or an email from our smartphone, we can cancel our appointment to meet someone.

Technology appeals to both genders. While one of the recurring themes of the male attitude is freedom, for women it's connection. (Again, "male" and "female" are meant as qualities of being not necessarily overlapping with gender.) It's ironic that while technology promises both freedom and expanded social connections, we end up chained in front of a screen –connecting mainly via keyboards and displays.

Earlier Exposure to Porn
Scientists at the University of Montreal began a study in 2010 to compare men who watched porn with men who didn't. But they changed the focus because they could not find any man who did not watch porn. So they explored how, when and how much porn men consume. They found that the average age of the first exposure to porn was ten.

We know that early exposure to strong sexual messages or, worse, being sexually abused, can trigger sexual dysfunctions ranging from strong denial to obsession with sex. When a child receives stimuli beyond his capacity to absorb, it can either trigger anxiety or diminish the reaction of his psyche. The first sexual messages can imprint in a way that affects the subsequent relationship with sexuality.

While parents can install family filters on computers, they aren't always used, don't protect every time, and can be easily bypassed by kids – who are generally more expert than their parents. Thus, kids can access sexual material through the Internet long before receiving guidance from the pivotal adults in their lives.

We teach sports to young people, we teach them technologies, culture, arts, enroll them in the most disparate courses, but very seldom, even in the most progressive nations, does anyone prepare them to face sexuality – one of the strongest energies that a human being can experience – in an honest and open manner. Schools don't give useful sex education, and few parents talk openly with their children, even if they have the time. Society leaves kids alone – abandoning them with hypocrisy and cowardice, so adults can avoid potentially embarrassing conversations.

At the same time, we pretend that teenagers don't act out the sexual messages they receive from the media – or, if we know they do, we expect them to be responsible and safe. Yeah, sure. Hormones aren't well known as sexual education experts. During their teenage years, the bodies of boys and girls start to secrete powerful sex hormones, so they are naturally going to be more interested in sex, while still insecure about their just-discovered sexuality.

Puberty is occurring earlier now, due to hormones in food, chemical pollutants like phthalates acting on the endocrine system, and, I'm guessing, because of increased mental stimulation about sex as well. Nonetheless, kids lack the basic knowledge – and self-knowledge – to correctly use a condom; to sense, recognize and express their yes's and no's clearly; to prevent sexually transmitted diseases; to respect their own as well as others' limits; to not be pressured by peers in their choices about sex; to feel comfortable about masturbation and sexual fantasies. At the same time sexual cyber-bullying and sex texting by mobile is increasing among kids, they seem not to be aware of the consequences of exposing their or others' bodies through the Net.

Polls about sexuality point up the basic ignorance of young people about sex-related issues. As much as youngsters are exposed to sexual messages, they nonetheless remain just as careless as they were decades ago about pregnancy and safe sex. Early teen pregnancies, a phenomenon that has been typical of Third World countries, are now on the rise in Western countries too. HIV is spreading mainly now among teens.

Today the first sexual curiosities are often satisfied through the Internet – much before having real experiences or even a clear idea of what sex is. The Internet is not new as the initial exposure to sex. When I was a boy we had sex comic books and magazines, but they were very mild compared with what is available today. Degrees of intensity do matter

The Digitally Divided Self

Desires

The Pandora's box of sex is already open and sexual messages are here to stay. In our society it is almost impossible to avoid sexual messages: they are omnipresent. Our desire for sex and associated products are continuously triggered and stimulated, giving us constant opportunity to become lost in them – or to find pearls within our awareness. Awareness can remain in the middle, between indulging in desires and repressing them. While all spiritual teachers talk about desire as a hindrance among the path to liberation, many are realistically saying that desires, because of their nature, have to be experienced in real life.

According to Nisargadatta Maharaj (1982), "The perennial desire for pleasure is the reflection of the timeless harmony within. It is an observable fact that one becomes self-conscious only when caught in the conflict between pleasure and pain, which demands choice and decision" (p. 97). One disciple asserted, "What the Yogi secures by renunciation (*tyaga*) the common man realizes through experience (*bhoga*). The way of Bhoga is unconscious and, therefore, repetitive and protracted, while the way of Yoga is deliberate and intense and, therefore, can be more rapid." Nisargadatta answered, "Maybe the periods of Yoga and Bhoga alternate. First Bhogi, then Yogi, then again Bhogi, then again Yogi. Weak desires can be removed by introspection and meditation, but strong, deep-rooted ones must be fulfilled and their fruits, sweets or bitter, tasted" (p. 97).

In order for our experiences to be lived totally, they have to fuel our awareness. Desires can be neither avoided nor bypassed. By stimulating the mind in infinite ways, digital media give desires – not only for sex – powerful leverage. This expansion needs to be matched with a parallel expansion of our observing awareness and the heart qualities that provide direction, grounding, and understanding of our inner reactions. In the absence of this balance, we end up with a strong inner drive that has neither steering wheel, reverse gear, nor brakes. We are carried along mechanically, driven by an infinite loop that we mistake for "freedom."

As to the condition of having no desire, Nisargadatta's wisdom was: "Then you are as good as dead, or you are the Supreme" (p. 66). And it's a long path of practice to merge into the Supreme condition of enlightenment, in which desires no longer drive us.

Cybersex as a Tantric Path

The desire for an attainable union, whether with a human partner or with God, has been the foundation of devotional longing, called *bhakti* in Hinduism. The longing itself is the path toward God. Similarly, in tantra, the energetic upwelling during non-orgasmic intercourse is the bridge to a deeper union.

Cybersex through chats and webcams is about self-stimulation and self-pleasuring. In this modality there is actually an opportunity, for brave souls who dare, to enter their depths. Self-love can become a tantric practice. The activation of sexual energy without a partner – through breathing patterns, meditation and solo techniques – has been a spiritual path in certain tantric traditions. The source of the sexual energy which can be reached and transformed is the very same source of love and awareness. Through tantra we can come to understand that we are ourself the source of sexual energy, and that the other is only triggering what is already in us. At the deepest tantric levels, then, there is no longer me, you, or the attraction between us. All is connected in a global Oneness (or in a cosmic orgy, if that is your preference).

So, in a way, whether our partner is human or a sex toy – or if sexual activity is mediated by cybersex – does not change much for our path to discovery. When we are engaged with other people, we can project our object relations, attachments, expectations, and sense of pride or worthlessness onto them. The less the sexual relationship offers hooks to attach our inner projections to, the more attention can go to our inner movements – our reactions as well as the flow of sexual energy. After all, Monkey Rocker, peddling sex machines, has touched upon a deeper truth.

Through cybersex meetings, which are almost exclusively with partners who are strangers, we can even approach a tantric attitude where young, old, beautiful, ugly, thin or fat no longer matter. We flow with the pure sexual energy. We can even export that same attitude to our offline life. Tantra is about "not choosing," merging with the sexual energy in itself. Preferences about body shape are seen as the mental constructions that they are. But widening our connection beyond the mental preferences can happen only after we have a matured heart center and the capacity to fully experience our bodily sensations. IT does not support either factor.

CHAPTER 6

COMMODITIZING AND MONETIZING

"All that once was directly lived has become representation... The real consumer has become a consumer of illusions" (Guy Debord, 1967).

T he Situationists, an international revolutionary group of the '50s critical of capitalist culture, spoke of "The Society of the Spectacle" which alienates people through a mediated and commoditized social environment. Media and products, in the Situationists' view, dull the audience and control desire. Half a century later, we have newly created media with greatly expanded scope – which reinforce the Situationists' principles. In the new digital millennium it seems that desires are not controlled, yet they are acceptable as long as they are associated with a market product, channeled through and stimulated by the media.

The Situationists perceived that in capitalism, emotions become transmuted into market products – and we have to pay up to redeem our emotions. The market, as they saw it, first takes away our real needs for connection and authenticity, then offers a pale reflection of the real – making us always thirsty for a real which will never come. The need for connection today is expressed through social networks which appear free and democratic. Yes, many Internet services are free of charge, but if we calculate hardware, software, the Internet connection – plus our time and attention – the cost must be reconsidered.

The market product now is us. We are being sold as targets to advertisers, according to the contents we view and produce on the Net. Moreover, the Situationists observed that people in our society are programmed to live a life that is merely a representation of a real life. Through technology, needs have been created in order to sell solutions. And the hi-tech market doesn't even require much in the way of commodities any more, since it is represented digitally – making blatant Debord's words about becoming consumers of illusions.

Replacing the Real

> Once we have surrendered our senses and nervous systems to the private manipulation of those who would try to benefit from taking a lease on our eyes and ears and nerves, we don't really have any rights left (McLuhan, 1964, p. 68).

Even babies now are deprived of bodily contact – for various reasons. Parents have little time and, even when they are with their kids, their hands and eyes are on their gadgets. There are no longer large or extended families. Adults are sometimes scared to cuddle kids for fear of accusations of pedophilia. Yet body touch is important for a balanced emotional and neurological life.

Oxytocin is a hormone and neurotransmitter. Apart from its well-known role in facilitating childbirth, recent research points to its absence in autism, personality disorders, depression, social phobias, psychosis and sexual disorders. Oxytocin is released during bodily contact, stimulating a sense of bonding, well-being and social participation. Some doctors promote the start of oxytocin treatment early in a child's life to improve her social skills. This paints the picture of our situation: first, the real (contact) is taken away, then to reclaim the emotions (bonding) a substitute is offered (drug) – in the form of market products.

The need for human connection now feeds a huge industry of mobile phones and social networks. Once the Net becomes indispensable, we buy whatever is required to keep our connection active. The idea of falling out of the flow is too scary. But then we can buy apps for our iPhone or iPad which provide the same data easily available on the Net. Since we can't sever the umbilical cord, we gladly pay for the nourishment it provides.

Playing with Feelings

> "Thoughts are the bricks of the mind; emotions are the plaster cementing the bricks together" (Chitrabhanu, 1980, p. 123).

Technology is now occupied with understanding, measuring, and driving emotional components – even to planning robots which can discern and interact emotionally with humans. On one side, the attention to emotions is welcome after centuries of dominance of the rational mind. However, feelings are basically thoughts which travel along the byways of the body. As Buddhism teaches, emotions are still part of the bigger "mind." Being more aware of feelings is a good thing, but from the wider perspective of spiritual development, we are not our feelings, just as we are not our thoughts.

However, both industry and politics can take advantage of the emotional world. The switch in politics from ideological to emotional battles leaves space for manipulation and irrational messages which leverage our primordial fears and instincts, while bypassing our attention. The surge of Nazism points out that those messages are effective even in culturally advanced countries.

A distressing example is in front of us in Italy in 2010. The ruling party dispenses messages emphasizing the "heart" and the "party of love" – interspersed with hate messages toward whoever will not bend to their rules, and fear messages toward designated enemies (immigrants, journalists, "communist judges"). These messages speak directly to the limbic brain.

Now that we have been emptied of personal narratives and meaningful content, we unconsciously perceive the emptiness of our lives. And technology promises to give back what has been lost on the social, psychological, and even spiritual levels. In our need to be filled, we let our inner self be invaded by products and information – continuously. Products and brands give us back a label, if not a meaning. Our profiles on Internet sites attempt to define us for the world – which invites others to acknowledge our tastes, self-image, ambitions, and so on from a modest number of available options (sharing links, writing short notes, commenting on other's notes, clicking on "like").

All of these externals cannot fill a void which is inner. But we try and we try – one click after another, one purchase after another. As Mick Jagger was singing in the '60s, we still have no satisfaction.

Since the gap between the promises of the market and the actual lives of people is huge, this system produces depression in many people – which, once more, is treated with products. Without adopting the attitude that "it was better when it was worse," let's see what economic growth has brought to Western society. The first question that comes to mind – embarrassing, but simple and revealing – is whether it has brought more personal happiness. Without a doubt, better economic conditions have created an improvement in education, life expectancy, and health in the last century. These aspects, necessary for adequate human and social development, have definitely come into being thanks to a Viagra-activated economy.

However, in the West, having gone far beyond our basic needs, are we happier or not? The answer is both Yes and No. Much research has been done on this in developed countries. As expected, poverty brings unhappiness. But once we've reached a dignified standard of living, an increase in income is no longer proportional to an increase in happiness. Beyond a certain point (quantifiable as the economic means of an average working person) the level of happiness does not increase. In other words, an office clerk has no reason to envy his overpaid manager.

In general, with the increased affluence since the '50s in developed countries, we find no parallel growth in collective happiness. People today are much more inclined to depression and mental diseases than our predecessors. A 25-year-old today is three to ten times more at risk of suffering from serious depression than a 25-year-old in the '50s. More than 20 percent of teenagers have anxiety and depression problems, and an average adolescent of today would have been considered a pathological case only a few decades ago. So the use of anti-depressants and psychotropic drugs continues to increase.

iMarket

Companies are interested in understanding, feeding and entering people's vulnerabilities and sense of insecurity. They feed our competitiveness as a way to silence feelings of insecurity, expand desires, transform desires into needs, challenge self-esteem, establish insatiability – so that the markets can keep running. Commercials – pasted onto every surface of modern life – have the sole aim of persuading us that such and such product is indispensable, that without it we would feel as if something were missing. Which then slips into a self-fulfilling prophecy.

What we have will, in fact, never be enough, because what we acquire are just products which, in themselves, cannot meet our soul's needs. Inner emptiness cannot be filled by owning something, much less a virtual something – but we try anyway. Various studies have shown that the most insecure people tend to identify themselves through material success. So the best message to stimulate purchasing is the one that makes buyers feel inadequate – comparing them with unreachable models. This has not changed with the online economy – where consumers are insatiable and the producing-consuming economy feeds on itself. In *Brave New World*, Huxley (1932) wrote:

> "We condition the masses to hate the country," concluded the Director. "But simultaneously we condition them to love all country

sports. At the same time, we see to it that all country sports shall entail the use of elaborate apparatus. So that they consume manufactured articles as well as transport."

The advertisement industry flourishes on similar conditioning. McLuhan (1964) wrote that:

Ads are news. What is wrong with them is that they are always *good* news. In order to balance off the effect and to sell good news, it is necessary to have a lot of bad news. Moreover, the newspaper is a hot medium. It has to have bad news for the sake of intensity and reader participation (p. 210).

Advertisers since McLuhan's times have learned the lesson. They know now how to induce the viewer to participate more. Shocking images – death, illness, war, sex and fetishes – are used to promote products, meanwhile redefining the boundaries of shock and compassion. The images become entertainment that leads to commerce. Even the '60s values of freedom, community, and anti-establishment views have been appropriated by the market – especially by IT gadgets which are promoted as tools of freedom, personal empowerment, and social connection.

In a depersonalized world we find our "personalization" in advertised products and from technology – customized cars, fashions that "express your real individuality," software that "adapts to your needs," custom themes for our blogs, software for "tailoring every detail of your website," customization of our social networking pages, and so on.

At the same time, less and less people have enough time and attention to listen to each other in an empathetic way. Human interaction is just another window in the attention deficit disordered multitasking craze. But with products and custom technology we can delude ourself into feeling cared for and understood again. The need for personal freedom and for connection are two of the most basic human needs. Technology promises to fulfill both.

Digital "freedom" then pushes us to redefine ourself continuously, playing with identities and prolonging adolescence forever. This redefinition, which happens only at the surface of the personality, is functional to the market. With every new lifestyle there's a total renovation of personal expenditure. Bloggers themselves are not out of the market game. The "State of the Blogosphere 2008" revealed that "more than four in five bloggers post product or brand reviews, and blog about brands they love or hate," while "one-third of bloggers surveyed have been approached to be brand advocates" and "of those, more than six in ten were offered payments of some kind" (Technorati, 2008).

Here we see again that our willingness to communicate and feed the machine with our "user generated content" is food for advertisers who target ads based on what we say on Twitter, Facebook – even in our email communications.

Brave New World

In *Brave New World*, every discomfort of old age was abolished. The character remained the same as a 17-year-old. People never stopped to reflect, always busy at pleasure and at work. Whenever a phase of reflection would emerge, the perfect drug – *soma* – was available in appropriate doses (Huxley, 1932). Eighty years after Huxley's novel, we witness life extension therapies, antidepressants to feed desire, Viagra to renew sexual vigor, commoditized entertainment in every moment of our lives. All of these militate against the growth of the soul.

In the preface of *Amusing Ourselves to Death*, Postman (1985) wrote that, "In *1984*, Huxley added, people are controlled by inflicting pain. In *Brave New World*, they are controlled by inflicting pleasure. In short, Orwell feared that what we hate will ruin us. Huxley feared that what we love will ruin us" (p. xx).

The move of marketing into the digital realm creates an infinite marketplace where needs are replaced by desires. Desires, fed by the mind rather than by finite biological needs like food and shelter, are endless. The digital world, qualitatively closer to the mind and its incessant cravings, is profoundly non-sustainable. The Internet, as it replaces TV, is ripe for social control of a class of the population that might start to question the whole system. It promises to be the new *soma* for a society experiencing economic and environmental decay.

Deconstructing Sense and Ethics

The inner void left by the infomarket calls forth either a nihilistic attitude or, conversely, a return to traditional or simplified ideas, as people attempt to make sense of the world. This prepares fertile soil for the seeds of populism and fundamentalism. The information society cares about efficiency, objectivity and velocity, a "childlike, essentially pre-ethical attitude" (Slouka, 1995, p. 26).

> When riding the will to power, human values are considered hindrances. Techno-nihilistic capitalism thus erodes the basis for compassion and the natural human capacity to care (Magatti, 2009, p. 265).

94

Capitalism, with its social climate dominated by confusion and speed, returns to what Marx considered its distinctive characteristic: evaporating everything solid into thin air (Magatti, 2009, p. 150).

Capitalism, deconstructivism, and the information society share an attitude of demolishing and redefining meanings. Living under their sway, identity of the individual becomes fragmented and superficial. Social connection, an important factor of identity, is then dismantled by the infomarket which tends to isolate people – even with the renewed sociality of the Web 2.0.

Toward the Denial of Truth

Technology, with its capacity to reorganize reality in infinite ways, can easily dissolve and redefine the relationship between things, as well as their meaning – until truth is no longer the fundamental bond which makes sense of information. After a TV appearance, the Italian journalist Travaglio, who has been active in denouncing Berlusconi's lies, wrote on his blog that on TV it is hard to explain things properly. True, but while it is easy to write elaborate and detailed explanations, on the Web it's hard to keep the focused attention of the reader. Both TV and the Internet are adverse to long narratives and deep reflection. Political accountability, while technically easily employed on the Net, becomes pointless in the absence of love for truth.

When what counts is the latest news with neither narrative nor a broad view, accountability – which requires a historical view – is weakened. Complexity and coherence give way to seductive words, simplified messages, and immediate emotional gratification. Being emotionally touched, then, becomes the parameter for evaluating truth. This creates an ideal ground for politicians who do not think it necessary (or have no capacity) to be coherent in their words and actions. They can afford to openly contradict themselves, because attention is weak, memory fails, and the ability to activate votes emotionally pays at election time.

Coherence and truth are no longer considered values. Berlusconi, for example, can publicly affirm anything one day and deny it the very next – without being called to resign or at least apologize. This means that the level of indifference to truth has reached pathological levels in Italian society (and in the U.S. as well – planted by Reagan and in full bloom under George W. Bush). It is only possible for this to happen when everything has been emptied and content is commercial, a joke, or a catch phrase. Slouka (1995) saw the perils of digital representations that deny truth.

This, it seems to me, is the threat we face: that soon, lost among electronic representations "just as good" as the real thing, we'll collectively lose sight of the fact that approximations and reenactments are a kind of lie, and that lies, even small ones, tend to create a climate increasingly hostile or indifferent to truth (p. 148).

Regaining the love of truth will be a long process in which rationality won't be enough to counteract our digitally fragmented awareness. Other cognitive channels are needed, among them insight-provoking inner silence and the development of the heart center which activates the curiosity needed for inquiry and finds delight in discovering truth.

CHAPTER 7

POLITICS, PARTICIPATION AND CONTROL

Google History keeps track of all the searches we do on the Net. Google Desktop and similar services index everything that is stored on our computers. RSS readers like Google Reader know our interests by managing our subscriptions to blogs. Tracing cancellations and new subscriptions, it is possible for them to map the way our interests evolve. Google potentially knows much more than we care to imagine. Analyzing our browsing speed of RSS articles gives information on where our attention falls. And both the sites we share publicly and the ones we don't convey something about what we want to hide from public view.

Even without future neurotechnologies, it is possible for Google to infer our emotional state by analyzing how fast we type our search information and how many mistakes we make. When we enter a search text in the Google toolbar, our entry is sent to Google "as is." So if we press the backspace to correct our typing, this too will be sent along. Google can know the threads of our mind better than we know ourself, and it can discern fairly accurate ideas of how the collective thoughts of our culture move as well. Such data in the hands of a politician or an advertising company would be invaluable.

On top of that, we expose ourself directly in social networking sites, forums, and blogs through our words and photos. In the global village of the Net, just as in landed villages, everything is known about everyone. We willingly offer ourself on the Net because we need to build an identity – to be mirrored, seen, recognized, to interact online. In doing so, we expose ourself to being controlled.

The Rulers of Our Psyches

From Bill Gates to Facebook, we watch people in their early 20s drawing hundreds of millions of people into their technological creations. This sudden success of young men reminds me of the sorcerer's apprentice. A website that quickly attracts millions of people requires a commensurate responsibility and strong code of behavior. It's a bit like suddenly becoming president of a country. But if elected leaders are inadequate, they are vulnerable to control by the opposition.

The impact on people's minds of a single site like Facebook, which engages hundreds of millions of users, is stronger than many laws and social institutions. But there are no elections in Facebook. The rules are made exclusively by the company. When we read about people whose Facebook accounts were disabled without notice, we are made aware of how powerless we are. We cannot expect the ethics of democracy from companies whose priorities are financial and whose skills are mostly technical.

The operating modalities and the social rules that derive from technical-structural choices have wide implications on the way we work, read, and relate with others – in other words, on the way we live. Every mouse click is not only an interaction with a site, it is an inner movement of our psyche as well.

The will to read our minds is not limited by our online activities. Neuromarketing uses the most refined equipment, such as functional Magnetic Resonance Imaging (fMRI), to understand how purchasing decisions are made and, consequently, how to direct their marketing strategies. Similarly invasive are Microsoft's projects for remotely monitoring productivity of employees.

> The Times has seen a patent application filed by the company for a computer system that links workers to their computers via wireless sensors that measure their metabolism. The system would allow managers to monitor employees' performance by measuring their heart rate, body temperature, movement, facial expression and blood pressure (Mostrous, 2008).

Digital technology and control are a perfect match. Norbert Wiener called computers a technology of "command and control." Anything we do on the Net can be controlled by government agencies. Every Web company – whether Google, Yahoo, or Microsoft – is subject to government control, and every Internet provider as well. In the US, the Patriot Act allows enforcement agencies to control communication by any media – and there are similar regulations in other countries.

Digital fingerprinting is a set of techniques which can identify a

98   *The Digitally Divided Self*

user based on the unique characteristics of every computer (for instance the software versions installed, screen size, and fonts installed). This information is sent when we access web sites. By analyzing those parameters, BlueCava has already identified hundreds of millions of computers and smartphones. Tracking digital fingerprints can be done, of course, without the user's knowledge, and so without any way for the user to opt-out or delete the tracks, which the more traditional tracking cookies allowed. Deep packet inspection, a technique which can be used for surveillance and censorship, is another intrusive tool set between the user's computer and Internet.

The need to control, being related to survival, is built into us – like the urge to attend to novel stimuli. The more control we have over the environment, the better our chances of survival. Even babies only a few months old delight in pushing buttons to activate a result. Predictability makes us feel safer. If we touch a certain button, we want a certain result.

Digital technologies give a feeling of being in command to the master and controller of the tool. (For programmers, this includes driving the behavior of people who use their software.) But at the same time we expose ourself to control by the modalities of interaction, by service providers, by government agencies, and by Web companies. Methods for tracing and controlling our Internet activities have become more sophisticated.

Governments
In 1996, John Perry Barlow wrote the "Declaration of the Independence of Cyberspace" in these terms:

> Governments of the Industrial World, you weary giants of flesh and steel, I come from Cyberspace, the new home of Mind. On behalf of the future, I ask you of the past to leave us alone. You are not welcome among us. You have no sovereignty where we gather.

Governments – not only in dictatorships, but also in Western countries – can control every piece of information that passes through the Net. One of the famous projects is Echelon, which allows access to the content of email, instant messaging, land lines and cell phones.

The Internet was supposed to dismantle nation-states and institutions. Individual governments are still carrying on their affairs and gaining increasing control over the Internet. According to critics in Congress, the National Security Agency monitors private phone calls and email messages of Americans in excess of legal limits – more than has been acknowledged previously, and despite legal and logistical problems (Risen, 2009).

In other words, governments can and will do anything. Internet providers and mobile operators give law enforcement agencies information about their customers' Internet activities and GPS locations. Almost every GPS-enabled smartphone collects location data. They know where we are, what we read and write, and whom we connect with.

Journalist Evgeny Morozov (2009) wrote about the political implications of the Net. In an article for the *Boston Review* he challenged the mantra of the Internet as a means of spreading democracy, declaring that it could even "subvert democracy." From Russia to China and Iran, governments are paying people to control and influence public debate. He said that "should the media dig a bit deeper, they might find ample material to run articles with headlines like 'Iranian bloggers: major challenge to democratic change' and 'Saudi Arabia: bloggers hate women's rights'" (Morozov, 2009).

Advertising and Our Attention

Attention is a valuable resource. The most important economic resource of the Internet is advertising, which feeds on people's attention to certain messages. The resource of attention is analyzed in detail and validated economically through sophisticated methods. The analytical systems of Web pages are developing in the direction of recording not only how many pages have been seen from which sources and from what type of users, but the movements of the mouse as well, the movements within the page, the parts selected, and on which parts we stop.

Once the Pandora's box of attention analysis is opened, there will be a race to develop techniques for securing this precious knowledge. We will witness more tricks to hook us into clicking and buying. Google has patented a method for analyzing what a user is interested in by considering factors like position of the cursor, amount of time the cursor rests on certain areas of the page, actions of the user, even the user's facial expression. In this way, it is possible to obtain a more accurate map of how, when, and what the user gives his attention to, getting ever-closer to reading the user's intentions, and interests – in order to feed him with tailored advertisements.

In place of the mouse, in the future there could be devices which measure our physiological states, perhaps even expand into neurological devices which can read our brain waves and the regions of the brain activated by specific stimuli. For instance, when a user is in an alpha-receptive frequency state, advertising broadcasters would likely be willing to pay more to the host site, since the user then is more receptive to the message of ads.

Myspace, the most important social network until a few years ago, is on the decline. In March 2010 there was news that Myspace was starting to sell subscribers' data profiles to advertisers, capitalizing on their users' willingness to give out information about who they are.

Google

Google's motto is "Don't be evil." It is self-portrayed of a nice company – cute logos, cool language in their blogs, investing in renewable energies, challenging China about censorship and control. But Google's motto guides the company like the Hippocratic Oath guides those doctors who prescribe medicines that harm their patients by their side effects.

On December 3, 2009 in a CNBC interview, Eric Schmidt, Google's CEO, said:

> If you have something that you don't want anyone to know, maybe you shouldn't be doing it in the first place. But if you really need that kind of privacy, the reality is that search engines – including Google – do retain this information for some time and it's important, for example, that we are all subject in the United States to the Patriot Act and it is possible that all that information could be made available to the authorities.

That's an honest statement which could have been expressed more succinctly as, "Forget whatever we said before about privacy." At the Techonomy conference in August 2010, Schmidt said that through artificial intelligence Google can predict human behavior, and that if we show Google fourteen pictures of ourself, it can even identify who we are – by comparing our photos with others' on social media, dating sites, etc. It's a boastful statement – but not far from the truth.

The ordinary human mind operates primarily on past conditioning. And it becomes even more mechanical through interacting continuously with machines. So there's little surprise that some well-written software can accurately infer who we are, what we want, which websites we will visit, and where we will go next as we shuttle about town. Google knows of every Web page we visit, every advertisement we click on and probably much more – with their mathematic and analytic tools that can interpret location, web navigation, connections with people, and email messages.

Besides predicting our behavior, Google can make decisions for us because, in Schmidt's words, people "want Google to tell them what they should be doing next" – via context-aware computing – like recommending a certain restaurant near our current location that would appeal to our tastes. As unnerving as his words are, one more time, there is more than a hint of truth in them.

Our will and inner direction are activated by the connection with our "belly center" – that place which martial arts practitioners are trained to move from. This center – which is also the ground for our search for truth – is weakened by overusing the mind without a felt, alive, and aware connection with the body. Lacking this connection, we seek guidance from technology even for the most basic decisions – just as we ask Google for information that we could retrieve ourself with a little effort of memory.

We are being made into helpless babies needing guidance and confirmation from Mother Google for all our activities – or at best into rebellious teenagers who ignore her suggestions but still turn up at dinner time.

Possessive mothers, wanting their children to be dependent on them, seduce them with their tastiest dishes (free and entertaining software tools), and provide for all of their needs – while resisting their children's efforts to leave home unsupervised. Yet everywhere we go we leave a trail of breadcrumbs so Google can follow us. A mother's children as well as Google's, then, never have to interface with the real world – nor their real Selves.

There is rightly a growing debate about the Internet and privacy, especially related to Google – and the company is facing a number of legal challenges. In 2010, after European regulators asked what kind of data Google's Street View camera-laden cars collected, Google admitted that for several years, because of a software bug in their system, they inadvertently collected private data from unencrypted wireless networks while collecting data about the location of Wi-Fi networks.

Intercepting private communication is illegal in most countries, but if it's a "software bug," it most probably will be forgiven. Data is king – beyond ethics and above the law. After further investigation it became clear that there had not been a bug, and that the collection of private data was intentionally programmed into the software running on Street View's cars.

Ben Edelman (2010, 2), an expert in Internet privacy and advertising, provided evidence that "even when users specifically instruct that the Google Toolbar be 'disabled,' and even when the Google Toolbar *seems* to be disabled (e.g., because it disappears from view),

The Digitally Divided Self

Google Toolbar continues tracking users' browsing." Google apologized for this "bug" as well. Besides managing data, Google has developed smart electrical meter that records consumption of electric energy which allow knowing the details about people's use of tools and technologies – and thus the details of their lifestyle.

A few months later, Edelman revealed something quite embarrassing for Facebook. Contrary to their privacy policy, when a user clicks an advertisement, Facebook "reveals to the advertiser the user's Facebook username or user ID. With default privacy settings, the advertiser can then see almost all of a user's activity on Facebook, including name, photos, friends, and more" (Edelman, 2010, 1). In October 2010 it was discovered that Facebook's FarmVille and Mafia Wars applications, played by tens of millions of people, were passing individual's data, and their friends' data as well, to advertisers and tracking companies – in violation of the company's policy. Mark Zuckerberg "apologized to users."

In February 2010 Google introduced Buzz, a would-be competitor to Facebook. To build an immediate base of users and connections, they used Gmail accounts to structure an automatic network of friends. Gmail users suddenly found themselves in an unwanted network of people with whom they had previously communicated by chat and email, exposing their connections with no discretion, posing major threats to privacy and even to personal safety, especially users living under totalitarian regimes. Issues of personal and professional privacy undermined trust in the confidentiality of their email addresses. Doctors' or lawyers' clients could suddenly see one another. People could be stalked, potential lovers tracked, connections with business competitors exposed.

As Morozov (2010) wrote in *Foreign Policy*:

If I were working for the Iranian or the Chinese government, I would immediately dispatch my Internet geek squads to check on Google Buzz accounts for political activists and see if they have any connections that were previously unknown to the government.

The need to colonize territory is founded in our primordial survival instinct. New territories open for conquest now are at the mental level, in the representation of reality. Google has maps of the physical world at Google Earth, and maps of the mental territory of millions of individuals. Since people today identify predominantly with their minds, it is not an exaggeration to say that Google is the colonizer of our mental territory.

Neil Postman reported in *Technopoly* that George Bernard Shaw saw his average contemporary as credulous as a peasant in the Middle Ages, believing as blindly in science's authority as his predecessor did in the Church. The situation is probably even worse today. We certainly have our high priests – from programmers to the engineers who set Google's mysterious algorithms which administer earnings or penalties – or even send sites to hell with zero page rankings. All under a preamble of objectivity and fairness.

"Google usually promises unbiased results, but occasionally admits otherwise," Ben Edelman (2010, 3) has discovered. He presented evidence that "Google has 'hard-coded' its own links to appear at the top of algorithmic search results." Even though Google's services, such as Google Finance or Google Health, aren't leaders in their areas, searching for a stock ticker or a health related word is likely to bring up Google services in the prominent positions.

Wikileaks

Even Wikileaks subscribes to the "data is king" attitude – the more data and information that is available, the more power we have against the big guys. At the end of 2010 we saw Wikileak's documents flooding the Net. Hundreds of thousands of raw secret documents, available for the first time to anyone with an Internet connection, were exposed to the media for interpretation. But without the awareness that understands in a broader narrative, information does not provoke any valuable change. After the initial reactions of surprise and general interest, the leaked documents were almost forgotten.

Perhaps the best way to have information ignored is to flash it on the Net, for it will soon be buried under a stack of new information. All information on the Net, from the most superficial YouTube video to the most resounding political revelation, is filtered by an inner "digital attitude." In front of a screen which divides our attention, and where the competition among disparate inputs is strong, political issues can only be short-lived.

That the Net makes concentration difficult is one more pressure on the mind as an organ of perpetual distractibility. The drunken monkey image of the mind is apparent when we try to concentrate. After a few seconds the mind is roaming elsewhere without our guidance.

Into Our Digital Persona

In a policy statement on children and advertising, the American Academy of Pediatrics notes that the ancient Code of Hammurabi:

> made it a crime, punishable by death, to sell anything to a child

without first obtaining a power of attorney. [It also reports on] numerous studies documenting that young children under 8 years of age developmentally are unable to understand the intent of advertisements and, in fact, accept advertising claims as true (*Alliance for Childhood*, 2000, p. 32).

Fortunately for the companies which developed Sentry and FamilySafe software for monitoring kids' activities, the code of Hammurabi is no longer applied. Those applications read private chats of children and sell data of what they write about movies, video games or music to companies that develop marketing messages for kids. Lower Merion School went even further, installing LANRev on kids' computers, a remote monitoring product that allows remote spying on students – for example, taking pictures through a laptops' webcams – without their knowledge.

In July 2009, some Kindle users had a surprise: Amazon electronically removed two books from their ebook readers, books these customers had already paid for. Amazon claimed those titles had copyright issues, applying a typical Orwellian Big Brother approach. Ironically, the books were George Orwell's *1984* and *Animal Farm*. It is technically possible that someday every copy of a title will be removed. And it is possible that our electronic bookshelf will also be scanned for "subversive" content.

In June 2010 Google announced the "remote application removal feature" as "one of many security controls [Google's] Android possesses to help protect users from malicious applications." Fatherly protection? No thanks! Any day now applications may be removed arbitrarily by a government. Apple's iPhone is also notorious as a walled garden where applications must first be approved by Apple itself.

You Can Tell What Somebody is Like by the Company They Keep

Even without access to our data, there are subtle ways to infer who we are. At the end of September 2009, an experiment done at MIT on social network analysis could identify which students were gay just by considering the data available on their Facebook pages. Through analyzing their online friends and the connections among them, their gender preferences could be inferred with a high degree of accuracy – raising more questions about online privacy. And social network analysis can tell more about us than our sexual preferences.

When there's no direct way to sneak into your digital persona, you must then be politely asked for it. According to city officials in

Bozeman, Montana (Hoffman, 2009), job applicants have been asked for their user name and password of any social networks they are part of, in order to investigate their background and character.

Linking the mechanical nature of the mind with the data which most people spontaneously expose on the Net is such that well-written software can predict our ideas, opinions, tastes and which products we would be willing to buy. Marketers are trained to catalog people on the basis of their personalities, attitudes, lifestyles and preferences, so social network analysis gives them powerful tools.

In April 2010, Facebook introduced an expansion of their social graph. People were no longer connected only to their friends inside Facebook's space, but on other websites and external applications as well. This allows other websites to make public our Facebook name, profile, picture, gender and friends list. This was automatically activated for 400 million users (a few months later, as I am writing, already more than 500 million) – unless they opted out, a procedure they did not make easy.

Most users will never even know that Facebook has introduced one more privacy challenge, and many others won't bother to act to protect their privacy. Even when we opt out, our friends can still share our public Facebook information on other websites unless we block their applications – one by one. With that information out in cyberspace, other companies have valuable information about our profiles and likes. Eventually Facebook apologized and said it would render privacy options easier to manage.

Is the Internet Empowering Us?
As early as 1991, Jerry Mander wrote:

> Computers have made it possible to instantaneously move staggering amounts of capital, information and equipment throughout the world, giving unprecedented power to the largest institutions on the earth. In fact, computers made these institutions possible. Meanwhile, we use our personal computers to edit our copy and hook into our information networks – and believe that makes us more powerful (p. 3).

Since the beginning, the Internet has been regarded as an instrument of democracy, and indeed Internet activism has grown over the years. The Net is considered a tool for decentralization that gives power back to small groups and individuals. It offers a place to distribute words, images, sounds and videos, a place to meet like-minded people and to organize groups for certain aims. Ideas can be spread easily through the Net, and anyone can do that relatively cheaply.

But something's missing. I am too young to have been part of the '60s political movements, but as a teenager I was part of the '70s student movement. The Internet did not yet exist, nor mobile phones. Faxes were only available to big companies. There were ordinary telephones, but we didn't use them that much. Yet whenever there was a gathering, assembly or rally, every student knew about it. We were posting flyers at the school entrance and talking in assemblies, but we mainly heard about things by word of mouth.

The dark side of the student movement was present of course, with some people degenerating into imposing their point of view. Egos were power tripping on every side of the political spectrum, but mostly the movement had genuine passion to act for a better world, a passion that was contagious. We could feel the collective energy and participate in the collective dream.

The student movement was very influential and well-organized, not in spite of the lack of technologies but perhaps because of it. We relied on personal connections. No cultural or social transformation in history has needed much technology. Obviously, the transmission of values and ideas through personal contact can light the inner fire much more easily than any forum, blog, Facebook cause, or YouTube video. Various online appeals and causes risk having as little impact in the real world as a discussion among prisoners during their hour of fresh air.

Perhaps we have pulled the wool over our own eyes, imagining that we could empower ourselves by airing our ideas through blogs, displaying our creativity on Youtube, building a community through social networking sites, transforming society through online causes. Were we deluding ourselves in thinking that we could be as influential as the big corporations? I don't see that central governments or big corporations have lost any power since the Internet arrived – and media giants look even bigger online.

Certainly the Internet can bring us together to raise our voices and be heard by many people. Yet information overload, emphasis on individual narcissistic representation, and a medium that fragments our attention work together to make the Net a difficult place to convey messages that breach our usual consciousness. Even when people are touched in their minds, this rarely matches their consequent action. Information tends to remain on the intellectual and mental levels. The medium, we are discovering, can also foster global indifference and detached participation.

Illusory Participation

As in Athens, important decisions will continue to be made by the elite: the bourgeoisie and the politicians, bureaucrats, and experts in their employ. Machines mediating between citizens and ruling institution would in no way enhance individual freedom: instead, this scheme would further naturalize the force of law, regulations, procedures, and other codes of conduct while further depoliticizing the administration of society. The "intelligent island" of Singapore points the way (Brook, 1995, p. xiii).

Blogs have been considered the best way to express opinions from the bottom, which could be giving democracy a powerful new tool. But, a 2009 Pew survey about offline versus online political participation found that the differences in participation between the rich and poor were exacerbated online (Aaron, 2009). In reality, every technology requires much technical expertise before it becomes easy enough for everybody to use without technical support.

Blogs have followed a similar evolution, and it is not surprising that among the most-read blogs are those on technology itself – written by people and companies with the skills to optimize their search engine visibility and thus the number of visitors to their sites. As Harkin (2009) reported, "A glance at the geography of the blogosphere is enough to show that a very small number of veteran bloggers have the vast majority of the readership entirely to themselves" (p. 121). And then, famous bloggers tend to link to each other, to read only each other.

Looking at the academosphere, the *Economist* in July 2008 included "Great Minds Think (Too Much) Alike" which pointed to research by University of Chicago sociologist James Evans. He found that more journals are providing online editions and that reference sections included fewer sources, predominantly those already well-known, and mostly recent ones – probably because they are easiest to locate through Google searches.

On the commercial level, "Online Shopping and the Harry Potter Effect" reported that successful sales become more concentrated. On a popular Internet music site, 0.4% of available tunes logged 80% of sales. The phenomenon is explained by the ease of rapid transmissions via readily available electronic technology that creates nearly instantaneous fads (Webb, 2008).

This has been confirmed experimentally by Duncan Watts, a sociologist at Columbia University, New York. He and his colleagues Matthew Salganik and Peter Dodds tested the effects of communication and peer approval on the musical tastes of 14,000 teenage volunteers recruited online (Salganik, 2006). A set of 48 songs was made available to all the volunteers, who could download whichever songs they wanted. The researchers split the volunteers into eight groups; in some, group members could see what their peers were downloading, but in others they had no such knowledge.

In the socially connected groups, the winner took all: popular songs became more popular, less popular songs were less in demand. This effect was much less pronounced in the socially isolated groups. Watts posits that information overload makes us more dependent on other people's opinions to find out what we like. Webb asks why, with information so available, people look to the choices of others.

In another article, psychological tests by Aldhous (2009) found Wikipedians grumpy and close-minded, "more comfortable online than in the real world."

Information – when detached from experience, from a felt inner view, and an ethical ground – mostly reinforces our conditioning instead of opening our minds to new arenas. "Information is dangerous when it has no place to go, when there is no theory to which it applies, no pattern in which it fits, when there is no higher purpose that it serves" (Postman, 1993, p. 63).

The mind's main job and natural inclination is to separate, discriminate, and judge. It gives us a powerful way to read and act on reality – which has given science and technology the strongest roles in our culture. Unless the mind is subordinated to a broader (we could say spiritual) awareness, it is non-inclusive by nature. From this perspective, it is not surprising that online we tend to stay in territory that already is familiar. Our social connections online certainly have the potential to broaden our mind – but mostly, as with other media, uniformity is promoted.

Lee Siegel expressed the paradox that we "must sound more like everyone else than anyone else is able to sound like everyone else" (2008, p. 73). The source of this apparently contradictory phenomenon is in the ego itself. It needs to be recognized and accepted, while at the same time it needs to feel different and special. Commercially, we are presented with millions of choices to help us feel unique, yet we tend to choose what is known – or at least chosen by somebody we want to be connected with and recognized by, much as teenagers are dependent on the peer group's opinions. When we are presented with millions of commercial options and we choose one, we delude ourself into thinking we are expressing our individuality.

Our choices about information can come from our depth only if we allow ourself to sense our own depth. The more we indiscriminately swallow information, the less we are able to make real choices that require listening to ourself. And we don't listen because we fail to exercise the muscles of our inner attention. Our capacity for focus is weakened by attending only to external inputs composed of short bits of information which cannot hold or convey a broad view. When we can't approach our inner self or when the skills of looking inside are weak, we can only consign our choices – along with the crowd – to whichever website pops up mostly quickly on our screen.

One of the mantras of the Internet is that there are no barriers of social status, religion, country, ideology. Yet the more we identify ourself with our mind's contents, the more we erect defenses against extraneous information which could shake our mind's structures – and, therefore, our very identity. Real broadening of the mind can only happen when we don't identify with our beliefs and ideas – which does not come through more information.

Slacktivism

Richard E. Sclove believes that technology is responsible to some extent for political disengagement. Residents of Ibieca, a small village in northeastern Spain, had to fetch water from the village fountain till the early '70s, when running water was installed in their houses. With pipes running directly to their homes, Ibiecans no longer went to the fountain. Families gradually purchased washing machines, so fewer women gathered communally to scrub laundry by hand where they had engaged in politically empowering gossip about men and village life. The places of social gathering became nearly deserted. Men were no longer connected with the children and donkeys that formerly helped them haul water. This was a crucial step in a broader process through which Ibiecans came to relinquish the strong bonds with one another, their animals, and the land that had knit them into a community (Harding, 1984, as noted in Brook, 1995).

It's not just painful in itself: the loss of community also carries a political risk. "As social ties weaken, so does a people's capacity to mobilize for political action" (Bowles and Gintis, 1986, as quoted in Brook, 1995, p.85). While technologies are not the single most important factor, they are important especially when linked with other factors such as legislation, the distribution of wealth, race and gender relations, and international affairs. This means that "we must learn to subject technologies to the same rigorous political scrutiny and involvement that should be accorded to those other factors" (Brook, 1995, p.85).

In Ibieca, introducing water pipes led to donkeys being replaced with tractors, since the fewer tasks a donkey is required to perform, the less economical it is to maintain them. As donkeys became superfluous, villagers had to finance and operate their new tractors and washing machines by turning to outside jobs. Sclove observed that the social effects of any given technology are often indirect and arise in tandem with apparently unrelated technologies. This implies that technology solely meant to address social needs is inherently suspect (Brook, 1995).

Good intentions expressed online are not necessarily transformed into real action and responsibility. If we can reside in virtual places, why should we be concerned about disappearing communities and environmental damage? We are willing to be universally connected by the Internet, but in real life we have become intolerant of differences of race and religion. And we often revert to our old conditioning as a safe haven.

Morozov said that "people can have lots of information and very little power to act on it." He reminded us that:

> East Germans who could not tune in to West German broadcasting had higher rates of opposition to their government than those who did. The idea that unfettered access to the Internet will bring democracy suggests one of the worst fallacies of cyber-utopianism. Once they get online unsupervised, do we expect Chinese Internet users, many of them young, to rush to download the latest report from Amnesty International or read up on Falun Gong on Wikipedia? Or will they opt for *The Sopranos* or the newest James Bond flick? Why assume that they will suddenly demand more political rights, rather than the *Friends* or *Sex in the City* lifestyles they observe on the Internet? (Morozov, 2009).

The Internet is too easy to crack down on, given the many weak links: service providers, Internet lines, could services, and the traceability of online conversations and email. As a last resort, computers can be seized.

Rallies and personal contacts are replaced by clicks and "likes," or by embedding links on our sites. We are becoming used to actions limited to the mental sphere. The pressure of one million participants in a Facebook group, or by one million emails to a prime minister can be easily managed by governments. Reduced into bits and bytes, such campaigns become as short-lived as the ever-changing electrical states of digital memories.

The Net as a tool promoting free speech and the dissemination of information on a grassroots level was paradoxically truer when it was much slower and we could access only words and a few images. The more the Net becomes visual and fast, the more it resembles TV. Substituting Web TV with traditional TV doesn't change much, if there isn't more depth or more attention. Depth is more easily acquired offline through real-life experiences that are supported by our less-distracted awareness.

The Yogic Geek

The power of controlling technology is unprecedented in history. HTML5, the new standard for the Web, allows even more opportunities for tracking. The data that is accessible ranges from the web pages we visit, to our location, pictures, and text from blogs. The appropriate response to this mental colonization is to develop – more than technical skills – a capacity to control our thoughts that has also no known precedent, a consciousness of ourself that is smarter than the software for tracing our preferences and mental tendencies. In other words, we need to know ourself, applying to our thoughts what in the Hindu tradition is called *jnana* yoga, the path of knowledge.

This means we must observe the train of our thoughts, what attracts us, what suggestions we are amenable to, and how we transition from one idea to another. Google's tools – which trace and store the course of our browsing, searches, and online activities – can also be used for deconstructing our mental conditioning, for letting go of our identification with our thoughts – a reverse engineering of our minds. By reviewing our Web history and searches, we can see what our mind might be prey to and how it can be dragged astray by suggestion.

Developers of free software generously offer their applications, using the Net to spread non-commercial tools – which often are better than commercial ones. The next challenge for technological freedom lies on the inner level. Our skills will have to be applied to observing our mind. It will be necessary to become master of our mind to protect ourself from manipulation by the exponential increase of inputs.

The less we are aware of the subtle mechanisms of our mind, the more we will react mechanically to the inputs presented to us. The more we react mechanically, the more predictable we become. And the more predictable we are, the more our mind is prone to be colonized by software, by market products, and by politicians. But the more we know ourself and observe the flow of our thoughts as if they were external phenomena, the stronger we are to choose whether to follow or simply to witness them. Perhaps, like yogis, we will need to control our physiology as well (heart rate, blood pressure, etc.) which can also be monitored.

The progressive manipulation and control of our minds by technology could have a positive side effect: it might motivate developing the discipline to keep our attention alert – to be aware of our intentions, mental mechanisms, and when we are about to slip into a state of vulnerability to manipulation.

Attention is an inner resource too important to be left to the Net and to advertisers. And our attention has never been attacked in such a massive and direct way before. Becoming masters of our attention allows us to "be here" fully – in everything we are doing. It invites us to activate our best resources and to make conscious choices. It allows us to treasure every experience for the maturation of our psyche. Attention and awareness go together.

When we are not attentive, we are dragged by external messages in directions we don't consciously choose – and often in ways which reiterate old mental conditioning. Without attention, we react mechanically in life.

With the refinement of spiritual development, the issue of privacy becomes meaningless. We are told that the individual personality is an illusion, a mental construction – and that once beyond duality, we don't perceive substantive differences between individuals.

The contents of individual minds that Google, Facebook (and others) want to know so badly in every detail – these are not the real thing. As long as we live in the ordinary world, in duality, the function of our personality must be respected and oriented toward the possibility of seeing the illusion. This is one of the many paradoxes of the human journey: that we need to create a "real" illusion in order to be aware of it and to contact truth.

CHAPTER 8

COME TOGETHER:
THE RISE OF SOCIAL NETWORKS

The external world has been impoverished by cars – which have directly changed the territory and massively shifted sociality. Children can no longer play in the street. Non-commercial public spaces for meeting and social interaction have been scattered – like the chickens that used to wander our byways. And regional commercial centers have been developed which we can reach only by car. The massive migration to cities and their suburbs during the last few decades has moved us away from an immediate and felt relationship with the terrain – which is now mostly seen as a road from one place to another.

The broad use of mobile phones has distanced us further from wherever we are located, distancing also from the people around us there. While roads boxed people into cars, the Internet has placed us in front of screens, indoors and out – with smartphones and GPS systems and their digital "augmented" version of the world.

While many things in life are free, including friendship, we are giving up the external world for a digital representation of it, buying products to reclaim digitally what we have lost.

Renouncing the World
The isolation of people did not start with the Internet. Isolation is functional to the market society. With more isolation, more products are purchased, and togetherness itself can become commoditized. We inhabit today a world where we don't know our neighbors, where face-to-face meetings are often usurped by the media, where

the media frighten us by exaggerating criminality and chaos so that people are suspicious outside of protected or formal venues. This is a world where social networks can rescue us with a relatively easy, cheap, fast and safe way to connect with people.

A US study of adults found that "cross-sectional models reveal that time spent browsing the web is positively related to loneliness and negatively related to life satisfaction" (Stepanikova, 2010). The correlation analysis of another study, "Self-Presentation 2.0: Narcissism and Self-Esteem on Facebook," concluded "that individuals higher in narcissism and lower in self-esteem were related to greater online activity as well as some self-promotional content" (Mehdizadeh, 2010).

One more study examined the relationship between social Internet use and loneliness, where the level of loneliness felt after online chatting was higher than that in face-to-face communication (Hu, 2009). Many Internet users regularly mock such studies for demonizing the Net and its users. They deny the validity of them, using rationalization as the predominant defense mechanism.

In the Western world dominated by economic crisis, social unrest could be tamed by glueing unemployed and poor people to the Internet. Even more than TV, the Internet can be a pacifier that weakens the capacity for social organization. *Dividi et impera* (divide and rule) works now as much as in ancient Rome. The trend toward isolation is increasing in the US. There are many more singles, and people have fewer friends and confidants. In June 2006, a study by the *American Sociological Review* found that the average American had only two close friends, down from three in 1985. And while 10 percent of people had no confidant in 1985, in 2004 such friend-starved people had grown to 25 percent.

The Inner Need of Connection and Facebook

The need to stay connected is a strong human force, so strong that even a digital connection is acceptable. So strong that people even neglect basic safety by texting while driving.

Among social networks which connect people to each other, Facebook has definitely come out the winner. After repeated resistance to signing up, I relented. My first resistance had been about the requirement of presenting a profile for introducing myself on my friends list. This somehow perplexed me. I like variety in people, and have always mixed with an array of artists, travelers, spiritual researchers, entrepreneurs, scholars, rich and the poor.

My life has many different facets, each of which resonates with similar characteristics in others. For instance, my interest into spirituality can flow better with people who've had similar experiences. If I "broadcast" messages to hundreds of "friends" on Facebook or Twitter, what we share cannot deepen. But if I focus on a specific color out of the entire spectrum of my personality, it can be the entry point to expand and inquire deeply with others, allowing the most creative, intimate and personal connections. Such connections are not possible online because they are as much experiential as mental.

The public profile which defines our digital persona in specified terms doesn't allow the subtle shades of our personality to be recognized and connected to. When we define ourself through a Facebook page, much of the inner quality behind that self-definition is lost. I am reminded of *One, No One, and One Hundred Thousand*, the last novel – a masterpiece – of Luigi Pirandello. Basically we are "One," but for the majority of people we are "No One," while among the multitude of people who know us we are "One Hundred Thousand."

We appear differently in the eyes of each person who knows us. Evoking the spiritual level, we can say that all of us are "nobody" and "everything" at the same time. But on the level of personality and object relations, Facebook is an interesting experiment. On the Net we are often anonymous (though potentially tracked by Internet providers and government agencies): in our Web surfing, in social networks and in forums, people mostly use identities which do not identify them precisely. Facebook is an attempt to reunify the various personalities and to give a center of gravity to the fragmentation of the online personality. It is an attempt to assemble – though limited to the digital arena – the various object relations.

Facebook may represent an evolution beyond the adolescent search for one's own self – the stage at which we attempt to find an identity through experimenting with the different facets of our personality, while often hiding online behind anonymity. Now I am to have my "real" me on Facebook – exactly the same in everyone's eyes – unifying the pieces of my history and therefore potentially the pieces of my psyche.

Facebook's first surprise to me was the instruction to update my status by writing in the third person: "Ivo….," which I could have completed with anything like "feels grateful," "has had lunch with friends," "is writing an article," etc. We are to write from the perspective of others, so we are seen and read as beyond their boundary. The third person potentially has a dual function: it supports inner observation as we propel our eyes to the other side, looking at ourself from the point of view of others. Yet speaking in the third person can feed the ego's need to be seen and recognized.

After a couple of months the suggestion became, "What's on your mind?" as Facebook was giving more importance to "Twitter-like" functions, stimulating a stream of messages in real time. The way of meditation is to let the thoughts pass by without holding on to them. In years of developing self-understanding, one of the few things I have learned is that the mind disgorges thoughts continuously; that the vast majority of them are not interesting; and that most of them do not even originate from me. Most thoughts arise from conditioning, and repeat the words and thoughts of others, with little variation.

I have begun to be less attached to my thoughts, letting them flow with a certain indifference. But now comes Facebook which elevates them to "news of the day" worth broadcasting to every "friend." Social networks capitalize on the mind's nature to be somewhere other than the present – planning, hoping, worrying, needing confirmation. Facebook would be nothing if people did not value their mental itches so much.

Experiencing for Others to See

The need for mirroring is inherent in everyone for their balanced psychological development. Through social networks, no experience has value any more if it's not made public – to be seen and commented upon by others. In an interview for *Digital Nation*, Sherry Turkle (2010) said:

> with the constant possibility of connectivity, one of the things that I see is... a very subtle movement from "I have a feeling I want to make a call" to "I want to have a feeling I need to make a call" – in other words, people almost feeling as if they can't feel their feeling unless they're connected.

Kids are on social networks during those delicate stages of personality formation when much-needed face-to-face connections are mostly supplied by clicks of a mouse. With development of the personality influenced by Facebook connections – which is hard to abandon as long as significant people in their lives are hanging out there – the network's rules of communication become a driving force of psychic formation.

Homogenizing the ways we interact with others and channeling the connection through Web applications and clickable options impoverishes the development of our personality. It impedes us from becoming aware of the subtleties, the challenges and the soul-growing potentialities of connecting with people in real life. Since social media distract us away from the feedback of reality, our imagination can fly unobstructed. The online world is well suited to feeding mental projections, transforming others into objects in our psyche.

We have become eager to participate in and contribute to the digital world. We are no longer merely viewers. Instead we are actors in the society of the spectacle as we feed social networks with our "user-generated content" that helps companies advertise specifically to us.

With real communities impoverished by cities, cars and the media, our sense of belonging is now readily managed by social networks and brands. For lack of anything better, Facebook groups – or owning an iPhone – can give a sense of "I" and "we." The authentic human need to belong and contribute to our community is exploited by marketing organizations.

I played around a bit with Facebook, wrote some notes, sent links, and uploaded a few photos of myself. Then I found myself on a tropical island taking pictures and thinking of how I would present them on Facebook. I had begun to move away from direct experience. Even the mind which interferes is part of the totality of the experience and I welcome it. But when it exaggerates, I set it aside. It reminds me of being a child: when something interesting was happening, adults would say, "When you tell this to your friends (or to your parents), they'll be amazed." That angered me because it pulled me out of the flow of my experience.

On Facebook I sense the risk of homogenizing the rich variety of ways with which I interact with individual people. With each friend I meet in person, a unique relationship is being created, almost an entity in itself, shaped over time by the alchemy of two souls interacting. People who develop a spiritual orientation pay attention to the role of each relationship in their lives so that each can evolve in an authentic way, free from past conditionings – or be severed if it cannot evolve. But interacting with icons as representations of people leaves space for the expansion of our inner representations and projections on them. This also increases our beliefs about them. Lacking real contact, there is no opportunity for a reality check to challenge those beliefs.

Empathy

In a world so interconnected, we might expect empathy to be increasing. But no. The "Me Generation" of American college students is actually more self-centered and competitive than previous generations, and less empathetic. "We found the biggest drop in empathy after the year 2000," said co-author Sara Konrath (2010), a researcher at the University of Michigan's Institute for Social Research. Measures of empathy were taken by standardized tests.

The authors suggested several reasons, including the massive exposure to media in the early years, violent video games, and a hypercompetitive society. Also, "the ease of having 'friends' online might make people more likely to just tune out when they don't feel like responding to others' problems, a behavior that could carry over offline." A detailed study by Twenge (2008) published in the *Journal of Personality* found that youth today are more egotistic and narcissistic than in the past.

Adolescents are known for lacking control over their impulsivity, exacerbated by underdeveloped frontal lobes and poor empathetic capacities. Technology now gives bullies powerful weapons for acting with a level of brutality which could hardly be matched in real life. In a society where the flow of vital energy is reduced to video games and initiation rites have died out, intense emotions have no healthy, soul-growing way to be channelled. And where kids are for the most part hyperprotected and confined to indoor life, that flow can only move through unhealthy channels.

In her August 2009 address to the House of Lords on the matter of empathy and social networks, neuroscientist Baroness Susan Greenfield reported that "the mid-21st century mind might almost be infantilised, characterised by short attention spans, sensationalism, inability to empathise and a shaky sense of identity." (Wintour, 2009). Empathy is possible only when our identity is strong and some parts of ourself can melt in meeting another soul. If our identity is weak, we cling to the little we have and become selfish.

In 1977 McLuhan talked about a return of the collective mind which lacks "any individual consciousness," like tribal people whose "main kind of sport is butchering each other." Far from being a place where love flourishes, according to McLuhan, the global village "is a place of very arduous interfaces and very abrasive situations" (2005, p. 265). In 2010 the Simon Wiesenthal Center found an increase of 20 percent over only one year in the amount of hate material on websites, social network pages, and forums.

We can say that the Net merely reflects reality, but the ease of expressing extreme points of view anonymously facilitates people being made into objects. In chat rooms, after a while it is easy to become unconcerned about leaving a conversation or deleting or being deleted by somebody (or being "Nexted" in Chatroulette). We are unable to perceive the human being on the other side as more than data and information, unable to see the full implications of the connection/disconnection.

In Tagged, one of the most popular social networks, I found in the instructions:

> Earn cash to buy other people as your pets! :) Earn $2000 just by coming to Tagged every four hours. When a pet is bought their value goes up by 10%. That profit is split between the pet and the previous owner!

Facebook has an automatic algorithm that can ban users. A number of them saw their accounts closed without notice or explanation by Facebook. Not even much empathy from Facebook – and no personal connection. Algorithms do their job, are much cheaper than people, and can't be questioned.

Recently a friend of mine commented on the difficulty of considering online people as real people with broad sensitivities. She said they have become ghosts in the eyes of others. I think that the "ghost-becoming" process is part of the mind itself. Technology then builds on this propensity and expands its impact. A real meeting with another, meeting them as they are, without projections based on inner object relations, is a rare event. We superimpose on others our experience with parents, siblings, sons/daughters, taxi drivers, politicians, assholes, sages.

Seeing a person in his real essence is an enlightened act. Sometimes we have a gleam of reality – but it is usually momentary. Facebook and similar sites accelerate the process of transforming people into "ghosts," which is the reason why I resist participating in them. I do not want to evaporate my friends.

Illusory Contact
Being able to choose the people we want to connect with through the Net seems to be an evolutionary step beyond traditional identifications with family, territory, religion or social status – but in reality it restricts the scope even more when we identify with ideas, preferences, or aversions. The mind is highly discriminatory in nature and tends to split mental hairs. We can contact like-minded people on the other side of the world about a specific interest, but mental specialization has a strong separating impact.

When we are engaged in mental activity, we have little tolerance for interruptions. Our mind can follow only one thread at a time. This is different from manual activity which leaves our mind free for talking with others or for reflection. If we are communicating on the Net, we must keep our lover or child on hold. We are very willing to befriend almost anybody on Facebook – but would we exchange our real life with our "friends" in Bangladesh who can access the Net from an Internet café – but only occasionally because it is a luxury?

The rhetoric about sociability and expanded communication on the Net does not stand up to authentic, straightforward, frank and direct expression of intentions and feelings. As much as the Net allows us to communicate easily with a large number of people, it also allows us all to withdraw into various hideouts when there's something uncomfortable looming. The basic detached nature of the Net then proves convenient. Not answering an email doesn't seem as rude as not answering a face-to-face question – and we can always blame the email system.

Another resistance I have to communicating with people I've known a long time but not kept in touch with is based on the recognition that what shaped our relationship is now absent, as we likely have evolved in different directions. It isn't easy through Facebook to find a new point of contact which fits our current inner condition. Nor can we re-enact the past. Once our psyche has been transformed, going back to an old form is impossible, like growing baby teeth again.

In the midst of my resistance, I rediscovered plain old email – which was the only way to communicate when I went online. From time to time I email updates about my life to those friends who are more part of my life. Email is simple and more environment-friendly, uses little bandwidth, and is accessible from any computer, even very old ones – and even with a very slow Internet connection.

Email is more direct and personal, almost carrying the feeling of letters. We could say that there's no difference in sending an ordinary email or a message through Facebook – but there is. With an ordinary email we are not in a crowded setting, which gives space to more direct expression of our inner states.

One of the reasons for the success of Facebook is that friends are supposed to be such. In reality, on social networks we are likely to meet people who are alien to our real-life narratives. Even though meeting people online can lead to interesting connections, mostly such contacts come and go and the relationship does not deepen. Facebook, however, developed as a way to connect with people we know, as well as those we knew in the past but lost touch with. Even though the invitation game of picking friends and friends of friends expands – so that I ended up befriending people I didn't know – with only a third of my Facebook friends I did share important events that shaped our lives.

I am especially resistant to participating in the limited communication on Facebook with those historical friends, for the very reason that some of them are real friends with whom I had such important connections. Since many of the friends who contacted me on Facebook know I'm a long-time Internet user and former computer book publisher, I need to explain that I rarely go to Facebook – I'm not deliberately ignoring them. And I'm left with a quandary: it doesn't look nice if I ignore them, but I also don't want further engagement in one more online toy.

Facebook built its base of users on such "hard-to-ignore" situations. For every level of communication there are different arenas, of course, and we can choose the medium appropriate to the depth and intimacy we want. For intimate people we would choose email, telephone, personal meetings and body/mind contact at every level from handshaking to lovemaking.

Facebook, like many Web applications, tends to expand its scope to include more and more aspects of our lives, until it can become a necessity. At first it's a cool way to connect, then it adds feature after feature, until it's essential to not isolate from our group of friends. Finally it swallows our time and attention. On Facebook I sense the risk of digitizing even the real and important relationships, transforming our rich histories into an orgy of trivia. I also see the risk of creating a cyber-elite that excludes friends who don't have the time, equipment, or desire to be involved in social networks.

Every time I connect to the site I find a number of updates about my friends. As I browse through those short updates, my attention is pulled to other Web pages and applications. On Facebook one friend is planning a trip, another quotes from a website, one more is sad (even though "negative" feelings aren't generally expressed), yet another has political opinions. It is like TV, where tragic news is immediately followed by gossip, everything melting into an anesthetized flow of information lacking real connection with our inner states. In the meantime, to make things worse, email messages arrive, websites are updated, and other applications are running on the PC.

I don't want to become numb to the felt connection with my friends, as happens with TV. Every message we get from a person who is valuable to us deserves time and attention to assimilate and respond to. But time and attention are scarce resources on the Net. Perhaps this is the reason why we share less about our difficult inner states on social networks – they require our full attention. It's easy to avoid a friend in need by writing a few words then clicking on the "send hugs and love" applications – or, paradoxically, clicking "I like." In participating in social networks, there's also the risk of exempting myself from direct contact with friends. Using Facebook then *decreases* individual contacts.

Instead of communicating, I found that I was broadcasting, transmitting to an audience. As the audience increases, the number of friends expands. The effect is seductive, gratifying to the ego. But it is different communicating to a public rather than to a single person. Each person has a unique story and a unique relationship. That very personal communication in which we can deepen mutual understanding receives a smaller share of our time.

I have noticed that after I passed beyond fifty "friends," I gave less attention to people's messages. I tend to scroll down my friends' messages like news items – as in those countries where everybody honks constantly, the meaning of the signal is lost, hearing is anesthetized, the signal merely background noise.

The nature of the mind is such that through repetition, less attention is given to similar stimuli. The mind chases novelties. I don't want to skim my friends' messages, but I do. We claim that one medium doesn't need to replace another, but our resources of time and attention are limited – and don't grow at the pace of technological evolution. The more time we give to social networks, the less is left for anything else.

The grand collective dreams of the last century are gone, though we are connected online, we are divided and isolated from each other. Online social and political aggregations are short-lived and don't require much effort. Offline engagements need continuity, participation, and sacrifice, something barely known in social networks. And we have been deprived of the need to be just with ourself. James Hillman (1993) wrote on this:

> The immense hypercommunication industry... all those oyster shell-colored, plastic-covered chip devices that turn the citizen into hacker, plugged into everyone everywhere – "I am because I am accessible" – does not, repeat, *not*, put an end to my aloneness but rather intensifies it. If I must be networked in order to be, then on my own I am out of the loop, out of communication, null and void, nowhere. I can't be reached. If to be means to be reachable, then in order to be I must stay networked. Result: the contemporary syndrome, communication addiction... When I sit down to write, I've stepped out of the loop, I'm no longer in the addictive pattern. I'm simply here, of this frosty, moonless night, alone – but I am not lonely. It is silent, a little scratching of the pen point or the hum of the machine. I am not spread out through the network, not so much connected as collected (pp. 95–6).

The Digitally Divided Self

CHAPTER 9

DIGITAL KIDS

W̲e are used to hearing that children are "naturally" at-tracted by technological gadgets. To every parent's amazement, even babies seem to grasp the functioning of remote controls and some computer functions. From this we infer that technology is natural and good for them, enhancing their knowledge of the world and boosting their creativity. What babies and children are attracted to are novelties, colors, sounds and a way to control their immediate environment. Computers give infinite entertainment to kids and a degree of control superior to any other toy.

Body/Mind Development in Childhood
Alliance for Childhood (2000) in their invaluable *Fool's Gold: A Critical Look at Computers in Childhood*, that:

> Infants and toddlers develop their visual-spatial awareness first through gross movements in space, such as crawling, and then by gradually fine-tuning their hand-eye coordination, until their eyes become adept not only at following their hands, but at leading their hands in finer and finer motions (p. 22).

It is only after many embodied visual and tactile experiences in three-dimensional space that young children recognize and appreciate visual forms as real objects, and develop the skill to visualize objects in the mind's eye. Then "too much time spent in passively looking at two-dimensional representations of objects on a computer screen – or a television set – may interfere with this developing capacity" (Alliance, p. 22).

In an interview, Joseph Chilton Pearce (2001) reported that:

Studies compiled by Dr. Keith Buzzell, Jerry Mander, Mary Jane Healy, and others show that the damage of television has little to do with content but rather with the pairing of imagery in synch with sound. This provides a synthetic counterfeit of what the brain is *supposed* to produce in response to language, as in storytelling. The child's mind becomes habituated to such sound-images, and the higher cortical structures simply shut down. Paul MacLean's work shows how in habituation an ancient reptilian brain takes over sensory processing and the rest of the brain idles along, doing nothing because it's not needed. The brain uses the same neural structures every time the TV comes on, and very few of the higher structures are developed. They simply lie dormant, and no capacity for *creating* internal imagery develops (p. 73).

All screen media, not just TV, have this effect on cognitive development. And it has been demonstrated that kids who are not told stories develop language later, and their linguistic skill is less refined.

Even on the physical plane, sitting for long hours can strain and injure the bodies of young children because "their bones, tendons, nerves, muscles, joints, and soft tissues are still growing. [Since their muscular and nervous systems are in the development stage,] it's not until about the age of 11 or 12 that their capacity to balance and coordinate the movement and the focusing of both eyes together is fully mature" (Alliance, p. 23). We know how much earlier their system is forced, through video games and repetitive use of pointing devices, to develop in a way not compatible with their slower biological pace. As a consequence, repetitive stress injuries, obesity and eyestrain are now common among kids.

Gary Small (2008) wrote that "underdeveloped frontal lobes [of teenagers] often impair their everyday judgment" and the massive use of computers and video games "appears to be stunting frontal lobe development in many teenagers, impairing their social and reasoning abilities" up to a point that "their brains' neural pathways may never catch up. [They are then] locked into a neural circuitry that stays at an immature and self-absorbed emotional level, right through adulthood." This is transforming humanity into a herd of frenetic teenagers with a diminished capacity to "delay gratification, reason abstractly, and plan ahead" (pp. 31–2). As Huxley described in *Brave New World*, we are headed toward the stunting of the soul's growth.

Denied Childhood
Childhood is not something to be hurried. Legend says that Lao-Tzu was in his mother's womb for 82 years and was born wise. The

maturation of kids, like wine, should not be forced. Time and the proper conditions are enough for proper development. The massive introduction of computers in homes and schools limits the broad range of kids' cognitive potential. For instance, emphasizing precocious analytical thinking actually delays cognitive capacity (Alliance, p. 10).

Since young children learn mainly through their bodies, pressuring them to develop mental skills which naturally come later interrupts development of their intellects – like the "failed experiments of the '60s in which preschoolers were pushed to learn to read and write. By the middle of grade school, they had fallen behind less rushed children in both academic and social skills" (Alliance, p. 10). Using computers instead of playing spontaneously inhibits even the capacity to play, as teachers report about children who use screen media a lot before entering kindergarten.

Another disruption of childhood comes from premature exposure to porn. Despite parental control software, porn is first seen at an average age of 10. This exposure interferes with balanced sexual development and can affect their view of sexuality dramatically, leaving imprints which are carried into later life.

Computers in Education

When somebody proposes the introduction or expansion of IT in schools, every door is going to open for its approval. Those who express doubt face strong opposition and are considered to be against progress. In reality, while the use of educational software is attention-getting and entertaining, it is not necessarily educational. Also, teachers are not as expensive as the composite cost of hardware, software, training, maintenance and frequent upgrades.

Kids develop computer literacy much earlier than book literacy – and they may never achieve the latter. Studies show that many kids have limited capacity to understand even simple texts and to express themselves with words. The qualities of analytical thinking which were supposed to be improved by computers have been the first victims. Creativity has followed quickly behind.

While the technology used in schools today will be obsolete in a few years,

> creativity and imagination are prerequisites for innovative thinking, which will never be obsolete in the workplace. Yet a heavy diet of ready-made computer images and programmed toys appears to stunt imaginative thinking. Teachers report that children in our electronic society are becoming alarmingly deficient in generating their own images and ideas (Alliance for Childhood, 2000, p. 4).

Computers, in other words, have a negative correlation with educational achievements. Research at Duke University in 2008 titled, "Scaling the Digital Divide: Home Computer Technology and Student Achievement," involved over half a million student/year observations of fifth through eighth graders. It found that:

> The introduction of home computer technology is associated with modest but statistically significant and persistent negative impacts on student math and reading test scores. Further evidence suggests that providing universal access to home computers and high-speed internet access would broaden, rather than narrow, math and reading achievement gaps (Clotfelter, 2008).

Lack of Mentors

The task of future teachers should be to convey essential human qualities, for students can easily access facts and concepts through the media. What kids need are mentors who can support skills for interpreting reality. Through real interactions with peers and guidance from adults, they learn empathy, emotional recognition and management, perseverance, attention, ethics, and a healthy connection with their bodies through play and sport. None of those qualities are developed better by using computers.

While kids need significant bonds with caring adults and with role models, technology takes them away from both adults and peers. The reality is that children today:

> are already spending far less time with their parents than in the past – according to one estimate, about 40 percent less time than 30 years ago. Now, even when parents are home, children are increasingly spending time alone. A 1999 study by the Fortino group in Pittsburgh estimated that children growing up today will have nearly a third fewer face-to-face interactions over the course of their lifetimes than the preceding generation (Alliance, p. 62).

Deprived of human interaction from the beginning, they may become a schizoid generation, withdrawing from people and reality, a condition in which social networks flourish. In this historical moment in the West, there are a lot of adults and far fewer young people. So adults can be available to mentor kids in the most effective ways. Unfortunately, life experience is not valued by the culture of digital newness, so kids end up isolated from that pool of potential guides.

Yet the human qualities of Joy, Inner Strength, Perseverance, Patience, Humor, Love, etc. are passed on by example, by direct contact and by inner inquiry. These essential qualities not only render our practical life more effective and our inner life richer, but are also tools which support the development of our soul.

Technology as an Answer to Social Fear

With the view of an increasingly dangerous world "out there," parents turn to technology. They often feel more at ease if their children have a cell phone or, even better, a GPS which can trace their position at any time. Children then have a permanent and direct connection with their parents, bypassing all connections with the people who live and work nearby – who, mostly unknown, are therefore seen as potentially dangerous. Even so, the availability of mobile phones and control systems has not brought more safety for children.

The massive use of such technologies is, instead, part of the problem. The tendency to ignore the people and social structures of the neighborhood does not build a safety net with familiar faces nearby. Disconnection from the surrounding environment has, of course, roots older than cell phones. A great deal of the landscape has been taken over by cars and other vehicles for the production, distribution and sale of goods. When kids don't know the territory and the people living in it, they will not turn to them either for necessity or for even casual, generic communication.

The best safety for children comes not from the cell network, but from the net of people known in the surrounding area who interact with each other. When I was a child we used to play in the streets, and the aunt or the father of one of us assumed the double role of protector and disciplinarian. When we got into mischief, we would often get a healthy cuff from these figures. Today they risk being sued by the parents. The world was not safe at that time either, but everyday life was not permeated by a general mistrust of people.

Nowadays an adult is perhaps more afraid of contacting a child than a child fears contact with an adult. In this culture of collective suspicion, an adult who communicates with a child risks being considered a child molester, so that the basic need for sharing and teaching between generations is mostly lost. Technology, in its attempts to resolve the problem, instead makes it chronic, and general withdrawal is accepted as normal.

The mobile phone, used as a solution to insecurity, actually alienates us further by reinforcing our insecurity, for we perceive the environment as hostile, which we are trying to control with this technology. We then fall into a mutual feedback between ever-more sophisticated technologies of communication/control and separation from the environment and the people who live in it.

Many only children – whose parents are often separated and lack extended families – have added prohibitions against playing outdoors or even in condominium courtyards – where adults who pass by might establish contact with the children and then be recognized in the streets, forming a supportive bridge between home and the outside. This situation impoverishes the quality and frequency of human relationships, which are essential for the development of the personality. Children end up with few people to connect with, though they may have hundreds or even thousands of digital "friends."

Wired Children

Kids are heavily wired to the computer today. A survey of 11–18 year olds, of whom 69 percent were between 11 and 13, revealed that: 62.2% first used or owned a computer before the age of eight, 80.2% first used the Internet between the ages of five and ten. 59.2% of them said that they inserted information from [the] Internet into their homework or projects without having read it in whole or part. On the question "How addicted are you to [the] Internet?", 62.5% answered they are "very" or "quite" addicted to the Internet and 53.2% to mobile phones (Kakabadse, 2009).

The Kaiser Foundation survey of more than a thousand parents of children ages 6 months to 6 years old found that "baby videos designed for one-month-olds, computer games for 9-month-olds, and TV shows for one-year-olds are becoming commonplace." In families where both parents often have busy lives, they increasingly "turn to media as an important tool to help them manage their household and keep their kids entertained" (Rideout, 2006).

Most studies on TV viewing have observed negative impacts, especially in heavy users and in children. While most people can agree on the negative influence of TV and video games, we delude ourselves in thinking that the computer is different.

The effect of most screen media on children is known to cause several mental pathologies, including hyperactivity and attention disorders. While the American Academy of Pediatrics recommends avoiding screen media for children less than 2 years of age, the Waldorf education model specifically does not expose children to screen media even longer, emphasizing instead play, arts, and a holistic approach to education.

Kids are often wired to video games more than to other screen activities. A study in 2008 explored "the different effects on hostility, physiological arousal, and state of aggression in those who played a violent video game (*Mortal Kombat: Deadly Alliance*) with differing levels of blood (maximum, medium, low, and off)." The research "showed that those in the maximum blood and medium blood conditions had a significant increase in hostility and physiological arousal" (Barlett, 2008). Violent video games also affect the speed of recognition of facial emotional expressions.

The Digitally Divided Self

Color photos of calm facial expressions morphed to either an angry or a happy facial expression. Participants were asked to make a speeded identification of the emotion (happiness or anger) during the morph. Typically, happy faces are identified faster than angry faces (the happy-face advantage). Results indicated that playing a violent video game led to a reduction in the happy-face advantage (Kirsh, 2006).

Barry Sanders (1995) extended the analysis to each of the electronic media. In his opinion, given the omnipresence of electronically generated images and sounds in contemporary culture, children grow up missing the oral experience of language critical to attain true literacy. Without the "technologies" of reading and writing, the development of the self is incomplete. Sanders also noted that the simultaneous passivity and arousal generated by electronic images engender frustration and alienation – which give rise to violence.

In an interview for *Digital Nation*, Clifford Nass expressed his concern about multitasking in younger and younger children. He reported that "when infants were breastfeeding and the television was on, infants were doing a lot of television watching."

> Breastfeeding evolved the way it did [because] the distance from the mother's face to the infant is the perfect focal distance. The voice is one that's very attractive. Well, if you think about it, what is television filled with? Faces and voices. What do babies love? Faces and voices. So now, at a time when we believe that children learn intense concentration, they're being drawn away. Then as they get older, as they get to 3 or 4, we started feeling guilty that we put kids in front of the TV as a baby-sitter. So what did we do? We didn't turn off the TV. We started giving them toys, books, etc., while they're watching TV. So what are we telling them? We're telling them "Don't pay attention; do many things at once." Well, it may not then be surprising that years later, that's how they view the media world (*Digital Nation*, 2009).

Kids are victims of technology even before birth. A study published in the journal *Epidemiology* in July 2008 titled "Prenatal and Postnatal Exposure to Cell Phone Use and Behavioral Problems in Children" tracked more than 13,000 mothers and children. It found that using a cell phone during pregnancy can significantly raise the risk of social, emotional and behavioral problems by school age – a risk on the order of tobacco or alcohol use (Divan, 2008).

Page (2010) discovered that the amount of time spent with screen media in kids correlated with psychological problems. Children who were engaged more than two hours a day in front of a TV or computer exhibited behavioral difficulties. The astonishing finding was that even when children were physically active, their problems remained.

Sleepless Children

Research by the Kaiser Foundation titled "Children's Media Use and Sleep Problems" (Zimmerman, 2008) found that both the quantity and quality of sleep of American children have deteriorated over the years, posing "major adverse implications for their cognitive ability, judgment, behavior and physical health... Inadequate sleep can bring or worsen a range of problems: obesity, aggression, hyperactivity." The total sleep time of children ages 1–5 diminished two hours a day between 1981 and 2005, and continued to decline in a more recent study.

Several important functions take place in the body and the brain during sleep. While the body is repairing and growing tissue and improving its immunity, the mind is consolidating memories and absorbing the learning of the waking hours, developing cognition and improving psychological health. The study reports that loss of only one hour of sleep per day for three days can impair neurobehavioral function significantly. During puberty children often need more sleep than before, though its timing shifts to later in the diurnal cycle. However, peer pressure and lessening of parental influence lead to adolescents averaging two hours less than the nine hours of sleep needed.

The interactivity of the Internet and video games that has become pervasive over the past two decades causes more engagement, increases alertness hormones, and inhibits users from limiting the activity. While TV shows have a defined beginning and ending time, this is not the case with the Internet, electronic games and phone use.

Most new forms of media are interactive, generate light, or (like social networks) involve more interpersonal and emotional involvement – all of which further delay sleep time of kids. Exposure to light decreases secretion of melatonin that supports sleeping. The nearer a light and the higher its intensity, the greater the melatonin suppression. Computers and video games are the biggest culprits. While good sleep is promoted by physical activity, this can be countermanded by media use. Disturbing to note is that sleep problems that arise in middle childhood tend to become chronic.

CHAPTER 10

LITERACY AND THE ANALYTICAL MIND

McLuhan (1964) saw that the advent of literacy arose at the same time as the phenomena of privacy and the individual point of view. Sequential attention and the solitude of reading invited rationality, planning skills, detachment from the group, a personal point of view, and the freedom of individuality. In contrast, preliterate societies are characterized by identification with the group or tribe.

He said that in the immediacy of the

electric age, when our central nervous system is technologically extended to involve us in the whole of mankind and to incorporate the whole of mankind in us, we necessarily participate, in depth, in the consequences of our every action. It is no longer possible to adopt the aloof and dissociated role of the literate Westerner (p. 4).

As literacy wanes – through the increasing attention to screen media which is creating a global tribal culture – we are seeing the end of privacy, as well as the rise in market-driven consensus thinking. Some authors call that "the wisdom of the crowd." But others, including me, see it as a weakening of individual critical capacity. Consensus arrived at through solitary reflection and patient, attentive, compassionate conversation – out of which wisdom may indeed arise – is very different from the rapid, shallow and undigested pointing-to information that the Net spews.

Literacy has a role broader than merely making us knowledgeable. The connection between our inner life, self-knowledge, and our external expression is mediated mainly by words. Words are the semantic bricks of our awareness. The fewer words we know and use, the less aware we can be of our intentions, feelings, and uniqueness as a person. There will be a stage in the evolution of our consciousness when words will be transcended – but probably not until we become aware of their power to shape and evolve our consciousness. Then we can enter the non-conceptual dimension of reality where we transcend words, along with concepts, and our soul expands without boundaries.

Alexander Lowen, the father of bioenergetics, from observing his patients wrote:

> Through the right words we see and know ourselves. We can consequently fully express ourselves. Using the right words is an energetic function because it is a function of consciousness. It is the awareness of the exact fit between a word (or sentence) and a feeling, between an idea and a sentiment. When words and feeling connect or dovetail, the energetic flow that ensues increases the state of excitation in the mind and body raising the level of consciousness and sharpening its focus... I believe that the energetic charge associated with the feeling excites and activates the neurons of the brain involved with word formation. When these neurons respond appropriately to the sense of the feeling, the proper fit occurs, and a light seems to flash in one's head (1975, p. 328).

Languages which have a refined discrimination of words offer more possibilities for accessing our awareness. Without the right words our inner or emotional experiences would remain as unacknowledged sensations, nebulous and disconnected.

Awareness and words are intimately connected in the human path to wisdom. Words can drive our consciousness up to a point where we step beyond words. As the soul is clarified or evolves, words and the conceptual mind, become superfluous – even though they can still be used to convey deep meaning. But prior to that condition, words as a medium and "technology" can greatly support the development of awareness.

Socrates, discussing the discovery of writing with Phaedrus, believed that it

> will create forgetfulness in the learners' souls, because they will not use their memories; they will trust to the external written characters and not remember of themselves. The specific which you have discovered is an aid not to memory, but to reminiscence, and you give your disciples not truth, but only the semblance of truth; they will be hearers of many things and will have learned nothing; they will appear to be omniscient and will generally know nothing; they will be tiresome company, having the show of wisdom without the reality (Plato in *Phaedrus*).

Nicholas Carr (2010), in *The Shallows,* narrated how our relationship with the written word has over the centuries shaped our present culture and attitude toward knowledge, and how this is being impoverished by digital media. Nobody challenges the importance of writing any more, not even philosophers who use it for elaborating their thoughts. Socrates, no ordinary philosopher but a wise and enlightened man who reached spiritual heights beyond conceptual thought, saw the threat of all media to our consciousness, even the noblest of them – literacy. Not only is literacy important for our inner and outer development, but it has been used as an instrument of power as well. The power of words is so vast that every socially advanced country rightly holds the literacy of its citizens as a basic human right.

Is the Internet expanding or inhibiting literacy? For sure, we read a lot on the Net – but *what* do we read, and what is the *quality* of our reading in terms of attention, depth, understanding and our capacity to develop our own insights and points of view? Blogs have triggered a renaissance in reading and writing, but if we look at the ten most popular blogs on the Internet according to *Technorati*, at the time I write eight are mainly about gadgets, technology, or software. Since most of the high-ranking blogs are dedicated to the IT world, this sets the agenda of the Net.

Adequate investment and good skill in search engine optimization (SEO) can drive a lot of traffic to a site, so even traditional media empires have had to stake out an Internet presence. While we are witnessing new, independent, and valuable blogs, the agenda is set by a small number of major sites which have a monopoly on online information – in a way even less pluralistic than traditional media. Today a great writer faces enormous challenges in being recognized, as her work is buried beneath millions of sites.

Since the advent of letters, every medium or technology has been welcomed in prophetic terms. The reality is that technology's role in our lives is quite unpredictable – and to know the actual implications, we need a higher wisdom. The mechanical clock, for example, was invented by monks during the Middle Ages to regulate the time for prayers. Yet without the clock, as Postman (1993) observed,

> capitalism would have been quite impossible. The paradox, the surprise, and the wonder are that the clock was invented by men who wanted to devote themselves more rigorously to God; it ended as the technology of greatest use to men who wished to devote themselves to the accumulation of money (p. 15).

The Internet was born as a military technology, but it became a medium for the advocates of freedom of expression and was coherent with the literate mindset. Now it is being transformed into an entertainment medium where words are suffocated by images, videos, and an infinite stream of information. Videos on the Net, with few exceptions, are no better than TV. A Pew Research Center study in June 2010 discovered that comedy and humor were watched on the Net more than news.

While images can be assimilated with no effort, awareness through words is more complex, and connected to our capacities for insight. Awareness derived from literacy is deeper and more revealing of truth than any image.

Analytical and Critical Skills

Maggie Jackson (2008), in *Distracted*, reported that the Organization for Economic Cooperation (OECD) tested the kind of problem-solving skills required for analytical reasoning today. Fifteen-year-olds in US ranked 24 out of 29 developed countries, with nearly 60 percent of them scoring the minimum or less on the *most basic* problems. Many US high school students lack critical thinking skills and are unable to express complex thoughts.

The weakening of literacy skills goes along with the disappearance of the individual point of view that is a by-product of literacy as McLuhan noted, along with the disappearance of privacy and even of individual identities. Blogs do have an important role in the analysis of politics and society, but I suspect that the capacity required for this is functioning because the critical skills to interpret reality were developed *before* the Net or *outside* the Net. Blogs like Beppe Grillo's, the most-read political blog in Italy and one of the most-read in the world, explicate things we could have inferred for ourselves thirty years ago as teenagers passionate about understanding the world.

The loss of analytical skills goes along with the *denial of the loss*, much as a drunkard will deny his state. Different studies from American universities have exposed a big gap between self-assessed literacy skills and skills calculated by tests (Maughan, 2001).

The constant stream of information makes it difficult to construct the whole picture behind any specific piece of information. Assembling historical facts and discerning their relationship is a titanic effort with the amount of information streamed in daily. Models for interpreting reality are outdated in this age when data is king. We no longer even need analysis.

With the developments of the Industrial Revolution the work of our bodies has been externalized to machines, leaving space for intellectual and cultural development. In the post-industrial information society we are externalizing our minds to information technologies. Just as machines took over our physical labors, IT replaces our mental effort. Instead we are fed small and more digestible chunks of information. As our bodies have become weaker and cardiovascular problems, obesity, degenerative diseases and cancer have increased, so our mental capacities and critical analysis skills are becoming weaker, along with a growth of mental pathologies like attention deficit disorder in children. Nor have we lost the "old-fashioned" physical diseases caused by the industrialized sedentary lifestyle.

Just as the body has lost part of its role with the advent of machinery, the mind is overshadowed by the arrival of digital technologies to which we outsource memory, thinking, and communication. As we needed medicines and prostheses for the body, we now need neuropharmaceutical prostheses for the mind. TV instigated the end of analytical and critical skills. The coherent, rational, deep discourse of books is much different from that of TV, which is incoherent, absurd, and switches rapidly between unrelated subjects. The Internet exacerbates that and mocks the gifts of literacy.

The so-called Google Generation is supposed to be smarter and have better inner tools for understanding reality. Not so. It is said that human beings can easily adapt to new media, get the most out of them, and improve their cognitive skills, but a study by University College in London debunks the myth.

> [Although] young people demonstrate an apparent ease and familiarity with computers, they rely heavily on search engines, *view* rather than *read* and do not possess the critical and analytical skills to assess the information that they find on the web. [The report] also shows that research-behaviour traits that are commonly associated with younger users – impatience in search and navigation, and zero tolerance for any delay in satisfying their information needs – are now becoming the norm for all age-groups, from younger pupils and undergraduates through to professors (Rowlands, 2008).

The study "Scaling the Digital Divide: Home Computer Technology and Student Achievement" demonstrated that universal access to computers and high-speed Internet is actually related to a diminishing of math and reading capabilities (Vigdor, 2010). *Wired* has reported the study by neuroscientist Ian Robertson which discovered that younger people were less able to remember general personal information than their parents (Thompson, 2007). And a test by the Royal Society of Chemistry revealed that the best contemporary students could not solve math problems which were easy for their parents. We have probably reached the peak of intelligence already, and are now witnessing the first cracks of degradation in our mental capacities.

According to Alliance for Childhood (2000), computers and other electronic media hinder richer face-to-face communication which involves both verbal and non-verbal communication. If the consequent delay in development of language is extended throughout childhood, it may permanently limit children's verbal and written expression, comprehension, self-understanding, and ability to think logically and analytically – all of which are based on language. The "inner voice" which originated from talking with adult caregivers – as well as unstructured time and quiet – are important for both academic and personal development.

A New Literacy Through eBooks?

eBook readers and availability of titles are multiplying. After at least fifteen years of false starts, it looks like eBooks are finally going to take over, driven by readers like Amazon's Kindle and the iPad. Since the early '90s there has been more than one wave of the craze for eBooks. In the meantime the Internet has come into our lives, and I noticed, starting in the US, that something was changing in traditional book publishing. Books were becoming smaller and the writing style more journalistic.

Some publishing colleagues have told me that "the reader doesn't have much time any more to read big, complicated books. They're used to Web pages." Or "the writing style should be more catchy and entertaining." I won't blame the Internet for this per se, but for sure it further lowers attention capacity – already weakened by the rapidity of TV cuts, by the remote control, and overall by the information industry. The new generation of eBook readers has improved readability, so it seems that this new wave will finally grow in popularity.

But books won't be the same any more. Even though eBooks won't replace paper books, they will get an important share of the traditional book market. We are already seeing traditional newspaper and magazines looking emaciated as the market goes electronic. eBooks will probably set different standards for length and writing style, and they already invite linking to related information, as well as visual and auditory complements. Soon, no doubt, they will connect us with other people who read the same book, making the reading experience more social and shared. Advertisements will come too.

eBook readers and publishers are going to compete by developing more and more features to "enhance" the experience. Wonderful: but some things offer up their best with less, instead of more. For instance, organic food is healthier because there are no preservatives, chemicals, GMOs, or colorants. eBooks won't lead to the extinction of books, but they will eclipse the inner experience of reading books.

People into the IT industry only focus on the technical issues of clarity of the screen, available memory, downloading procedures – giving no attention to the subtle inner changes. What matters for them is what we can *do*, not what is *being done to us* by technology. Being alone with a book – whether electronic or paper – without Internet, links, images, videos, nor anything or anyone else popping up on the screen while we read, will probably become rare. But it is that very intimacy which allows uninterrupted feedback between words as the semantic bricks of our awareness and our inner world.

The claim that the physical platform on which words are written doesn't influence our reading experience reflects, one more time, the Cartesian position that pure thought is detached from matter – that concepts, therefore, can be transmitted independent of the medium, like pure electrical states of *0* and *1*. eBooks also bring an end to the privacy of reading, for when somebody knows what we download and buy online, and we share our notes with a network of readers, the intimate experience of reading is over.

Digital books depend on both hardware and software which we can't be certain will still be available in the medium or long term, while a paper book can last hundreds of years. I already can't read from magnetic storage devices just twenty years old. Nonetheless, the rhetoric that books can be better preserved digitally is used to discourage paper printing. However, digital formats will quickly become obsolete as hardware and software change, leaving behind all that eTrash to deal with.

The Reading "Technology"

In the midst of Twitter-mania – with its push toward speed writing and reading of up-to-the-minute (and short-lived) information, it is good to be reminded about different ways of reading by two spiritual teachers from very different paths. Carlo Maria Martini (1987) wrote:

> The Christian tradition developed *lectio divina* (divine reading), a method in four steps: *"lectio, meditatio, oratio, contemplatio"* (reading, reflecting, oration, meditation). Those successions are the products of theological and anthropological reflections on the way the believer approaches God's words, in order to assimilate them and transform them in real life, in action (1987, p. 217).

And from the Indian mystic Osho (1997):

> To read is to know a certain art. It is to get into deep sympathy. It is
> to get into a sort of participation. It is a great experiment in medi-
> tation. But if you read the Gita the same way as you read novels you
> will miss it. It has layers and layers of depth. Hence, *paath* [study of
> holy texts] – every day one has to repeat. It is not a repetition; if you
> know how to repeat it, it is not a repetition. If you don't know, then
> it is a repetition. Just try it for three months. Read the same book –
> you can choose any small book – every day. And don't bring your
> yesterday to read it: just again fresh as the sun rises in the morning
> – again fresh as flowers come this morning, again fresh. (p. 122).

This is a very different way than the fast browsing of news and
streams of messages on the Internet. We chase new information,
forgetting that the value in newness is in the freshness of our view
which produces the burst of understanding. This new mode of
being with words takes a toll on our concentration (Levine, 2007).

Digital Writing

Reading books and writing are associated with a different inner
state than online activities. Reading and writing in a focused way
are "technologies" of knowledge, but also of introspection and self-
knowledge. The pace is slower and more balanced, giving time for
information to sink in, to percolate deeper. Book pages don't blink,
pop up, or refresh.

The PC was not much more than a writing tool in the beginning,
but nowadays it is difficult to keep away from the Net, for its "call" is
loud. Yet even when not connected to the Net, writing on computers
has been found to be less efficient than with the traditional pen.

A study by Virginia Berninger at the University of Washington
revealed that children in second, fourth and sixth grade – with and
without handwriting disabilities – were able to write more and
faster, producing longer essays with more complete sentences using
a pen than with a keyboard, irrespective of spelling skills. The keyboard was better only for learning the alphabet, while for sentence
structure results were mixed. Many children don't grasp what a sentence is until third or fourth grade. Writing is not simple, having
several levels: letters, words, sentences and paragraphs. With a keyboard a letter is selected by pressing a key, while formation of a letter with a pen requires complex motions of the entire hand. Brain
imaging studies with adults have shown an advantage of forming
letters over selecting or viewing letters, while a brain imaging study
at the University of Washington with children showed that sequencing fingers may engage thinking (Berninger, 2009).

When the big picture is needed, when we need to mentally organize sentences, computers are not of much help, despite word processing tools for organizing thoughts. In writing without a word processor, we create a mental image of the conceptual structure. Lacking tools for quick edits, deleting, and moving words, we need to paint a larger structure in our mind. At a certain point in the writing of this book, I used the word processor but only for copying what was already written and edited on paper by hand. Likewise my editor transcribes his hard copy markups to the computer for my approval.

Even though word processors have powerful tools for the organization and layout of a book, I have found that a white page which doesn't flicker and doesn't reorganize my text was a better place for insights to arise. And I could write in any setting – lying on the sofa, sliding around in a taxi, or sunning on the beach. And screens (even the best ones), like vampires, are not comfortable with strong natural light.

A Pew Internet survey found that since 2006, blogging has dropped among teens and young adults (Lenhart, 2010). Blog articles are being replaced mostly by shorter writings on Facebook, Twitter and other social media, with blogging now following that trend toward brevity.

Blogging is still connected to a literate world and produced for a general public. Writing for social networks, instead, addresses our "tribe" of friends – with shorter discourses, less analysis, and colloquial expression that is more intimate, but less complex.

Communication and the Transformation of Consciousness

In my opinion, words are the best "technology" for becoming aware of inner states and communicating them – like bridges to our inner world. Words are worth a thousand images.

Words can bring us a long way toward the expansion of our awareness: however, they are slippery, and cannot bring us to the most elevated levels of consciousness. Furthermore, words are heavily influenced by the interpretations we superimpose on them through our cultural beliefs and our individual conditioning.

Much in the communications industry, the Net included, is based on the assumption that more communication equals more understanding equals a better world – on the assumption that ideas, concepts, meanings and feelings can be expressed and transferred by language. According to Michael J. Reddy's conduit metaphor:

Ideas are objects that you can put into words, so that language is seen as a container for ideas, and you send ideas over a conduit, a channel of communication to someone else who then extracts the ideas from the words... One entailment of the conduit metaphor is that the meaning, the ideas, can be extracted and can exist independently of people. Moreover, that in communication, when communication occurs, what happens is that somebody extracts the same object, the same idea, from the language that the speaker puts into it. So the conduit metaphor suggests that meaning is a thing and that the hearer pulls out the same meaning from the words and that it can exist independently of beings who understand words (Lakoff, 1995, p. 115).

For the conduit metaphor to work properly we would need to share a very wide set of attributes: the same language, the same interpretation of words, a compatible level of culture, a similar background, a similar kind of sensitivity. (So similar that perhaps the real point of communicating by words is actually to get closer to our own self-understanding.)

The conduit metaphor is what makes us write in blogs and social networks, thinking our message can be sent and "uploaded" to other minds to reach them in the way we intend. We can't actually know about how our message will be interpreted, yet we are surprised when there are misunderstandings.

Experiments in 2005 demonstrated that:

without the benefit of paralinguistic cues such as gesture, emphasis, and intonation, it can be difficult to convey emotion and tone over e-mail. Five experiments suggest that this limitation is often underappreciated, such that people tend to believe that they can communicate over e-mail more effectively than they actually can (Kruger et al., 2005).

Funny or sarcastic emotions were especially difficult to convey, but anger and sadness were as well. The authors concluded that "this overconfidence is born of egocentrism, the inherent difficulty of detaching oneself from one's own perspective when evaluating the perspective of someone else."

The digital culture believes in the power of electronic communication and feedback as a tool for expanding participation, and even consciousness. The origins of the conduit metaphor lie in the belief that we can separate information from the person who receives it. "Pure" information is something we can separate from the "noise" of our interpretations and feelings. This is the Cartesian dream of separating pure thought from the person in his wholeness – which also replaces essential human qualities with knowledge and information.

CHAPTER 11

LOST IN THE CURRENT

uman beings evolved with a terror of predators, so that visual or audio signals are associated with something potentially dangerous. When threatened, the instinctual brain mechanisms, located especially in the amygdala, become activated.

First described by Ivan Pavlov in 1927, the "orienting response" is our instinctive reaction to any sudden or novel stimulus, visual or auditory. This ancient survival mechanism is one of the reasons why it's difficult to sit in front of a TV and ignore the moving images. Each time we attend to a new stimulus, the mechanism of reward is activated. On the neurophysiological level, dopamine is released, leading to a sense of well-being and euphoria – thus reinforcing our reaction and improving our chances of staying alive. Though we rarely encounter predators any more, the mechanisms remain in the brain. Whatever facilitates survival of the species is gratifying – like the pleasure of sexual engagement.

Attend to This!

The events on the Net which anticipate and activate the reward system are numerous: new email announcements, instant messages, Twitter or Facebook updates, new articles in blogs, video games, news. The amygdala is stimulated by all the media. And the Internet has multiplied the stimuli by concentrating the textual, visual, auditory, and interactive channels in a single medium.

The inner reward system makes us attend to information. By interacting with it we produce new information ourself. The reward system is activated even when we *anticipate* a reward. So a simple sound that signals an incoming email or IM text releases dopamine – even when a spam message is delivered. Any action that activates the reward mechanism also activates another mechanism: that of addiction.

Even if they are not badly addicted, many people – myself included – experience difficulty stopping online activity. Stimuli which previously evoked a certain neural response, over time produce less effect. So, it's necessary to have more stimuli that are more intense, more varied, and more frequently.

To achieve this, we need more computing power and faster Internet to manage the increasing number of events running simultaneously on the screen. Technological development is pushed by the greed for "more" and "faster." The brain, particularly the amygdala and the hippocampus, mistakes the continuous stimuli with survival, so it becomes difficult to turn away from the source of stimulation.

While it's difficult to ignore a nearby TV, the computer is even more powerful and complex, because it adds the frenzied activity of chasing and producing information to the passive staring at a screen. Besides the neurological triggering of the survival mechanism, much web content actually relates to survival – being sexual or financial, including online gambling, auctions and stock investing – which activates the dopamine shots.

Seeking social stimulation is not traditionally considered compulsive or addictive, but as technology co-opts social life as one more window present on the screen, it is possible to become a Facebook addict because of the dopamine reaction.

Fundamentally, both TV and computer screens are about moving images. Seeing something new moving activates the orienting response. While TV editors increase the number of cuts and edits in order to hold attention, the Internet generates an even larger number of interruptions as we open multiple windows, run several programs simultaneously, and communicate by instant messaging.

Since it would be nonsense to react physically to an image on a screen as if a beast were threatening us, like we did in ancient times when a potentially threatening change took place in our surrounding, we have learned to suppress emotions and inhibit our reactions. But they aren't really gone, building up as tension in the nervous system. In bioenergetic terms, there's a charge but no discharge. In other words, stress and frustration build, even though it's often not perceived consciously.

Attend to it Now and Forever!

The real killer application of the Web is "Now." The real-time, fast stream of information is what hooks people to screens. Many websites and applications are built on a stream of frequently updated information. Twitter opened the way, and Facebook and Google followed.

When I was young my grandfather would suddenly jump up from his armchair, shouting "Tutte balle!" (just a pack of lies), and turn the TV off. For twenty years now I've lived without a TV, but the Internet is much harder to resist, so it requires extra strength to turn off.

Because the Internet, smartphones and video games have no temporal structure, there is no clear "beginning" or "end," as in traditional media like TV, where programs start and stop on a schedule. Thus there's no inherent end to online interaction. Also, online we expect answers immediately, and with that expectation reinforced, our endlessly curious mind is pulled further into the current.

New is Cool

Information once traveled at terrestrial speeds – at a horse's pace at best. With the advent of the telegraph, information and its transmission were dissociated for the first time. At that moment, novelty took on the meaning of improvement, advancement, and progress.

Postman (1993) pointed out that shortly after Morse's historic demonstration of the telegraph, the fortunes of newspapers ceased to depend only on the quality or usefulness of articles, but, also on the quantity, distance, and speed of dissemination of information, establishing the basis for the current model of real-time news and the race to be the first to broadcast it.

The constant flow of new information prevents us from having a meaningful relationship with events. Every input is immediately superseded by another. Staying with the same thing for a long time does not satisfy our desire for novelty. We don't want prolonged or deep connection with things, for that slows down the flow of juicy neurotransmitters.

Even blogs, initially instruments for the expression of thought, are mostly oriented now to the latest novelty. The shorter the article the better, so as not to detain or strain the reader. The more frequent the articles, the more the reader will be engaged.

Instant Gratification

In Huxley's *Brave New World* the governor asks the youth if they ever faced an insuperable difficulty or if they'd endured a long gap be-tween a desire and its fulfillment. After a lengthy pause (which made the governor nervous), one of them confessed that he'd once waited almost four weeks for a woman he was attracted to to ac-quiesce. The intense feeling was "horrible." The governor reported that ancient people were so stupid that, when the first reformers came to save them from those horrible feelings, they rejected them. In the New World people were conditioned even before birth, and life was engineered to quickly satisfy every desire. For unpleasant feelings, there was *soma*.

"Silence is weird," a 1999 cell phone billboard proclaimed across the plains of Texas. The whole world of technology strives to avoid idle time and silence. Efficiency and speed are the most cherished qualities. Internet technology introduced new levels of speed to the acceleration of traditional media like radio or TV, where pauses or silences are assiduously avoided.

The Internet experience, being interactive, is even more extreme. Our attention is split among many sources, and the flow of infor-mation accelerates. Most people will leave a website in less than one second, if they can't figure out what the page is about. With the fast pace of video games and the Internet, kids grow up expecting im-mediate responses in real life as well.

Walter Mischel of Stanford University in 1972 carried out the "marshmallow experiment." Children between four and six were invited to eat a sweet, but told that if they waited fifteen minutes, they'd be given a second one. The older children were more likely to gain the reward. But ten years later the patient ones were more competent, and later still they had higher SAT scores.

If any time in history needed long-term vision, it is now. Both in the environmental and financial arenas we are paying heavily for the cost of instant gratification that depends on energy and re-sources.

Neurological Changes Related to Instant Gratification
Neuroscientist Gary Small (2008) reported that the underdeveloped frontal lobes of teenagers often impact their everyday judgment in seeking instant gratification. The massive use of computers and video games tends to stunt frontal lobe development in teenagers, impairing their social and reasoning abilities to the point that the neural pathways may never catch up. He expressed concern that this would lock them in an immature and self-absorbed stage right through adulthood.

Without the ability to delay gratification, he worried, the emotional centers of the limbic system, which are not able to plan for the future, will dominate. The frontal lobes – associated with attention, planning, long-term memory, dopamine reward, and recognition of future consequences of our actions – reach maturity about age 25 as the myelination of white matter progresses. A poorly myelinated forebrain has been associated with onset of schizophrenia in young adults.

The frontal lobes also determine the capacity for clear mental discrimination, which allows us to make subtle distinctions and to recognize truth. On the spiritual plane, discriminating awareness is an important capacity for the path toward expanded awareness. On the social dimension, it is the foundation of critical skills. When people no longer see the big picture, have limited memory, and focus only on the latest novelty, there is no need for governments to threaten the press, for anything they write is quickly forgotten and buried beneath more information.

Damage to the frontal lobes produces distractibility, poor attention, poor memory, poor planning, and indifference to people and the world around, as well as euphoric and uninhibited behavior. I may be going too far if I point to those same symptoms with the use of technology. However, there's a strong resemblance between those symptoms, Internet addiction and attention deficit disorder – which can be triggered by heavy use of electronic media, and is indeed rising among youth.

Neuroscientist Susan Greenfield expressed her fear to the *Daily Mail* that technology is "infantilizing the brain into the state of small children who are attracted by buzzing noises and bright lights, who have a small attention span and who live for the moment" (Derbyshire, 2009).

Fulfilling human experiences need time to be internalized. To pursue scientific research, to master a skill, and to enter a state of meditation all require time. The ability to tolerate frustration is an exercise in bringing awareness to our feelings and in creating a bigger container for them.

Meditation itself is an exercise in the acceptance and transformation of frustration. There are few things as frustrating as sitting without doing, observing thoughts arising along with judgment, boredom, and impatience. Ecstatic states can also be reached, but usually not until after some inner knots have dissolved in the waters of awareness.

Accepting Emptiness and the Eureka Effect

Even the process of writing requires a patient and empty attitude. Many writers – and probably many bloggers – face writer's block.

People who depend on the spark of creativity to express something bright and new often are afflicted by it.

Creative expression has its cycles – and the similarity between creativity and procreativity is not just linguistic. The process of creative revelation and the eureka effect has been documented by neurophysiological research. Joseph Chilton Pearce (2002) cites Margharita Laski's work which illustrates the six stages of the discovery process: (1) asking the question; (2) looking for the answer; (3) hitting the plateau; (4) giving up the search; (5) eureka! and (6) translating the discovery in a way that can be understood and shared with others.

These stages involve different parts of the brain – both hemispheres as well as the emotional-limbic brain, which is connected to the heart. Without the passion of the heart, the creative discovery seems difficult to attain. "Love of truth for its own sake is actually the expression of essential heart," wrote Almaas (1988, p. 191).

The fourth stage – giving up the search – is usually not accepted in our hyper-productive culture that is afraid of silence and emptiness. This is so, even though everybody has had the experience of finding a solution or an insight when the mind was not actively looking for it. "The corpus callosum can complete the circuitry only when the left hemisphere is inactive, when the analytical and critical processes of mind are suspended" (Pearce, 2002).

Most spiritual teachers describe the stage of giving up the search – even without formal knowledge of neurophysiology – and that the acceptance of not-knowing is necessary for insight. The eureka effect applies to the scientific and artistic arenas, as well as the spiritual. Given this, if writer's block is accepted, then the creative spark is likely to ignite.

The eureka effect has been documented by Tufts University researchers, coordinated by Sal Soraci, using an electroencephalograph which can register the moment when the fog surrounding a problem melts and shows the passage toward insight. Researchers presented sentences to subjects that at first glance made no sense. For example, "The girl spilled her popcorn because the lock broke." Subjects became mute and a bit confused. After a few seconds the researchers gave them the cue, "lion cage." The eureka effect activated about 400 milliseconds after the cue was given. Electrodes on the scalp can pick up that pulse, which is designated "N400."

In another experiment, Soraci displayed a blurred object which subjects attempted to interpret. The image was slowly brought into focus. ("Is that a doughnut? A wheel? Ah, no, it's a watch.) Soraci hypothesized that the more the brain attempts to discern a concept, the better it remembers it. (He proposed that this discovery could lead to more effective methods of teaching.) If this is so, then the immediacy we expect of Google actually inhibits learning, removing us prematurely from the inner source of knowledge. In the spiritual realm, Zen points to the importance of an empty mind, as do other paths of self-knowledge. The mind should not have much to say, nor can it even know what to say.

In body building it is known that for optimal results, it's necessary to alternate activity and rest. The growth of muscles takes place during the night when they are relaxed. Excessive exercise brings the opposite result. So it's surprising that there are still few studies regarding the physiology and psychology of knowledge, given that most people are spending much more time with information than at the gym. So, too, is it surprising that even people whose focus is learning and knowledge don't know when to stop in order to maximize their resources.

The love of truth demands times of not-knowing. While the heart feels at ease with emptiness, it is a threat for the ego-mind greedy for novelties, which is attracted to a hyperactive state. The mind isn't interested in deep insight – though that is the heart's delight.

Faster and Faster, but just Apparently

The greedy consumption of information requires faster and faster computers and Internet connections. The expansion of bandwidth and the computing power required create the real digital divide by forcing everyone who can afford to to sign on – with great personal and global environmental costs. Just as the cessation of growth of the physical body allows the growth of consciousness to begin, perhaps slowing down the physical expansion of technology would provide more space for deepening.

Faster Internet connections feed a huge market for cables, routers, computers, smartphones, software and online services, but this hasn't translated into deeper contents. Even though computers and Internet lines have grown in power and speed, this hasn't always meant a parallel growth in efficiency. In the mid-80s with a humble PC running on an Intel 8086 processor, I was teaching UNIX (Xenix), which was adequate to handle four people working in multiuser and multitasking mode from their individual terminals. Now hundreds-fold computing power is not enough for certain applications, and we experience delays in many of them. Something has gone wrong in this.

Jaron Lanier expressed his concerns about software in *One Half a Manifesto*:

If anything, there's a reverse Moore's Law observable in software: As processors become faster and memory becomes cheaper, software becomes correspondingly slower and more bloated, using up all available resources... There are various reasons that software tends to be unwieldy, but a primary one is what I like to call "brittleness". Software breaks before it bends, so it demands perfection in a universe that prefers statistics.

Kris de Decker (2008), in "Faster Internet is Impossible," wrote that "faster connections inevitably bring new applications, which eat up the extra bandwidth." While the Internet transports twice the volume of information every year, "that's not the consequence of a growing amount of internet users, [but rather] the spectacular growth is mainly the result of an increasing bandwidth consumption per user. Every year each of us downloads (and uploads) almost twice as much digital information as the year before."

The main reason for the yearly doubling of traffic is the growing importance of multimedia. Music, pictures, and especially video need much more bandwidth than other media. Faster connections in themselves are not threatening access to the Internet. The problem is that most websites will adapt to the ever-faster connections, which makes them gradually inaccessible for people with slower connections. Today, most websites are impossible to download with a dial-up connection – because they have become so corpulent.

According to most people writing about technology, the expansion of Internet broadband throughout the world would be the answer to almost all the world's problems that involve the right to knowledge, the digital divide, and the opportunity to establish human rights. This is the updated hi-tech version of the need to "civilize" the world through Western values, believing that bringing the information economy system everywhere will bestow welfare and comfort to all.

When I look at advertisements showing kids in the developing world smiling in front of their computers, it reminds me of the missionaries who have carried the Bible everywhere to "civilize" the world. Bill Gates himself, in his humanitarian efforts, said a few years ago that the problem of developing countries certainly isn't lack of computers or the Internet, but the scarcity of potable water and research for eradicating illnesses like malaria. I thank Uncle Bill for this statement – and might even forgive him for pissing me off all the years I've used his software.

The race for larger bandwidth arises with the development of more complex websites and software. Just consider antivirus updates or operating systems. Finding myself often in countries where there is no fast connection to the Net, it is impossible for me to update my operating system – not even carry out some simple tasks. New versions of free software like Open Office are of the order of 150 megabytes, which challenges even an ordinary ADSL connection.

The more bandwidth expands, the more the Net resembles hyper-TV – with videos and animated worlds to immerse us, and which are hungry for speed and resources. We move further away from words and narrative in favor of visual communication.

As applications and sites require greater computing resources, memory jams in the attempt to manage the applications – just like rush hour traffic. Solving auto congestion by constructing or widening roads only promotes more car and truck traffic to the detriment of other forms of transportation – and it's harmful for the environment. It also encourages non-local production of food and goods, the loss of non-urbanized territory, and the disappearance of local traditions. We can only begin to see the collateral costs of expanded computing resources.

Into the Loop
James Harkin (2009) traces back our present obsession for remaining in and feeding the information cycle to Wiener's work on communication loops during the Second World War. "When inhabitants of cyburbia return there compulsively to check for updates, they are not only trying to be more efficient and more productive, but to ward off a persistent fear of falling out of the loop" (p. 169).

Staying in the loop doesn't come without a price. A study at Loughborough University, England, found that it takes more than a minute to get back on track with our thoughts after we've been interrupted by email (Jackson, 2002).

Since the loop can't stop, we feed it by carrying our connection everywhere through smartphones. It is estimated that ten percent of smartphone users are constantly checking email, Facebook, SMS, and news. These people are considered addicted.

Katie Hafner (2009) reported in the *New York Times* that teenagers' obsession with texting doubled in one year, to an average of nearly eighty each day. She noted concern about distraction, inadequate sleep and anxiety.

No more vacant time for kids, no more staring out the window or at the ceiling and daydreaming. Texting and Facebook updates don't allow time for being with ourself, for fear that being out of the loop for too long means exclusion from the group.

When I first learned programming, the most common language

was C, based on a paradigm of procedures and structure – carefully planned, sometimes with elegance. However, this type of programming made managing the exchange of information with external events or other programs and procedures quite complicated.

Eventually programming shifted to event-driven languages, with procedures activated by messages from other software or from inputs such as the click of a mouse or a stream of events from the Net. This type gained prominence when graphic interfaces like Windows, and later Internet communication, appeared. The execution of software then became an exchange of data between programming modules which affect each other circularly.

As software responds to events, so users have started to react the same way – becoming servomechanisms of technology that fit as one more module responding to events. The ego-mind is made in such a way that it easily slips into a never ending jumping between goals and desires. It is restless by nature, its very existence depending on running after something. But its objectives, once reached, can have no value - which provides impetus to pursue another. The mind can never be in the present since it is always chasing future goals.

IT simulates instantaneous fulfillment with novelties dosed out in a "real-time" stream of information. The effect is that it takes us further away both from the real and from available time. The good news is that we are not just the mind as we know it, even though few people in our society at this time would acknowledge that.

Technological Updates and the Right to Silence

I created my blog at indranet.org just two years ago, and I've already had to update Wordpress several times, install dozens of versions of many plug-ins, and configure the site in technically challenging ways to present it in both Italian and English. Having been out of the programming world myself for years, I needed the help of technicians.

A blog requires updating not only with new articles, but in exchanging information with other sites, in visitor analysis, linking to social networks, SEO techniques, and so on. Blogs, like every technology, keep expanding their possibilities and producing new versions. For a long time I've been stuck with an old Wordpress version, since the technician who wrote the first multilanguage plug-in I used was no longer available to update the plug-in for the new Wordpress version. One day he told me that he had changed his technological focus, and having stopped updating even for a few months, he was now too far behind to catch up. Before I could find somebody to update my site, it was hacked by advertisement robots that exploited the old version's vulnerabilities.

If blogs can become outdated so quickly, archived images won't last much longer. With digital technology the images of today will be hardly accessible through technologies of the near future. In ten years the Internet sites where we display our images will be purchased, closed, transformed or merged. Our old computer where we stored them will have obsolete standards for storing and exchanging data. To ever be able to access images, online or on the old computer, they will need to be copied to different memory supports than the current ones, maybe converted to different graphical formats (but will the concept of "format" even still be in use?) – and who knows what else.

While grandma's digitally scanned photos risk disappearing, the original prints on paper will continue to exist – perhaps a bit yellowed. As our jobs, personal finances, and social contacts depend more and more on the Internet, only people who work in the technical fields have the time to keep up to date. The rest of us will be left behind, or spend most of our time keeping updated and resolving technical problems.

This is a cyber-enslavement of sorts. While the cloud computing of Google, Microsoft and other companies promises to take away the burden of updating software versions and managing our data, we pay with our privacy in exchange. To be aware of every privacy issue and how to set our profile or opt out of standard settings is another time-consuming job we are forced to undertake in self-defense. As updates make it both fashionable and indispensible to have the latest technology, we support the IT industry. The right to non-information, to non-update, and to silence will be, in the future, a privilege – and one of the indicators of quality of life. Staying out of the loop, out of forced technological consumerism will be an act of liberation.

Cogitus Interruptus through Multitasking

With the explosion of digital gadgets, it is common to see people multitasking, attending to many inputs at the same time, in order to be more "efficient." But it comes at a price. An experiment by the Institute of Psychiatry in London in 2005 found that the IQ of people who checked messages on their mobiles while taking a test dropped more than people smoking cannabis.

A study by *CyberPsychology & Behavior* entitled "Electronic Media Use, Reading, and Academic Distractibility in College Youth" found that:

activities that require focused attention, such as reading, are declining among American youth, while activities that depend on multitasking, such as instant messaging (IMing), are increasing... [Also] the amount of time that young people spent IMing was significantly related to higher ratings of distractibility for academic tasks, while amount of time spent reading books was negatively related to distractibility (Levine, 2007).

Digital Nation (2009) interviewed Clifford Nass, professor at Stanford University, about his studies on multitasking. He and his colleagues were shocked to find that "multitaskers are terrible at every aspect of multitasking," whether ignoring irrelevant information, switching from one task to another, or keeping information well organized mentally. With multitasking increasing among younger and younger kids, they are "worse at analytic reasoning, which is extremely valuable for school, for life." The multitaskers "seem to think they're great at it," but "they get distracted constantly. They are very disorganized in keeping their memory going." Yet, "virtually all multitaskers think they are brilliant at multitasking," irrespective of gender. The strong denial by multitaskers is typical of every addiction.

Stephen Talbott (1998) observed that while it is true that we can do several things at the same time,

> our conscious attention is single and indivisible. We may be able to switch it rapidly from one thing to another, but at any given instant it is consumed by one thing alone... Everything may be taken in sensorially, but only one thing at a time is attended to... The point where we exercise our attention is the point where we manifest our highest capacities. It is the only point where we can gain mastery over technology (or anything else) and the only point where we can deepen understanding. Moreover, if we are not masters of our own attention, we are tools of our surroundings and of our own subconscious.

As Talbott implied, when our attention is divided among numerous inputs, we easily become servomechanisms of technology. Just as our internal organs need enzymes to be able to digest food, our psyche needs the enzymes activated by attention and awareness in order to grow, understand, and integrate its qualities. We achieve inner growth when we recognize ourself, when external experiences are associated with inner observation.

While experiences lived without awareness do not consciously transform our soul, they still impact us. They lodge in us undigested in the form of conditioning which we mechanically reproduce without knowing where they came from.

The volume of information we receive simultaneously is limited only by the capacity of our computer's memory and the speed of Internet connection, so it expands proportionally to technological development. With the current speed of online communication, full assimilation of messages is obstructed. Split and fragmentary attention has become the rule for online activities, and this habit has been gradually shifting to our life offline.

After engaging online in many simultaneous activities, if we feel as if we've achieved nothing, it is because nothing has been touched by our presence and awareness. When we give only partial attention, in reality we are never truly anywhere. The mind cannot give its attention to more than one thing at one time; multitasking means, as with computer processors, jumping from one activity to the next. While a computer processor jumps from one activity to the next in milliseconds, biology is much slower.

Machines do not need awareness or a psyche that grows with experience. The time needed for the soul to mature runs much slower than electronics. For the psyche to be deeply touched by anything, it is necessary to stay with an experience for a certain time – to sense it and allow it – which expands our awareness not only to mental processes, but also to the sensations and emotions connected to it.

For the psyche to grow, we need to nurture it with time, awareness and attention. A society in which individuals have fragmented attention hinders not only deep analysis and complex thought, but maturation of the soul as well. Complex thought, contemplation, and wisdom require prolonged attention. It is not by chance that every meditation technique requires time for concentrating attention.

Slowing down of mental activity leads to awareness of the empty nature of the mind. And this is exactly what the ego does not want to face. Our impatience seems tied to Western monotheism with its concept of a single lifetime to earn eternal life, so we hurry onward – with a Plan B to extend our life through biotechnologies and immortality projects.

A common mantra of technophiles is that "it saves time." Every new software promises to make things simpler and faster, better than before, more automated. The problem is that for every task made simpler, more tasks are added. We can never save time through technology, because *the nature of the mind itself is to keep busy*, more so when our bodies are immobilized in front of a screen. So we welcome new ways to keep the mind busy and overload it with more time-wasting procedures supposed to manage data better and "save time".

We have lost the capacity to be in empty space where our mind is not busy, but where our attention is strong. Our capacity for conscious attention and presence does not grow according to the amount of information available. It actually becomes scattered. We can "be here" with just one thing at a time. We can be "here" even better with none. Then we can just "be."

No History, No Narrative, No Past
In 1959 McLuhan wrote:

> When news moves slowly, the paper has time to provide perspectives, background, and interrelations for the news, and the reader is given a consumer package. When the news comes at high speed, there is no possibility of such literacy processing, and the reader is given a do-it-yourself kit (2005, p. 8).

Since the mind's content is transitory, we can easily understand why websites and applications have a transitory nature as well. What was hip and "wired" a few months before quickly becomes "tired." Once the novelty is gone, neurophysiologically, we don't get the same "high." Being a mirror of the hungry mind, the Net privileges anything new over historical narrative.

The clearest examples of the disappearance of narrative are technology news, which are mostly announcements of added features with no broader perspective. Not only is history unimportant, it is intentionally ignored. Previous software versions are mentioned only to compare features. Software applications themselves urge us to quick action, which discourages a reflective attitude. Even scholars have noticed that their concentration capacities have become weaker by interacting with online material (Carr, 2010).

There is no point writing an online article a few days after an event, or commenting on an article a few days after it was posted online. Leaving an idea to sink in overnight – to be touched by the wise archetypes of our psyche – is already too late. Nobody is interested in anything but the latest event – even and especially in blogs, where the emphasis is toward New and Short. SMS, Instant Messaging, chat systems, Twitter, Facebook – all are engineered for managing short texts with frequent updates. Links in themselves do not create connection. In fact, they tend toward dispersion. Or worse, when there are several interruptions.

The end of narrative also affects the development of music. We can have thousands of tracks on our tiny iPod, and easily download many more. We can skip tracks and fast forward through the assemblage. How much time we take to decide whether we like a piece of music becomes shorter. The era when we listened to a complete album has gone, and probably most people don't even bother to listen to a complete song if they don't like it immediately.

My first contact with Pink Floyd was at a stall at the *Fiera di Sinigallia* in Milan when I was about 13. I bought a pirated cassette of *Atom Heart Mother*. I'd heard something about Pink Floyd's music through older friends, since neither Italian radio nor TV broadcast such music then. At first I didn't like their strange music and long tracks that contrasted with catchy popular jingles of mainstream media, so I put it aside. But since I didn't have much other music, after a while I gave it another chance.

Eventually there came a revelation. I grasped their boundless, sometimes disquieting music. Had I approached that album in a 'digital' way, I wonder if I would have had the patience to hear it through, even listen a second time, or third.

Good things take time to reveal themselves, to pierce our mental structures which tend to automatically reject what's not familiar. (In March 2010 Pink Floyd won a legal battle and a small but significant victory toward respecting artists' narratives. The judge stated that EMI can't sell individual songs digitally if not part of a complete album).

Digital and Human Memory

When we save a file on a digital device we expect it to be available any time we want it, but that's not guaranteed. Alexander Rose in *The Long Now Blog* pointed out that the newness of technology is directly proportionate to its fragility. Yale librarian Paul Conway studying the longevity of records from ancient Mesopotamia onwards, found that the durability of media has been decreasing progressively, while the quantity of information being stored has increased. Ancient cuneiform clay tablets of Sumer still exist. "Many medieval illuminated manuscripts written on animal parchment still look as if they were painted and copied yesterday." Paper records of the Renaissance are faded but still in good condition. Ironically, "books printed on modern acidic paper are already turning to dust." One would think that old black-and-white photographs would not last long, but they can last a century or more. However, the much newer technology of color photographs cannot prevent them from fading after thirty years or so. Celluloid movie film lasts about twenty years, videotapes less, and the latest digital storage media only about ten (Rose, 2009).

Likewise, our human long-term memory is weakening. The sheer volume of new information even prevents neural consolidation into memories, leaving the contents of our mind as volatile as computer RAM.

Sitting close to the screen affects memory as well. Remember when our parents told us not to get too close to the TV? Then the PC moved us even closer. Then laptops. Now smartphones. Our field of vision and eye movements have become very limited, and the frequency of blinking has dropped.

An experiment showed that a medical problem was solved spontaneously when people could move their eyes at and away from a picture of a human body. This "embodied cognition" occurs when some part of the body externally reflects a mental process (Thomas, 2007). Studies indicate that the communication between the cerebral hemispheres is improved by moving the eyes in different directions, which could be a support in psychotherapy. Rotating the eyes leads to an improvement of memory, an increase in creativity, as well as a greater exchange of information between the brain hemispheres.

When we spend hours in front of a screen, something is bound to change on a neurophysiological level. Information overload and limited movements of the eyes decrease creativity and memory capacity – a familiar feedback loop with screen media. Personally, maintaining my gaze on a screen for long periods decreases my ability to perceive things in a broad perspective and to observe the correlation between apparently unrelated information. I tend instead to focus on details. To reflect, relax and unfocus, I need to look into the distance for a few moments or rotate my eyes each way.

Studies reveal that short-term memory improves when we walk in nature, or even just by looking at scenes of nature (Thomas, 2007). Marc G. Berman and colleagues (2008) at the University of Michigan tested the effect of scenery during a walk on cognitive function. Cognitive abilities improved by viewing scenes of nature, but not of streets or industrial areas.

Addiction

In his blog article "Technophilia," Kevin Kelly (2009) wrote that an acquaintance of his has a teenage daughter who spends her day texting her friends, anywhere, anytime – as many other teens do. He recalls that when her parents wanted to ground her, "to reinforce the seriousness of her misconduct, they took away her mobile phone. Immediately the girl became physically sick," as "if her parents had amputated a limb. And in a way they had. Our creations are now inseparable from us. Our identity with technology runs deep, to our core." Kelly concluded that "we are embarrassed to admit it, but we love technology."

Those look more like symptoms of addiction, not of love. Or, love in the way that an alcoholic loves his bottle. As people who are addicted to alcohol or hard drugs would rather die than abandon their addiction, our attachment to technology can accompany us even into the grave. An MSNBC article reported that people, especially under 40, now ask to be buried with their cell phones. Neither death nor toileting can part them from their mobiles, as they take them everywhere. Noelle Potvin, family service counselor for Hollywood Forever, a funeral home and cemetery in Hollywood, California found "a trend with Blackberrys, too. We even had one guy who was buried with his Game Boy." It can be any tech device.

The Future Laboratory, a London-based think tank, has observed this also in the UK, Australia and South Africa, but it's happening mostly in the US. Ed Defort, publisher and editorial director of *American Funeral Director* magazine, reported the trend of being buried with iPods or Bluetooth headsets, but especially with cell phones. "A fairly common occurrence... in the last five or six years," said Frank Perman, owner and funeral director of Frank R. Perman Funeral Home, of Pittsburgh, PA, a trend he "expects to grow exponentially, especially with the price of technology getting so low." He added, "A lot of people say the phone represents the person, that it is part of their legacy. It's an extension of them, like their class ring" (Mapes, 2008).

Like any addiction, even Internet addiction is exacerbated by problematic psychological conditions. A study by *CyberPsychology & Behavior* showed that:

> individuals who were lonely or did not have good social skills could develop strong compulsive Internet use behaviors resulting in negative life outcomes (e.g., harming other significant activities such as work, school, or significant relationships) instead of relieving their original problems. Such augmented negative outcomes were expected to isolate individuals from healthy social activities and lead them into more loneliness (Junghyun, 2009).

Neuroscientists have also documented that the learning and the pleasure centers of the brain are the same. Having a new idea causes the reward system to release euphoria-producing neurochemicals such as dopamine and endorphins, probably because learning increases survival chances. Hunting for food has been transformed into hunting for information – though the former involves the totality of our senses.

The dopamine release, which we chase even more frequently than food, shelter and sex, drives our goal-oriented behavior. The problem is that the dopamine system has no brakes built in. There's never enough, so we seek more and more in an endless loop. This ancient neurophysiological heritage is well understood by the market society. Manipulation of desires in traditional capitalism is a way to control the individual and the social classes. With the advent of what Magatti called "Techno-Nihilistic Capitalism," desires are continuously stimulated in order to feed a market that would otherwise wither away.

The neurophysiological reward system is also activated by natural rewards like food, water, sex. These are intrinsically pleasurable in order to ensure survival and preserve the species. Sometimes those natural rewards can become addictive too, but the simple activation of the brain's reward system is not an addiction in itself. Addictive behavior is defined as the inability of normal rewards to direct behavior. For instance, food, work, family, and health might be neglected due to an addiction.

With the enormous expansion of technology bringing to the Net more and more people who spend more and more time online at faster and faster connections, there are a growing number of people that are caught in repetitive activities. People can get addicted to online gambling, gaming, porn, cybersex, auctions, chat, Facebook and Farmville – even to news and to surfing itself, actually to anything that displays frequent change and triggers the seeking modality.

In South Korea, a country which experienced rapid advances in Internet connections, there are hundreds of centers where children are being treated for addiction, especially to games. A similar situation is happening in China and Taiwan. Addiction to video games has been studied for pathological symptoms in a Harris poll of a random sample of 1,178 American youth. Video-gaming habits and parental involvement were noted. About 8 percent showed pathological patterns, spending twice the time non-pathological gamers did, accompanied by lower grades, and attention problems (Gentile, 2009).

The Journal of Adolescent Health reported on research at Kaohsiung Medical University in Taiwan on Internet activities and behavior of 9,405 teenagers. It found that those addicted to the Internet exhibited more aggressive behavior than those not addicted. Even accounting for factors like exposure to TV violence, 37 percent showed signs of aggressive behavior. Whereas those who devoted time to online research and study were less prone to violence, those engaged in "online chatting, gambling, gaming, and spending time at online forums or pornography sites" were more prone to aggressive behavior (Ko, 2009).

The Digitally Divided Self

Every study about the negative influences of Internet addiction is immediately met by a loud chorus challenging both the methods and the evaluations. These resemble the familiar rationalizations of addicted people: offering apparently logical motivation to deny or minimize their dependence. One typical response is that the medium in itself is not addictive – it depends on how it is used. As in every rationalization, there's a kernel of truth. The Internet medium in itself may not be addictive, but its continuity depends on the same continuous feedback loop that feeds every addiction.

Psychiatrist Jerald Block (2008) postulated that Internet addiction is a mental condition. In an article for *Standpoint* magazine, he noted that patients addicted to the Internet resemble "schizophrenics in whom there is a similar loss of grounding... Given enough exposure to virtual reality, people cannot help but begin to question whether their real lives are merely simulations of life." He detailed how the challenges to psychiatry of compulsive computer use

> are tremendous. Recognition and treatment are both difficult. Patients downplay their computer use. It is either a topic of shame or a valued asset, a prize not to be put at risk. Thus, it is usually the practitioner that needs to raise the issue. But most mental-health providers became therapists because they like people, not technology (Block, 2008).

When talking about the limitations of current treatments which involve restrictions on computer use, he found that "after restrictions are lifted, many people seem to binge," concluding that "until we learn more or have better clinical tools, our best approach may be to work on prevention."

Preventing Internet addiction will be difficult. Banning computers is not an option, but at the same time we can't allow children to use screen media as much as they want, just as we don't allow them to binge on chocolate. What is too much? Lacking consensus, the best we can do is to teach emotional awareness, training them to recognize the emotion that drives the need to be in front of the screen and to recognize when the compulsion takes charge. They can also learn the value of silence – perhaps if it is called prayer or meditation.

Jerry Mander (1991) documented the problems related to TV, at a time when that was almost the only screen people were staring at:

> The hyperactivity of TV imagery, while pacifying the brain, simultaneously speeds up the nervous system: TV makes us both dumb and speedy. In the end, television viewing just prepares us for the appropriate mental state for video games and computer fixation (p. 66).

Mander's point cannot be accepted by Internet enthusiasts, who believe that TV is evil and the Net is good. They don't see that all screen media are affecting us.

Small (2008) observed that "as Internet addiction takes hold, the brain's executive region, known as the anterior cingulate, loses ground" (p. 49). And Ko (2009) concluded that "the neural substrate of cue-induced gaming urge/craving in online gaming addiction is similar to that of the cue-induced craving in substance dependence... [suggesting they] might share the same neurobiological mechanism."

Awareness of Feelings and Addiction

Alexithymia, a term coined by Peter Sifneos in 1973, is a condition which causes difficulty in understanding, differentiating and communicating emotional states. It is considered a personality trait, not a clinical condition, affecting about seven percent of the population, slightly more prevalent in males. Subjects usually lack imagination, have little intuition, and limited introspective capacity. One of the predominant characteristics is a limited capacity for emotional connection with people, since they are not able to sense – either in themselves or in others – subtle shades of emotions, being limited to "feeling good" or "feeling bad." The cause – whether genetic and neurochemical, or psychological, such as a traumatic experience that leads to detaching from feelings or lack of reflection of their emotions by the parents – is unclear.

Another characteristic is limited capacity to control impulses. The discharge of tension caused by unpleasant inner states can be compulsive, such as abusing food or substances, or distorted sexual behavior. De Berardis (2009) found that alexithymics had more dissociative experiences, less self-esteem, more obsessive-compulsive troubles, and greater potential for developing Internet addiction. In particular, the study specified that the difficulty in identifying emotions is associated in a significant way with an elevated risk of developing Internet addiction.

That study demonstrates the link between an emotionally impoverished world and Internet addiction. Alexithymia may be a precursor of addiction, but excessive use of technology in turn can lead to a "second-hand" emotional life and a disconnection from the place where the emotions are activated, recognized, and can mature – which is the body and in real-life relationships. Lack of awareness of our inner states can, then, lead to acting mechanically and becoming servomechanisms of technology.

If we do not understand what we feel and we don't heed our inner experience, we will not know ourself, leaving us dependent on external stimuli – which will trap us repeatedly. Our identity will depend on external input, since we lack any identity apart from the one projected on us by the Net. Awareness of our feelings is an embodied process as much as a mental one. The Internet limits us to the mental plane which takes us further away from connection with our body and awareness of feelings.

An alexithymic's limited introspective life is a condition shared by everyone who lives in a continuous flow of information, giving attention only to external sources. The inner life and the capacity for introspection become impoverished, and it becomes more difficult to switch attention from the external to the inner. Titanic effort is needed for "self-remembering," to use a term dear to Gurdjieff.

Awareness of emotions can prevent the dissociative experiences typical of alexithymics because it "anchors" us to the body. The best "technology" for expanding awareness of our emotions is meditation, in which the flow of inner events is witnessed, felt, acknowledged, and not acted out. And not clicked away.

Human physiology hasn't changed much since ancient times, nor has it caught up with the huge cultural development that our minds have undergone over the centuries. At a bioenergetic level, when we sit at the computer our mind is impacted by powerful stimuli while our body is mostly still. Since the input cannot be balanced and released through the body, the energy gets stuck in the mind – where it circles in loops, looking for rewards.

From this perspective, porn and cybersex can be considered attempts to release tension and regain awareness of the body. Unfortunately this kind of release has only a short-term effect, since it is mostly driven by the same reward mechanism that generates the tension. Internet addiction is a challenge to break. First, because it is not easily recognized, since it is so enmeshed with the need to work.

When someone is addicted to illegal drugs, it is necessary to avoid any contact with the substance – as well as the setting, places, people and objects associated with it. It is extremely difficult to avoid any contact with the Internet, since contemporary life requires an online presence.

When our muscles are sore after hard work, we naturally stop and rest. That is not the mode of the mind which is unable to naturally slow down – for the dopamine system is never sated. We have to employ conscious will to stop swallowing information. The mind counters with every reason for needing more information. Web pages, links, IM and social networks provide food for bulimic minds – and no mind is willing to diet.

Only in the past few decades have we come to know the deadly consequences of saturated fats, sweets, and excessive consumption of red meat, which were greedily eaten in previous decades to celebrate abundance and improved economic status. With regard to information intake, we are now exposed to excess – the ramifications of which are just beginning to be clear. We did not reform our eating habits until we saw the tragic consequences for our bodies. Hopefully, we won't delay modifying our computer behavior until there are tragic consequences for the human mind.

In both the food and IT industries, enormous financial interests are involved. Awareness of the possible dangers of excessive food spread very slowly – and it is accordingly slow with technology. We need "information dietetics." Even if our society becomes damaged by Internet addiction, the fast pace of technological development will not slow or stop unless environmental or economic catastrophe forces it to – just as we did not put the brakes on the automotive industry despite car accidents and global warming. (About 1.3 million people die each year on the world's roads, and tens of millions sustain non-fatal injuries.)

The reward systems in our physiology were created for survival, not addiction. Food and water and sex give us positive rewards to ensure survival of our bodies and the species. Addictions that have to do mainly with the mind follow a similar mechanism in order to ensure survival of the ego-mind. A silent mind means no-mind. Silence and stillness are the worst enemies of an ego that generates thoughts continuously, and feeds on them.

This never-ending activity is a defense mechanism of the mind in order to preserve its role as sustainer of the ego – that false personality built by beliefs and conditioning. Thoughts, both conscious and unconscious, build and maintain the personality, giving the illusion that there is somebody directing the show.

Those who practice meditation have seen, through personal observation, how the mind seduces us, always trying to draw our attention into a net of thoughts and images. Meditation techniques, such as *vipassana,* that focus on concentration and observation have been developed as a way to notice our thoughts and emotions in a detached way, in order to strengthen our witnessing and observing capacities, while weakening the distractive power of alluring thoughts. Historically, we have appropriately asked for freedom of thought and speech. Now we need the freedom for non-thought and the right to silence.

CHAPTER 12

THE DIGITALLY DIVIDED SELF

Attention

> In any single moment of awareness, which may be as brief as one millisecond, attention is focused in only one sense field. But during the course of these momentary pulses of consciousness, attention jumps rapidly from one sense field to another, like a chimpanzee on amphetamines. In the blur of these shifts among the sense fields, the mind "makes sense" of the world by superimposing familiar conceptual grids on our perceptions. In this way our experience of the world is structured and appears familiar to us (Wallace, 2006, p. 37).

The mind compensates for the gaps in continuity by mechanically recalling our previous experience and conditioning. Spiritual teachers speak of this in various phrases: that we create reality; we are asleep; we do not see things as they are in their essence. The more the inputs we receive without attention from our part, the more the structures of our mind are unconsciously activated to make sense of the world.

Attention is one of the foundations of awareness. Without it, we have no protection against information which is poured into us. Without attention our real identities and human values have no role in transforming information into wisdom. Then without choice we ingest whatever is put in front of us.

Without attention we risk becoming servomechanisms of technology, clicking compulsively with no direction. An open mind without goals is very different from the lack of direction of a mind frenzied with the longing to be filled. Lacking attention we have no control over our intentions nor critical perspective for interpreting information.

Attention is an ingredient of mindfulness – the awareness of our inner state which includes our body, feelings, and sensations. Meditation techniques begin with focused attention and concentration.

With attention, awareness, mindfulness, "presence" and a quiet mind, we are nourished by our interiority instead of force fed by external stimuli. As attention is connected to our identity, weak attention produces a weak identity. A scientist of the Rational Psychology Association, studying changes in the brain from overstimulation, defined "the new indifference" as the capacity to cope with contradictory stimuli without being concerned (Talbott, 1997). If we add to this the pervasive difficulties with prolonged attention, the lack of inner awareness, the weakening of literacy, and the absence of strong ethical and ideological ground, we are easily manipulated by messages which simplify the world. We are then prey to fundamentalisms and populisms with their promise of rapid solutions and return to the "certainties" of the past. Without attention nothing makes sense and there's no motivation to delve deeper.

"It is worth noting that Ted Nelson, the maverick who first coined the term 'hypertext' to describe our ability to navigate our own path through electronic information in 1965, has suffered since childhood from what later became known as ADD" (Harkin, 2009, p. 135). Attention disorders are expanding parallel to the expansion of information, leaving us vulnerable to unbalanced external guidance. Short attention span and lack of inner guidance work together to create a weak identity.

The Construction of the Self
The ego personality, though born as a defense mechanism that lacks substance, is nonetheless an unavoidable and important development of the soul. Without ego we cannot have the qualities or capacities needed to go beyond it. The Net encourages us to have a personality that is "liquid," ever ready to change shape as the flow of information pulls us in different directions.

Without a well-defined personality built by real relationships, mentors, and life experiences combined with inner awareness, we identify loosely with transitory mental stimuli. Lacking a narrative and continuity, our personality is never well-defined and solid. Such a condition can feel free from rigid mental structures, more open to existence. But this is a mere phantom of a spiritual state. Yet it attracts our soul because of their superficial similarity.

This looseness of mental structures before a solid personality

The Digitally Divided Self

has been established leads to a fragile inner state that is prone to insecurity. An insecure ego will either turn to old territorial, racial and religious conditionings in its search for a solid home (even though it's more like a cage), or will split pathologically. Only a strong personality based on real human qualities can welcome the new and integrate it into its soul without feeling threatened.

When there was strong guidance from the state, religions and ideologies, the ego crystallized mainly through ideological, ethical, and religious impositions, rather than deeper, felt, and original human qualities. Though some messages were in competition, a personality could form – one built on concepts and sand castles.

Personality shaped largely by the printing press culture greatly advanced human knowledge, understanding, and social development. This culture invited development of the capacity for structured and complex thought; logical, linear structures and interpretative models of reality; and sustained attention. The contemporary ego is still conditioned by ideologies, religions and even by the theories of science, but in recent years we have witnessed the softening of those messages. Ideologies are no longer shaping inner values. Religions are showing their darker side. Even science seems to have reached its limits in guiding humanity out of the problems it's facing. Reason and rationality themselves, though important advancements from the darker ages of blind faith, cannot offer clear direction any more.

Human relationships and direct contact, the most important elements in forming the personality, are more and more mediated by the Internet – where "friendships" can be established and ended by a simple click, and personal profiles, connections, and sites themselves can change, be born, and die capriciously. With this instability, it is difficult to develop authentic and long-lasting relationships which allow us to know ourself more deeply through interacting with others.

Family guidance has become less possible today, so kids are now mentored by peers, TV, pop culture and the Internet. Singly nor together can these give coherent or consistent direction for the formation of a personality. Parents themselves are busy with their work, lives and gadgets. With less opportunity for real human relationships, the construction of personality is not a linear process any more. And different from the culture of the press, visual media today present contradictory nonlinear messages that lack structure and narrative, so that construction of a personality is forever "in process." True flexibility is a quality only available once our personality is well established and strong enough to accept and integrate contradiction without feeling destabilized.

This lack of structure and narrative began with TV, and the Internet has established it. Even though its links give the Internet an appearance of connection and structure, its nature is nonlinear and scattered. Most of the time links don't connect any discourse into a larger and deeper narrative, rather they mainly dissipate attention.

The printing press culture created not only a new process of cognition, but personality came to be defined as a structure. In the post-printing press culture, the ego personality has become fluid, but only apparently more open. Exposed to greater volumes of information that all compete for our attention, we are split by multiple inputs without a director to integrate the personality at the center of consciousness.

If this tendency toward a collective loosening of the structures of the ego by media and technology progresses, can human psyches jump into an egoless state beyond the conceptual mind, bypassing the construction of a stable ego? Will there be a superior entity to take charge of the psyche? Will the psyche slip into a state preceding ego? Will it collapse into psychosis? Or are we witnessing the evolution of the psyche itself, so that traditional ego formation will find a new path?

I cannot see an anthropological change in the human psyche as possible, even if supported by neurotechnologies. While we know from the latest research that the brain has a high degree of plasticity, the way the soul develops and unfolds has not changed much since the Buddha observed his own. The ancient paths to self-realization are still valid today, even though every epoch may have added to the understanding of the soul, teaching the path in ways more comprehensible and effective to its contemporary minds.

The hope that the Internet could overcome central governments and the one-to-many broadcasting models was perhaps a projection onto the external of something that will take place within us, dis-integrating the central organization of our psyches. The media and technology are reshaping our psyches to a degree we have not yet understood – perhaps because we are too distracted by the stream of information to notice the shift, or even to care.

The external pressure of stimuli is stronger than our capacity to digest them through the enzymes of our inner awareness. We no longer can resist external input. Like a spiritual egoless state, we flow with existence, but our minds are not empty – a condition necessary for flowing with the higher intelligence of existence. We are instead emptying our soul.

Addiction to the Net seems to offer another path to a pseudo-center of gravity for our soul. Then we flow with the endless loop of information, linked to technology that never pauses to reveal our emptiness, maintaining a cluttered mind to hide its insubstantiality.

As a "digital native" once said me in an email: "Paradoxically, for my generation's sense of loss and confusion, what the Net offers is like an anchor." Technology is taking charge of shaping our identities. Years ago we started with e-something (email, ebooks, etc.). Then it became i-somethings – iPhone, iMate, iPad. The name of the tool is now capitalized and the "I" is not, representing the move from something we might own to something that defines our identity. When we come back to our Facebook account it feels like coming back home – with all of the people who shape our lives presented in an orderly manner.

Identity then becomes defined by the flux of information we receive. The succession of thoughts gives the sense (or the *illusion*, as spiritual teachers say) of an individual recognizable identity. Though our personality is perennially under construction, it still feels the need for a defined identity. Overwhelmed by a quantity of information we cannot process, we are unable to – nor do we *want* to – make order of it, we skim, simplify, revert to the known, and regress to a mode of thought which neither requires nor accommodates nuances and complexities.

While the state of spiritual enlightenment accepts contradictions and chaos, it is beyond ego, beyond the mind and its confusion. In contrast, the mind processing scattered inputs of IT has weak attention and lacks a center of awareness. The information society enormously accelerates the stimulation of the mind – which can either move into a pathological decline of capacities or evolve toward its transcendence.

One of the appeals of Facebook is that it provides a neat and orderly way to integrate our various online sub-personalities. It is a collector of our object relations that offers us a feeling of a rounded, connected personality that is supported by the people in our friends list. With kids and teenagers spending so much time on social media, part of the process of personality construction takes place inside Facebook itself. Their attachments and object relations – the very building blocks of personality – are being shaped by Facebook which, not metaphorically, can reshape and manipulate their personalities.

Having massively invested in such an online personality, people cling to its shape. Any slight change in Facebook's user interface is met by a loud chorus of complaints from users who feel lost without their familiar references. Basic to the construction of personality is also the amount and quality of body contact. This is the first generation of children who have had less body contact. Furthermore, we spend more time indoors – whether at school, home or offices – in front of a screen which demands little of our body. Apart from the obvious problems of cardiovascular disease and obesity, our soul lacks the integrated connection with our body. When our body screams for attention, we respond with technological solutions like fitness programs and cosmetic surgeries.

Essential qualities of the personality are developed through involvement of our body with matter. Peter Nitze, global operations director at AlliedSignal (an aerospace and automotive-products manufacturer), talking about his practical education, said:

> If you've had the experience of binding a book, knitting a sock, playing a recorder, then you feel that you can build a rocket ship – or learn a software program you've never touched. It's not a bravado, just a quiet confidence. There is nothing you can't do. Why couldn't you? Why couldn't anybody? (Alliance for Childhood, 2000, p. 69).

This quiet confidence is the consolidation and acknowledgement of an inner quality born of hands-on experience. When inner confidence is alien, there is a lack of direction – which we try to compensate for with a digital measurement of our presence through technologies like GPS.

Technological Development
as a Metaphor of the Psychological One

The very name "personal computer" conveys an exclusive, unique and intimate relationship between the user and the medium. We don't refer to our cars or our digital cameras as "personal." In psychological terms, the relationship between a user and his computer follows the stages of development of the relationship of a baby with his mother or caretaker, starting from the early symbiotic phase. The first sub-phase of the symbiotic stage is what Almaas defines as "merging love."

> This aspect is present from the beginning of life but dominates especially between two and ten months of age. This period of life generally coincides with the period of ego development, called the symbiotic phase by Margaret Mahler... In this state of ego development, the child is not aware of the mother or himself as separate individuals in their own right. The ego has not separated itself. Mother and self are still a unity – a dual unity. In infant observation we find

that when the infant experiences the dual unity without any frustration or conflict, his essential state is that of merging love. It is a pleasurable, sweet, melting kind of love. The baby is peaceful, happy and contented (1986, p. 92).

Every heavy user of computers knows that he can lose his sense of time and enter a state of merging with the computer. Computers can even soothe us. And like the baby with its mother, there is an instinctual compulsive quality in this merging. The computer gives us the continuous attention that the baby needs from his mother. It always gives feedback and responds to our requests. As with infants, there's no need to talk to have our needs met – we just subtly move our fingers and relate to our immediate environment (the screen) through our eyes.

The merging stage between mother and child in recent decades has been disrupted by bottle feeding, earlier daycare, and the massive distraction of screen media. Babies no longer breastfeed enough, nor adequately develop the bonding that comes from prolonged body contact. It has been demonstrated how early separation affects the developing brain in a way that fosters mental pathologies. Without enough body contact they are cheated of the vibrant connection with their own bodies as well. When a stage of development – whether in our physiology or our soul – is skipped, we spend our lives looking for ways to correct and restore what is still missing.

The symbiotic phase is by no means constant perfection. Almaas wrote about the impact of difficulties:

> When the infant's needs are not met adequately or immediately, he cannot but experience frustration, rage and other painful affects. But the infant's experience of this negativity is not experienced as his own or his mother's; it is part of a merged relationship. There is still no clear concept of self and other, and no clear boundaries between the two. Thus the frustration and suffering can only be experienced as what we call "negative merging," in contrast to the positive merging of the experiences of gratification (1988, p. 245).

Everyone has experienced the frustration that computers can trigger – set off by delays, interruption of our work, lost Internet connection, no response from the person we are communicating with, viruses, lost and corrupted files, hardware crash. We then crave the smooth, sweet feeling of the original symbiotic phase. Negative merging "manifests as many kinds of desires. Since it is a state of painful undischarged tension, the desires are ultimately for discharge, though the objects of desire will vary greatly" (Almaas, 1988, p. 258).

The feeling of undischarged tension is common with computer users. So how can this tense frustration be discharged while we remain in front of the computer? The Net redirects desires and offers many surrogates for discharging the tension: bloody video games, porn, funny and weird videos, or participating in flame wars. But all of those discharges are short-lived, and prone to trigger an addictive effect.

Beyond the period of dual-unity, development enters the separation-individuation phase. Margaret Mahler has described how it opens the way for the first tentative autonomous steps into the world while the baby still feels the safety of caretakers. Hardly anyone remembers when the PC was not yet connected to the Net – an exclusive merging object with no one at the other end of the screen. With the Internet, we entered the separation-individuation stage. We can go out to "meet" people and seek any information – safely, from our computers.

The separation-individuation process accelerates the structuring of the ego. We recognize that ourself and others have separate existences and identities – just as the Net establishes a constant identity, open ID, unambiguous IP address, personal blogs, and real names in social networking. Part of the success of Facebook depends on connections among people with a defined real name and identity – what in psychological terms is called "object constancy."

The structure of our soul is based on authentic qualities of essence like Will, Peace, Strength, Love, Compassion, Joy which can be achieved through a path of self-understanding. But the normal construction of a personality consists of false qualities that strive to mimic the authentic ones. Almaas (1987) has written that

> the personality [is] the "false pearl." Each person retains the memory of what [of our original nature] was lost and will try to imitate it, will try to act, believe and feel in ways that are so close to the essential states that after a while the person fools himself, and other people as well. Some people do this more than others, and some people are better at it than others. The personality is really nothing but an impostor trying to take the place of essence (p. 127).

Here is found the origin of the need to create virtual worlds. Our psyche is from the beginning equipped to deceive. The first primitive ego structures are created when, from unavoidable experiences of separation, hunger, and physical pain, we split our perceptions, imagining that we are still receiving the love and comfort that is lost. This is the beginning of a fantasy world and of the constant search for fulfillment.

Millions of MP3s and the Missing "My Personality"

During an Italian conference dedicated to music on the Net, one boy asked the speaker, "We can download the complete recordings of any artist, but the problem is: What do we like?" This question summarizes the entire journey of the technological society which offers countless choices – but does not provide tools for creating a solid individual identity.

In *The Paradox of Choice: Why More Is Less* Barry Schwartz affirmed that the great variety of choices present in rich societies create paralysis instead of liberation (2004). A decision feels unsatisfactory, the more people can regret it. Unrealistic expectations lead to self-blame when the results are not perfect. The explosion of choices – and disappointment – may contribute to depression. Submerged in front of many options with a comparison of their features keeps us at a superficial informative level, without entering the depth behind our need. When our choice is driven by the market, at that very moment we are deluded yet believe that we know who we are and what we want.

We feel then like unique people making original choices. The choices and personalizations offered by industry simulate an acknowledgement of our identity. In order to be accepted and successful in society we have to be unique – but only within acceptable parameters.

So how are personal preferences created? Our musical predilections reflect our individual nature. Music passes through and connects the body, mind, emotions, and spirit. What we like in music depends on who we are as human beings – which is hardly to be found by downloading gigabytes of music from the Net.

Music resonates with our essential human qualities. An energetic kind of music cannot be appreciated deeply if we do not recognize and accept our inner strengths. Sweet and moving music cannot reverberate in us if we do not feel our own vulnerability and tenderness. In the same way, music can help us recognize and nourish the growth of these qualities in reciprocal feedback.

True freedom allows us real choice. But this authentic need of the soul is manipulated by industry when it offers choices from an infinite number of MP3s, or when we are creating our online image. Because we identify with what we know, think, and believe – in other words, with those fragile and unreal aspects that fill our mind – we believe that information can help us define our personality.

Attachment to the Machine

The ego personality somehow keeps itself whole by bonding with the objects of its attachment. If our anchor and life reference is the Net, then we will become attached to it.

When gmail introduced another feature to its email system, it was introduced this way (italics mine):

> How often do you try to chat with somebody and *they don't respond* because they just *walked away* from their computer? Or maybe you're in the middle of chatting with them just as they *need* to leave. But you still *need* to tell them something – something really important like you've moved, where you're meeting... or *ice cream*! We *need* ice cream! This is why we built a way to chat with your friends even when they're away from their computers. Now you can *keep* the conversations going with a new Labs feature that lets you send SMS text messages right from Gmail. It combines the best parts of IM and texting: you chat from the *comfort* of your computer, and your friends can *peck out* replies on their *little keyboards* (Direc, 2008, for Google Blog).

It's amazing to read in a single paragraph so many words which convey the meaning of need, abandonment, attachment, nourishment. The whole passage sounds like an infant who resists being separated from his object of care and attention. Our object relations have been transferred to technology with Mother Google who is nourishing us through her infinitely long umbilical cord anywhere a mobile phone can reach. The aspect of love and sexuality that engenders psychological attachment is replicated online. The cybervirgins described in chapter 5 and the whole industry of dating sites and porn thrive on this need.

The Monkey Rocker sex machine site writes: "Though it can't hug you back, or cuddle, it's perfectly understandable for you to develop feelings for your Monkey Rocker." Japan is beginning to use robots to take care of and provide companionship to elders. And it has been observed that the elderly develop feelings for them. Now even care, affection and sexuality are being mediated by machines. This is part of the accelerating digitization of reality.

The Need for Mirroring
The psyche has a natural need for mirroring by others. In building a sense of identity, being seen and recognized as our real nature helps us recognize our true self. So sharing our lives online feels like being seen and understood, a reflection that most people do not adequately receive – either in childhood or later in life.

On social networking sites and in chats there is a tacit agreement to give each other mostly positive feedback. If not, we can quickly block a person from contacting us, removing anything that doesn't support our expectations. Most Internet users are accom-

The Digitally Divided Self

plices in the violation of their own privacy. Google and Facebook know that people need to show, share and give feedback. Internet users are exposing more and more of their ideas, pictures and intimate lives through blogs and social networking sites. It seems that an act or thought has no value if it is not seen or uploaded and if it has no audience to confirm its existence.

Giving up our privacy on the Net looks like a good deal in return for the opportunity to show ourself to the world and fill the void left by inadequate mirroring in the past. However, this can become just another inner self-image – as inconsistent as any other, if driven merely by mind, since self-representations are considered obstacles to self-understanding.

The construction of our personality and self-esteem online can only go so far, leaving us feeling destabilized and insubstantial. So we crave more confirmation because those external inputs never cohere into a solid identity for us. After the necessary stage of being seen and appreciated by others and recognized for our inherent value, we need to look at ourself through introspection. We indeed create a deeper identity by sensing and recognizing our inner worlds, turning away from external confirmations.

Maternal Feeding and Paternal Limit Setting

With the headline "Stop sending mail you later regret," Mail Goggles asks a few simple math questions "after you click send to verify you're in the right state of mind." In other words, it prevents you from sending email while drunk or in any other unclear state. Google Labs offers Mail Goggles to "prevent many of you out there from sending messages you wish you hadn't... By default, Mail Goggles is only active late night on the weekend as that is the time you're most likely to need it" (Perlow, 2008).

In addition to being motherly, by feeding us with infinite information, Google now has acquired the paternal role of regulating and setting limits. This simple software is being introduced – in Google's style, as usual – in a low-profile way, but it marks the beginning of an intervention in our intentions and inner lives. It would be interesting to know if Google keeps a record of our test results, and what they would do with that information. Perhaps they'll advertise alcohol addiction recovery or food supplements to protect against alcohol toxins? Of course, the tool itself is valuable. The time it takes to solve a simple math problem can provide a healthy pause and could divert our thoughts, giving us space to reconsider our intention (though I doubt that people who indulge in drinking will enable the feature, or keep it enabled for long).

However, there's no technical way to help people stop the fast flow of thoughts and the actions they generate. Any software is bound to feed the mental chatter, rather than stop it. Only the development of our awareness "muscle" can stop our impulsiveness. The last thing that the unawareness condition of alcohol wants is to stop, reflect, or stay in an empty space where running thoughts might be transformed through very low-tech activities like meditation and self-inquiry.

Associating math capacities with moderation is indicative of a culture which associates rationality with anything good. But those are not necessarily connected. For instance, I have always been adept with numbers and would have no difficulty answering the questions correctly even if drunk. And correctly answering simple math questions reveals nothing about my inner state. I can still be impulsive, angry, hurtful, or irrational. But slowing down to take a test could help us be more aware of what exactly we are sending. If our message was sent by post instead of by email, there would be time for organizing our thoughts. Also writing with a pen forces us to reflect more, while finding an envelope, stamp, and mailbox gives more time to consider our words.

I'm not saying that we should go back to snail mail, but the procedures involved in letter writing provide a ritual which gives time to digest our intentions, ideas and feelings, thus allowing us to distill the value of our connection with the person. The ease of online communication is not compatible with the slow pace needed for reflection – which involves our thoughts, memories, feelings, and sensations. Physiology does not observe Moore's Law that processing speed doubles every two years. Connecting with our heart is a process far slower than ranting out an impulsive idea.

The Sand Castle Crumbles: Toward a Schizoid State

R. D. Laing was a controversial psychiatrist who led the anti-psychiatry movement. Combining existential philosophy with psychiatry, he gave new perspectives on the nature of mental illness. In his best-known book *The Divided Self* (1959) he describes an increasingly common personality:

> The schizoid individual exists under the black sun, the evil eye, of his own scrutiny... The "self-conscious" person is caught in a dilemma. He may need to be seen and recognized, in order to maintain his sense of realness and identity. Yet, at the same time, the other represents a threat to his identity and reality... He is, therefore, driven compulsively to seek company, but never allows himself to "be himself" in the presence of anyone else... The self is related

primarily to objects of his own fantasies. Being much a self-in-fantasy, it becomes eventually volatilized... Losing reality, it loses its possibility of exercising freedom of choice in the world.

Fifty years after Laing's book, findings from a research study entitled *Virtual Reality Induces Dissociation and Lowers Sense of Presence in Objective Reality* "indicate an increase in dissociative experience (depersonalization and derealization), including a lessened sense of presence in objective reality as the result of exposure to VR" (Aardema, 2010). Kelleci's (2009) study of more than 2,000 students entitled *Psychiatric Symptoms in Adolescents with Internet Use: Comparison Without Internet Use* found that "Internet use in adolescents was associated with more severe psychiatric symptoms."

Considering the study as supporting dictatorship, techno-enthusiasts could ironically say that we should then ban the Internet to prevent such symptoms. While banning the Internet is no solution, limiting screen media for people who escape reality and live a predominantly mental life is advisable. I am not suggesting that kids who are thoughtful or have active imaginations be suppressed – that would not support the development of artists and geniuses in the future. Real art is not just a product of the mind, but the integrated work of body, mind, and heart as well as deep qualities of the soul. But a kid who spends much of his time in front of screen media needs to ground himself in reality. Encouraging him is like filling an obese kid's refrigerator with junk food.

The building blocks of a strong identity also come from our connection with others and from the knowledge that others have about us. Without this, we suffer from an existential insecurity. In Laing's words I can recognize the heavy Internet user who needs to be connected and seen through social networks – but only to a certain point and at a safe distance. His profile and the people he is connected to are mostly objects of his projections and the self-images he wants to feed. The world of chats, forums, blogs, and social networking support his identity in a very fragile way. Whether conscious or not of the underlying emptiness, he clings to the digital representation of the world in fear of losing it.

The digitization of reality is being applied to every human activity, so that we live predominantly inside our own mental projections, mediated by digital technologies. Offline reality is slower and perhaps boring, while online only a click separates impulse from fulfillment. Our identification with our presence on the Net resembles identification with our ego. Both are constructions of the mind. Both lack any substance. And for both, we are dismayed by the idea of losing them.

Danna L. Walker (2007) reported in *The Washington Post* the difficulties her students have in unplugging from the Net. "There was a moment in my day when I felt homeless," one student said. "I was walking down the street literally with nowhere to go, and I just didn't know what I was going to do." This sense of loss is what chains us to the medium. If our identity is created and maintained mainly on the Net, the fear of losing access to it is a real threat. The crash of a hard drive with no backup, a virus subtly destroying our data, somebody stealing our passwords – these are a catastrophe.

Alexander Lowen classified people according to bioenergetic psychological characteristics. What Laing described is similar to the schizoid character which tends to reduce contact with his own body, to live essentially on the mental level, to separate thoughts from emotions, and to avoid direct contact with people.

The schizoid personality, one of the earliest-formed character structures, derives from emotional deprivation going as far back as the first months of life. It is rather common in advanced market societies where worklife rhythms deprive children of the physical and emotional contact necessary for adequate psychophysical development. The schizoid character lives in the mind and imagination, disconnected from the body. Withdrawn from the world, it is compatible with the current separated life in which every need is individual – which feeds the market industry. There we can still connect socially, but behind a screen through gadgets and social networks – which capitalize on our participation.

Even our technology has become more "schizoid" – more detached and less physical. Wireless connections, Bluetooth, Wi-Fi, and GPS provide a way of communicating that is disconnected from the world of matter. The division that the schizoid state has imprinted on our personality calls for a unifying agent. Information itself, paradoxically, is the apparent glue and it also keeps our mind always identified with something. Since information can change the shape of our identification, the frail schizoid personality can be morphed (and manipulated) by it continuously. The unification, however, is illusory – through information we cannot establish a core of felt identity. A split personality needs a continuous stream of input to identify with in order to avoid the threat of emptiness. For while emptiness is a blessing in advanced spiritual states, it is the terror of the ego mind.

The Other as Image
The Internet is moving toward a culture of images and videos. People in social networks and in chats have become concepts repre-

sented by small pictures scrolling on the screen. "Friends" come and go with a click. These tools can connect people, but they cannot give the sense of a "community." Considering people as objects – once the exclusive domain of pornography – has been extended online to other kinds of connections.

The Net has highlighted a tendency of the psyche. We project attributes of our internalized object relations on the other – mostly unconsciously. The Net may make evident that others are objects for our psyche, but it cannot make us aware of our internalized objects and how they were formed. Mental health depends on a healthy personality which the schizoid type can't properly build, living primarily in a fantasy world that lacks real connection either with others or his own body.

Detaching from the Body

In *Sexual Reality* (1992), Susie Bright interviewed human-computer interaction expert Brenda Laurel who expressed her views on the body and gender orientation of people into IT.

> I know from fifteen years' experience with computer guys that we have a class of people we call nerds who are radically uncomfortable with their bodies and their sexuality. I've had men tell me that one of the reasons they got into this business was to escape the social aspects of being a male in America – to escape women in particular. These are nice guys – not nasty, just shy, dweeby guys. When men talk about virtual reality, they often use phrases like "out-of-body experience" and "leaving the body." These guys are not talking about out-of-body experiences in the way that some Eastern mystic or Peruvian Indian would. They are talking about it in the sense that if you slap a screen over your eyes you won't have to see air pollution. That is a Western industrial let's-dominate-the-earth kind of mentality. When women talk about VR they speak of taking the body with them into another world. The idea is to take these wonderful sense organs with us, not to leave our bodies humped over a keyboard while our brain zips off down some network. The body is not simply a container for this glorious intellect of ours (p. 66).

In my own experience with people into IT, I witnessed some who don't shift out of their "digital" attitude for any life event. I saw successful people who could not reconsider their life attitudes even when facing life-threatening illness, or when their son was addicted to the Internet. Others manage by swallowing psychotropic drugs. They look everywhere but inside. Any problem is approached as a technical issue. At best, they can consult a doctor who administers some chemical to alter the information system of our neurotransmitters.

Overcoming identification with the body has traditionally been a mystical path, but that took place after fully integrating the body-mind connection and becoming aware of the full range of emotions and bodily sensations. Even saints in the Christian tradition, whose religion promoted disconnection from the body, in their path toward God could not escape facing the fullness of bodily sensations, even if it was the "Devil's temptation." The historical split between body and mind in our society is ruptured further by long computer use which involves our body only minimally.

Mystics say that when a person reaches elevated spiritual states, the identification with his body/mind fades, and is replaced by a wider identification.

> When a man falls madly in love with God, who can he call his father, his mother, his wife? He loves God so intensely that he is now crazy for him. He no longer has duties, he's free from his debts. What is this love frenzy? When a man reaches this state, he is no longer aware of his body to which in normal times he is so closely connected (Ramakrishna, 1963).

Much before the advent of the Internet, McLuhan (1989) foresaw that the new technological man would lose touch with nature as a direct experience, so that "with or without drugs, the mind tends to float free into the dangerous zone of abstractions" (p. 95). He envisioned a man who sits in front of his "informational control room," processing information from any place in the world, blowing up his ego and becoming schizophrenic, with his body in one place and his mind scattered in many. This splits the connection with his body and threatens his identity.

> A discarnate man is as weightless as an astronaut but can move much faster. He loses his sense of private identity because electronic perceptions are not related to a place. Caught up in the hybrid energy released by video technologies, he will be presented with a chimerical "reality" that involves all his senses at a distanted pitch, a condition as addictive as any known drug. The mind, as figure, sinks back into the ground and drifts somewhere between dream and fantasy. Dreams have some connection to the real world because they have a frame of actual time and place (usually in real time); fantasy has no such commitment. At that point, technology is out of control (p. 97).

We can easily recognize Internet addicts and virtual worlds like Second Life in McLuhan's description. Alexander Lowen (1995) lamented that over the years he has seen a continuous deterioration in his patients' bodies in terms of integration and aliveness. The old-fashioned hysterical patient

> is almost never seen. The hysterical person couldn't handle his

feelings; the schizoid individual hasn't many. Most people today are dissociated from their bodies and live largely in their heads or egos. We live in an egotistic or narcissistic culture where the body is seen as an object and the mind as the superior and controlling power (p. 291).

The Schizoid State is an Ontological Condition

Human beings *had* to become schizoid with the loss of the wholeness of the body/mind/soul. Historically the body had to be protected from predators and the dangers of the environment. Thus it had to be armored by muscular and outer protection – which disrupted awareness – and extended through technologies, whether spears or cell phones. Much as in a traumatic reaction, the terror of ontological loss required withdrawal from the body.

Wild animals do not lock traumatic symptoms in their bodies. While they quickly regain their force once the danger is gone, humans risk withdrawing, numbing and freezing the body. We are prone to our traumas becoming chronic in our psyches if we don't work them through with specific trauma-healing techniques like Peter Levine's Somatic Experiencing (1997).

The Eye, the Ear, and a Global Tribalism

In 1964 McLuhan had foreseen the connection of the whole of mankind where, "in the electric age we wear all mankind as our skin" (p. 47). Skin is the border between us and others, that last layer that defines our corporeal identity. "To wear all mankind as our skin" means that our identity becomes collective and is no longer anchored to a well-delimited "I." During embryogenesis both the skin and the nervous system develop from the ectoderm, the external layer of the embryo, and both conduct electricity.

In astrological symbolism, Neptune governs Pisces, the skin, the nervous system, the faculties of imagination and illusion – which extends to psychedelic drugs. Neptune also addresses the movement of the masses, and of the collective consciousness which is opposite and complementary to the individual's. Industrial society has prized individual identity and choice more than anything else, but historically identity was not always perceived as it is today. Individualism and the emphasis on individuals is a relatively recent phenomenon.

In primitive and tribal societies, as well as some developed nations (like China and Japan), the relationship between individual and collectivity is more important than individuality. McLuhan defined a human being dissociated from his sensory world as "literate man," in contrast to the tribal man connected with a cosmic perspective. Nevertheless, this very dissociation gave him the freedom to separate from the constricting environment of clan and family to obtain new powers through specialization and the freedom to develop individual identity separate from clan, family, or tribe.

McLuhan also defined as "tribal" those societies connected to auditory space, instead of the visual space stimulated by literacy. In auditory space the center is everywhere. This creates broad participation, but renders goals impossible since there is no clear direction. According to McLuhan, visual space is continuous and convergent. It tends to create a perspective, a point of view, and an objective. "It's hard to have a fixed point of view in a world where everything is happening simultaneously. It is hard to have an objective in a world that is changing faster than you can imagine the objective being fulfilled" (McLuhan, 2005, p. 237). Tribal man lived

> in a much more tyrannical cosmic machine than Western literate man has ever invented. The world of the ear is more embracing and inclusive than that of the eye can ever be. The ear is hypersensitive. The eye is cool and detached. The ear turns man over to universal panic while the eye, extended by literacy and mechanical time, leaves some gaps and some islands free from the unremitting acoustic pressure and reverberation (McLuhan, 1964, p. 156).

The extended global village accessed through the Internet, where we are continuously connected with all of humanity, seems like a return to "unremitting acoustic pressure and reverberation" through the explosion of information. Different authors have spoken of the Net in almost mystical tones, hypothesizing global minds and highly interconnected consciousnesses. In the mid-'90s I was also an enthusiast of the Net in similar terms, publishing books and writing in magazines as if the Net were the much-awaited enzyme for raising global consciousness.

But the world of the ear of tribal beings represented a tyrannical cosmic machine. While on one side it opened the doors to the cosmos, on the other it contained the individual experience within the restricted world of the tribe. Tribal people can experience shared states of consciousness through collective rituals (which happens nowadays in spectator sports, raves, and enormous collective events like Burning Man and political rallies), but their social experiences are limited by the tribe to social rules that are tightly defined. The tribal being actually fears leaving the tribe as a threat to his identity.

In the wider tribalism of the electronic global village we reproduce the tyranny through the omnipresent connection to the Net. While this extends the range of relationships to the whole of mankind, it squeezes us into a world of informational "pressure and reverberation" that we cannot avoid. In the enlarged tribe of the global village our nervous system needs to be numbed to the overflow of information – creating the same lack of focus and of individual perspective typical of preliterate man.

Digital tribalism does not allow the definition of a clear individual identity. The formation of identity, necessary even when we "wear the entire mankind as skin," needs more than the online feedback which reflects us in the Internet mirrors where we interact and share through digital means. Human connection, an authentic need for forming the personality, is being replaced by technology. Like any reflection of what is real, these mirrors are insubstantial and can only produce fragile personalities.

Just as in tribal societies everything about everyone was known, now in the social networking sites we broadcast much of our ordinary, social, professional and intimate lives. The proof of the existence of our lives and emotions is no longer within us: it is on the Net. Internet companies profit from our presence of the Net, and they study the tendencies of the collective mind in order to direct their advertisements more efficiently.

Far from being a participatory and democratic society, in the extended tribe we have leaders and chiefs. Google is like the medicine man of the tribe who keeps secret his magic potions – represented by the algorithms that determine page rankings – and dispenses power to sites according to its proprietary rules.

The Mind as a Medium

McLuhan (1964), considering technologies as extensions or self-amputations of our physical bodies, saw Narcissus as

> numb. He had adapted to his extension of himself and had become a closed system. Now the point of this myth is the fact that men at once become fascinated by any extension of themselves in any material other than themselves... This is the sense of the Narcissus myth. The young man's image is a self-amputation or extension induced by irritating pressures. As counter-irritant, the image produces a generalized numbness or shock that declines recognition. Self-amputation forbids self-recognition (p. 41).

Every technology has a role in both the extension and numbing of our organs. The computer gathers up all pre-existing media and extends them to become an extension/amputation of the whole mind. Computer technology expands our mental possibilities in terms of research, information, and knowledge processing – but numbs other capacities like self-recognition. With the pervasive accessibility of information, there is no necessity to remember, nor to analyze in depth. Following years of uninterrupted growth, in the last few years we seem to have reached the peak of intelligence.

In dealing with information technologies, the mind tends to be compulsively busy finding, communicating, and elaborating information – which in turn produces further information. What the computer numbs in the process is the capacity to observe our minds from the perspective of a witness.

We become less aware of both our mental mechanisms and our whole body/mind system. The body literally is benumbed and the mind turns exclusively to external stimuli, obstructing the capacity for self-observation and inner focalization, and weakening mindfulness that might lead to self-understanding. The computer as an extension of the mind externalizes the mind's work and prevents recognition of *mind* in the Buddhist sense – as the wholeness of thoughts, emotions, and sensations.

The computer medium charms us by reflecting our mind on the Net, and like Narcissus we become a closed system, numbed by our reflection in the ocean of the Net that we "navigate." We are fascinated by our reflected images on blogs, social networks, dating sites, forums where we are stuck in the information loop. Since we don't recognize ourself from the inside, we look for external mirrors and lose the sense of who we are in an infinite game of mirrors, like Narcissus who became oblivious even to the love of the nymph Echo.

When the conceptual mind is born, we lose our original self-realization. As soon as mind is present, our experience is shaped by past impressions, and we lose the immediacy of knowing. This happens very early in life. We, unconsciously or consciously, struggle for the rest of our lives to regain that condition. But we translate the original drive toward completeness of the soul into the search for external fillers.

If the computer is a tool for outsourcing the mind's functions, the mind itself can be considered a "medium," since it both extends the soul and induces numbness in our awareness of what the mind really is – an external reflection of the soul's qualities. The mind is born from an amputation – the shock of separation from the condition of merging with existence. This creates a numbness which does not allow us to recognize our real nature. Spiritual teachers say we are asleep. To awaken it is necessary to observe the mind itself – with the discrimination and introspection acquired through meditation and inner exploration.

The Digitally Divided Self

Just as dreams protect us from awakening by including external noise as part of the dream story, the virtual world's dream keeps the introspective capacities of the soul in a "sleeping" mode which makes self-observation difficult. This prevents our soul from transcending the mind. Perhaps, perceiving a distant echo of the fact that the conceptual mind itself is nothing more than a medium created by our soul, we try to outsource it to the computer to free ourself of it.

But anything which can be simulated and brought outside is not really "us." If we can reproduce some faculties of the mind through technology designed by the human mind, it means we are something more: specifically, the awareness that stays above that. Similarly, if we can observe the mind, we can step beyond it. Spiritual teachers say we are part of a global awareness which is connected to our specific body/mind. This global awareness certainly cannot be externalized in a medium, and it is not the hive mind of the Net – which simulates it only at the mental level.

The mind, created by the separation from the wholeness of existence, is an extension/prosthesis of the soul which is trying to regain what it lost through incessant mental activity, and through simulating essential qualities with fake ones. The mind has created, as an extension/prosthesis of itself, information technology which simulates the mind and outsources it to technology. Thus IT dazzles us like a reflection of a reflection of the original soul, a double illusory layer of *maya*, which offers both opportunities and risks. Perhaps we will be able to use IT to become aware of the unreality of our mind mechanisms. If not, we lose ourself in the delighting unreality of IT itself, which will distance us even further from the truth.

No Identity
Besides supporting our schizoid condition, IT promotes an ever-changing identity shaped by the information we absorb and by the huge number of people we are connected to. As the fast spinning of a color wheel appears white, our rapidly morphing identity can bring us to a state of no-identity.

Since the beginning, the Internet has been associated with collectivity rather than individuality, giving it a transpersonal promise. The creation and spread of information looks like the action of a collective mind. Software is developed by collective efforts, often in the public domain. Projects like Wikipedia depend on the cooperation of millions of eager people. Social networks like Facebook or Myspace, though offering space for individuals to express themselves, often form an aggregation of identities into loose collective groups. Several cyberculture experts talked, especially during the '90s, about the emergence of a global mind through the Internet.

McLuhan (1964) forecast that "electric technology" would create a global embrace beyond words, a "Pentecostal condition of universal understanding and unity" (p. 80). "Because they become profoundly involved in one another in an all-at-once simultaneous field of happenings, [they] begin to lose their sense of private identity because identity used to be connected with simple classification and fragmentation and non-involvement. In a world of profound involvement, identity seems to evaporate" (2005, p. 79).

The apogee of social networking produces the weakening of individual differences, homogenizing people in a common modality of interactions. Perhaps the appeal of being connected in such a pervasive way reflects a state longed for by our souls, where individual egos melt. But that state can only be reached through consciousness processing rather than information processing, as Peter Russell (1995) defined it.

In *Out of Control*, Kevin Kelly (1994) introduced the concept of the "hive mind," a superorganism emerging from the interaction of individual minds. The individual mind recedes to the shadows, since "life is a networked thing – a distributed being. It is one organism extended in space and time. There is no individual life." This led Mark Slouka (1995) to write, "The whole elaborate metaphor of the global superorganism, like most monstrosities – like the Third Reich, say, or the utopia of the proletariat – is based on a solid foundation of reasonable premises and hard facts" (p. 98).

Since the birth of the Internet, there has been an emphasis on collective intelligence, the wisdom of the crowd – which is a pale reflection of the morphing of individual consciousness into the universal which comes at the advanced stages of the spiritual path. What actually happens is a regression to a state preceding the formation of a solid, unique self. Sherry Turkle (1984, 1995) explored the personality in role-playing games and later on the Net, noting that object relations are transferred to the computer, with an effect on the formation of identity in young people. One aspect of our online identities, explored by several experts, is the attenuation of inhibitions in online life. The superego, that part of our psyche devoted to restraining our actions and desires, grips us with less strength in the online environment. Without the pressure of the superego we can explore parts of ourself which are usually kept in the shadows.

Using false identities – a phenomenon more frequent in the first years of the Internet than now – hides our public identity (partly from our own self as well), and the superego is hidden along with it. There are two complementary tendencies on the Net: one which encourages keeping multiple online personalities, and the other which tends to gather them into a central personality.

There is also the tendency toward reunification, as on OpenID – a "way to use a single digital identity across the Internet" – or on Facebook, where most users choose their real names. Anonymity is still possible in relationships with other users (though we can be traced by service providers and governments), but since we are connected in a tight net of relationships, anonymity does not serve the construction of our social identity that we work so hard to create.

Both spiritual and scientific literature indicate that there is no "I." Neuroscience has not found anything that can be labeled a "center of consciousness" or our "I" location. Yet every part of the brain seems to communicate with the other parts even in the absence of a coordinating entity. Artificial intelligence scientist Marvin Minsky (1998) wrote:

> But if there is no single, central, ruling Self inside the mind, what makes us feel so sure that one exists? What gives that myth its force and strength? A paradox: perhaps it's *because* there are no persons in our heads to make us do the things we want – nor even ones to make us *want to want* – that we construct the myth that *we're* inside ourselves (p. 40).

Minsky's paradox inadvertently reveals a deeper truth. The spiritual teacher/non-teacher U. G. Krishnamurti (1982) asked:

> Is there in you an entity which you call the "I" or the "mind" or the "self"? Is there a coordinator who is coordinating what you are looking at with what you are listening to, what you are smelling with what you are tasting, and so on? Or is there anything which links together the various sensations originating from a single sense – the flow of impulses from the eyes, for example? Actually, there is always a gap between any two sensations. The coordinator bridges that gap: he establishes himself as an illusion of continuity. In the natural state there is no entity who is coordinating the messages from the different senses. Each sense is functioning independently in its own way. When there is a demand from outside which makes it necessary to coordinate one or two or all of the senses and come up with a response, still there is no coordinator, but there is a temporary state of coordination. There is no continuity; when the demand has been met, again there is only the uncoordinated, disconnected, disjointed functioning of the senses. This is always the case. Once the continuity is blown apart – not that it was ever there; but the illusory continuity – it's finished once and for all (1982, p. 65).

Neuroscience also holds that there's no center of consciousness – but it doesn't see anything beyond that, relegating human beings to the level of a software program where the various modules exchange data and actions. The ego, as the teachers of awareness say, is an illusion, an entity which keeps together our personality artificially, a collection of thoughts, ideas, hopes and feelings which, through its unending activity, creates the illusion of a director. The constant flux of information on the Net interacting with our sub-personalities also creates the illusion of continuity.

Even though spiritual teachers say there's no "I," most of them recognize the necessity of building a structured personality in order to go beyond it. Assagioli, the father of psychosynthesis and one of the inspiring figures of transpersonal psychology, applied the concept of different psychic parts and their integration to a spiritual context. And in Almaas's Diamond Heart school, there's a stage in the path when the Essential Self, the *Pearl Beyond Price*, develops as a balanced, rounded, whole personality.

The Pearl, essentially differently from ego, is something real – based on real qualities which integrate in an individual, with a personal, distinctive flavor. The Pearl is not a cluster of mental images nor object relations inside our psyche. The Pearl grows with the support of the essential qualities of Will, Compassion, Strength, Intelligence, Joy, Peace and others, which have to be recognized, felt and explored in order for them to integrate in our soul. It is funny to see that some of the essential aspects of the personality are listed as attributes in the avatars of online games where we can score points for "endurance," "intelligence," "strength" and "willpower."

CHAPTER 13

THE PROCESS OF KNOWLEDGE

S cience is grounded in a particular approach to knowledge. Scientists believe that knowledge has value only if it is objective. The myth of objectivity is so pervasive that it applies even to a subjective and inner science like psychology. Subjective experiences are usually considered "isolated cases" and not worth further investigation since, being unique, they can't be reproduced in a laboratory.

In his scientific inquiries, Descartes looked for a "clear and distinct perception" as the foundation for the scientific method independent of previous subjective ideas and emotions. His procedure involved a meditation technique, though different from the accepted scholastic methods of his time, and different as well from the Eastern forms of meditation such as *vipassana* or Zen. Descartes suggested that every scientist begin any inquiry by first emptying the mind of all preconceptions.

History praised him as the father of the scientific method – or blamed him for being the one who split body and soul. However, scientists never actually adopted his meditative method. Too bad Descartes stopped his inquiry at, "I think, therefore I am." Had he gone just a bit further, he would have reached "I witness my thoughts, therefore I am not them."

The Reign of Objectivity
Modern science, based on reproducibility and objectivity – which are fundamental to understanding Newton's world of physics – led to enormous technical and scientific development, but never developed the tools to understand awareness, the soul, the psyche it-

self, or existence. The problem of locating consciousness (which is nagging the neurosciences today) seems to be elusive to the research method which negates any role for inner life.

According to modern science the individual's subjective qualities would pollute the "purity" of scientific discoveries. The original reason for the dominance of objectivity has to do, again, with Christian scriptures. Since human beings have been created in the image of God, they can approximate God's view of nature.

According to the scriptures, humans were created on the last day of creation, set apart from the rest of creation. Thus, nature is something humans can know objectively. And the human mind, created in the likeness of the divine, has the potential to understand the universe as created by God. Humans, then, should be able to attain this comprehension by adopting as purely objective a perspective as God brought to creation, thus maintaining our separation from the natural world. (We should not forget that Descartes developed his method in order for human beings to appreciate and discover God's creation.)

But there is another element that I feel discredited subjectivity even further. When in the beginning Adam and Eve used their very subjective capacities to choose, instead of obeying God's rules, they acted out the original sin. Better, then, to not trust subjectivity, but rely instead on objectivity, data, and accurate digital equipment. The West thus excluded the inner subjective channels of exploring knowledge from science, leaving them to philosophy or religion – and without crediting them as reliable channels for reaching truth. Religion and science portioned out the territory: to science the outer, while to religion the inner. Sometimes they've had their border skirmishes, but this non-written agreement has worked fine for centuries.

Alan Wallace (2000) analyzed the history of the ascendancy of objectivity. He delineated the difference between scientific and contemplative discoveries. While the former are objective and public, the latter are subjective and private. Even between scientists, there is no complete guarantee that the research which led to certain discoveries was accurate and reliable, thus trusting the work of colleagues is still essential. A complete guarantee could be possible only by repeating the same experiments in similar laboratories. Wallace asserted that if scientists had always doubted their colleagues' work, science would have developed very slowly. He concluded that the same discourse could be applied to contemplative research. If societies valued the contemplative experience, people would simply trust the authenticity of the best souls of their times and of the past.

The Digitally Divided Self

When I explore the writing of spiritual teachers, I understand that, using different metaphors and words, they describe a common state of elevated consciousness. This motivates me to embark on my own exploratory path. The spiritual path, in spite of the availability of precious teachings, has to be experienced personally – and from the beginning – by every researcher. There will be little inner progress only from reading spiritual literature. Spiritual paths, though often considered somewhat vague, irrational, or even re-quiring psychiatric care (and there are such cases), are actually more "scientific," because they require one to experience the journey from the beginning, while science is based on a sort of *faith* in the validity of experiments.

The spiritual journey is never linear, in spite of wise men having lit a torch along the path. The journey is both universal and indi-vidual at the same time. The difficulties of the path necessitate a guide who has already traversed it. But in the West, where the spir-itual teacher is held in suspicion, the researcher first needs to over-come the barriers of social acceptance to become a disciple. We accept the authority of science in statements about life, perhaps from people who have no personal experience with what they say (though they often have economic incentives), but we suspect the authority of a spiritual teacher who has personally traveled a path!

The rejection of spiritual teachers has different origins, among them the monopoly of institutionalized religions on the soul. The Christian message is that Christ is the only one designated to em-body the connection with the divine, and thus the only one who can speak with the voice of God's authority. Then there is the em-phasis on individualism in our culture, as well as a lingering '60s counterculture stance against authority – which misunderstands true authority, derived from the wisdom of life experience, with au-thoritarianism. In general, in the West there is no acknowledge-ment of the spiritually enlightened being. Yet on the spiritual journey, guidance can only come from those who have matured the qualities and inner states which must be transmitted. Though it is possible to become spiritually realized without teachers, such cases are rare.

While the scope of intervention of science in society has ex-panded to involve the social, moral, and ethical implications of find-ings, those aspects are often not supported by the scientist's inner life. It reminds me of the Buddhist story of the mother who had a son who ate too many sweets. Worried about his health, she con-sulted a monk whose wisdom would convince her son to stop. The monk told her to come back in two weeks. The mother returned and the monk said to the son, "It's no good to eat too many sweets." The mother, perplexed, asked the monk why he waited two weeks to make such a simple statement. He replied that it had taken time to conquer his own indulgence.

Joining Inner and Outer Knowledge

There have been scientists who combined inner research with the external – Pythagoras, da Vinci, Swedenborg, Tesla, and the ancient scientists of the Vedas. Their states of consciousness sometimes led to discoveries in the natural sciences. But interiority is needed even more in order to understand the nature of the psyche, the soul, and consciousness.

To have an effective theory of consciousness it is necessary to study it from the inside and maybe even from beyond the mind, from a space where it can be observed by a broader awareness. Cognitive sciences and neuroscience, refuting the existence of a state beyond the mind, try to find consciousness through neurotechnological mappings of the brain. They discover everything but the presence of consciousness itself. Or they become even more obscure than mystics by saying that consciousness "emerges" by the complex interaction of neuronal connections – which paves the way for even considering the Internet a "conscious entity."

While the teachings of enlightened teachers regarding consciousness have been valid for thousands of years, those of science tend not to stand up to paradigm changes. Nevertheless, only a few scientists welcome the mystics' discoveries as hypotheses worth investigating. When the authority of science is challenged, it seems we must choose between scientific reason and faith. But there's a third way. A connection between scientific research and inner states is possible – a connection which might even enrich science. A. H. Almaas, originally trained as a physicist, has developed a path whose method is inquiry, a technique for inner exploration which joins the mind, emotions, and sensations in the search for truth. I have interviewed him twice for my *Innernet.it* online magazine on the matter (Almaas, 2008, 2009).

He does not deny the validity of science, as far as scientists' objectivity is concerned, "in the sense that our subjectivity tends to cloud our perception and knowledge, because of personal beliefs and biases." Nevertheless, in his opinion science has had an incomplete intuition about subjectivity because "it neglects to notice that this biased subjectivity is the subjectivity of the ego, and that the human soul can be free of the ego" (Almaas, 2008), free from the filters which obscure the pure perception of reality.

The evolution of a scientist's inner life is not important for science, which does not distinguish between the subjectivity of the ego and the one which comes from wisdom. Almaas holds that, "the truly subjective and personal – meaning one's own [independent of] influences coming from beyond one's true being, is a rare and hence precious development." I asked him whether a new scientific method including both subjective and objective approaches is possible. What is available when our soul matures, he answered – "in terms of inquiry, research, discernment, analysis, synthesis, and so on – can be very useful in any field of research. But it will require that the researcher integrates this spiritual faculty in their functioning for it to operate in any field" (2008).

Almaas regards knowing (*gnosis* or *nous*, the higher intellect of the Greeks), as having a mystical or intuitive ground in which knowing and being are inseparable. Ever since Western thought separated the experience of being from the objects of knowledge, the source of being has been relegated to the rubric of mysticism, and is considered mysterious, irrational, non-scientific, and even anti-scientific. Almaas agrees that objective knowledge should be free from the distortions of the knower, but the path toward objectivity cannot be reached by "sterilizing the situation of inquiry, by removing the subject from the field of inquiry" (2009). He thinks that the scientific understanding of objectivity:

> is not real objectivity, it's a schizoid isolation. It is the result of trying to arrive at objectivity through schizoid withdrawal. Because we don't know how to deal with our subjectivity, we shut it off. That has been the accepted way of science, and some people have been advocating this approach even for psychology and spirituality... The best way to understand personal experience objectively is through inquiring not only into the object of inquiry, but also into the inquiring subject at the same time. The physicist does not include his own impact on results when observing an experiment. He merely tries to interfere as little as possible and works on improving his instruments. However, when we inquire into our personal experience, we do not try to avoid interfering, we simply include our interference as part of what we observe. Our exploration is not only into the nature of our experience or state, but also into the totality of who we are, including the nature of the part of us that observes or explores (2002, pp. 356 and 358).

Heisenberg's principle of indetermination also tells us that the observer and the object observed cannot be separated on the fundamental level.

> We cannot, because the knowing subject is nothing but the collapsing of the field of presence and awareness into a knowing self...

Descartes' philosophy of science is an approximation, similar to how Newton's classical theory of physics is a good working approximation, to the laws of physics. Now we know that Newton's physics collapses at the two extreme ends of the scale of physical measurements, where the general theory of relativity and quantum theory have replaced it as more accurate in the domains of macro and micro distances respectively (Almaas, 2009).

The inadequacy of Descartes' method is clear in the understanding of consciousness, the soul, and transcendence, which all necessitate a first-person experience. Almaas believes that mysticism, in its turn, contributed to negating the fundamental unity of being and knowledge, by considering spiritual knowledge as

> vague, intuitive, mysterious, non-conceptual, incommunicable and so on, [while] direct mystical knowing and the knowing of specific forms in precise details can be wed, because they are originally one and non-dual. This means that we can have a mystical knowledge – which is knowledge by identity – that can be precise, clear, specific and detailed (Almaas, 2009).

This channel of knowing brings the possibility of "scientific knowledge that is direct knowledge, meaning precise and detailed gnosis of forms of manifestation" (Almaas, 2009). In the same way, the subject who knows by observing his own reactions, prejudices and attitudes during the act of exploration, engenders fewer and milder subjective distortions, and comes closer to objectivity.

> We find different degrees of objectivity, where each degree is objective within the subjective framework we work with. In other words, if we use the framework that we are separate individuals in the ordinary world, then objective truth means something different from objective truth in a framework that does not hold such assumptions of separate individuality. Again, objectivity means something different depending on whether we assume existence and nonexistence are two antithetical opposites or inseparable and co-emergent (Almaas, 2009).

The process of clarifying distortions is like a distillation. "Objectivity is complete when there is no more separate self to hold biases" (Almaas, 2009), thus transcending any dichotomy between the observer and the observed. This approach unites again scientific inquiry based on objectivity with direct knowledge. Such a new method could progress toward the discovery of existence.

Pure knowledge, the *nous*, exists and is grounded in the mystical union of being and knowledge, beyond the experience of a separate self.

Not Knowing

"The Edge Annual Question 2010" asked 170 scientists, philosophers, artists and authors, "How is the Internet changing the way you think?" Among the answers which grabbed my attention was Anthony Aguirre's (Associate Professor of Physics, University of California, Santa Cruz) "The Enemy of Insight?" which resonates with my reflections on knowledge and the inner mechanisms underlying insights.

> I, like most of my colleagues, spend a lot of time connected to the Internet. It is a central tool in my research life. Yet when I think of what I do that is most valuable – to me at least – it is the occasional generation of genuine creative insights into the world. And looking at some of those insights, I realized that essentially none of them have happened in connection with the Internet... I've come to think that it is important to cultivate a "don't know" mind: one that perceives a real and interesting enigma, and is willing to dwell in that perplexity and confusion. A sense of playful delight in that confusion, and a willingness to make mistakes – many mistakes – while floundering about, is a key part of what makes insight possible for me. And the Internet? The Internet does not like this sort of mind. The Internet wants us to know, and it wants us to know *right now*: its essential structure is to produce knowing on demand. I don't just worry that the Internet goads us to trade understanding for information (it surely does), but that it makes us too accustomed to instant informational gratification. Its bright light deprives us of spending any time in the fertile mystery of the dark (2010).

The attitude of not-knowing is shared by both good science and by spiritual inquiry. Descartes himself started his philosophical investigation with a not-knowing attitude which led him to find his first principle, "I think, therefore I am." Let's see what the spiritual teachers have to say about not-knowing.

Sri Aurobindo said of the enlightened mind: "One is in an unutterable state of truth without understanding anything about it – simply, it is" (Satprem, 1974, p. 208).

Nisargadatta Maharaj: "When consciousness mixes with itself, that is samadhi. When one doesn't know anything – and doesn't even know that he doesn't know anything – that is Samadhi" (1985, p. 6).

Then Osho:

> This is the ultimate paradox of mysticism: with not-knowing you can reach knowing and through knowing you lose it. Not-knowing is superior to any knowledge. Universities make you learned but when you enter into the Buddhafield of a spiritual Master you enter in an anti-university. In the university you harvest more and more

knowledge, information and you accumulate. In the anti-university of a Master you unlearn more and more... until the moment you don't know anything anymore (1983).

Meister Eckhart, considered a heretic by his Church, was, however, influential in the fourteenth century and later:

Teachers say that God is a being, a being gifted with intellect, who knows everything. But I say: God isn't a being, He doesn't have an intellect and He doesn't know this or that. That way God is free from all things – therefore he is all things (1995, p. 72).

And Almaas:

Why am I here? Where am I going?... These are questions that you cannot answer with your mind. These are questions that should remain questions. Do not try to simply answer them mentally. These questions are like a flame. If you answer them with your mind, you will put out the flame, because the mind doesn't, the mind can't know the answers to these questions. When you answer them with your mind and you think you know, the question is gone. When you believe you have answered such questions, the flame is gone and there is no more inquiry (1990, p. 1).

Even neurophysiologically a stage of not-knowing is needed to reach the "Eureka effect" (Pearce, 2002). Being in the unknown is uncomfortable for the mind, since our ego identifies mostly with what we know. Knowing reassures us. So whenever we have a thirst to know anything, we quench it on Google. But this way, as Almaas says, "the flame is gone." Good meals sometimes require slow, long cooking – better if directly over the fire, rather than electricity, while Google works hard to avoid any "fertile mystery of the dark" or delays in offering its answers.

When I was a kid I believed that somewhere, somebody had the answers to all my questions about the world and about existence. I was confident that sooner or later I would have access to that knowledge, and this quieted my cognitive anxiety. The very fact that knowledge was present somewhere, however hard to reach, made me feel that it was certainly obtainable, as if it was in the air and only needed the proper antennae to pick it up. The Web did not exist then, nor did Google, which now provides almost the entire repository of human knowledge. Nor did I know Rupert Sheldrake's morphogenetic field theory, much less the spiritual view of universal consciousness, nor had I heard of the Akashic records.

But what happens to the process of discovering knowledge when we get it instantly on Google? Google is simultaneously an extension and an amputation in our answer-finding capabilities. Through Google we deceive ourself in thinking we are getting answers. Restless if they don't come quickly, we risk quenching the flame of the quest. Knowledge gives us a false idea of control, a protection against the anxiety of the unexpected that is inherent in the mystery.

The very nature of mind is uncomfortable with the unknown. Trying to know – or at least knowing that there is an answer – comforts us, as I experienced. One of the capacities of adults is staying with the feeling of uncertainty. But when we are satisfied with the answers given by search engines, the passion for searching further is extinguished.

Even though we can actively jump online from one query to another and from one link to another, this can inhibit the prolonged attention that is necessary to connect inner and outer knowledge. Search engines are now used for scientific, cultural, philosophical, and even existential or spiritual searches. The Net points our attention from one piece of information to another without allowing it to root in our inner world where it can morph into inner knowledge.

The trend of search engines is to make queries more user-friendly and recognize common patterns of languaging. Still, a Google query requires the user's intuition to find the precise terms that lead to the information desired, calling on capacities of discrimination, focused attention to the problem, and understanding of the subtleties of the language – skills which are rare – according to what every site owner sees from the way people write Google queries to arrive at their Web pages. Far more than Google, it is our passionate and focused attention which ensures that we will attract the knowledge we seek.

Passion and concentration support discovery and invite *synchronicity* to contribute to our knowledge. (The term, coined by Jung, describes two apparently unrelated events that coincide to yield something meaningful.) By focusing our attention, our awareness meets another. Actually, it is awareness that meets itself. Attention that attracts discoveries happens in arenas as diverse as science, police investigations, and inner knowledge. Nisargadatta Maharaj (1982) said:

> Once you are inwardly integrated, outer knowledge comes to you spontaneously. At every moment of your life you know what you need to know. In the ocean of the universal mind all knowledge is contained; it is yours on demand. Most of it you may never need to know – but it is yours all the same (p. 385).

Searching the Net is made as simple as possible. However the effort in searching is exactly what brings us in connection with the search field. The "I'm Feeling Lucky" button on Google allures us with the idea that our quest is about to end. There is an instinctual attraction to arriving at the end of a quest, to finally quiet the noise of the mind – the same phenomenon that accompanies spiritual re-alization. Google's search is a reflection of this quest on the mental level – but mind soon becomes restless again.

The mind wants answers and wants them with immediacy, while our spiritual nature is comfortable with not-knowing – a state of wonder associated with babies is rediscovered and integrated with the adult quality of awareness. U.G. Krishnamurti (1982) described it:

> This state is a state of not knowing; you really don't know what you are looking at. I may look at the clock on the wall for half an hour – still I do not read the time. I don't know it is a clock. All there is inside is wonderment: "What is this that I am looking at?" Not that the question actually phrases itself like that in words: the whole of my being is like a single, big question mark. It is a state of wonder, of wondering, because I just do not know what I am looking at. The knowledge about it – all that I have learned – is held in the background unless there is a demand. It is in the "declutched state." If you ask the time, I will say "It's a quarter past three" or whatever – it comes quickly like an arrow – then I am back in the state of not knowing, of wonder (1982, p.62).

However valuable Google's answers are, it is equally important to remain with wonder and not-knowing. Mystics have not given knowledge the role that we do in modern life, especially the sepa-rating knowledge of duality.

> The knowledge of the ancients was perfect. How perfect? At that time, they did not know that there were things. This is the most per-fect; nothing can be added. Next, they were aware of things, but they did not yet make distinctions between them. Next, they made dis-tinctions, but they did not yet judge them. When judgments were passed, Tao was destroyed (Chuang-Tzu).

Words are Second-Best After Silence

Spiritual teachings often affirm that the ultimate knowledge is to be found beyond words and concepts. A spiritual researcher decon-structs his mental frameworks, which are predominantly made of thoughts, words and concepts that form a dense net which over-shadows truth and reality. We connect our identity to words and concepts – which can become heavy structures of consciousness that mistake the map for the territory – so we approach life guided by conceptual maps.

About the end of their first year children learn to voluntarily let go of objects from their hands. At the same time they start to talk. This suggests to me that children can let go of attachments to physical objects because they are being replaced by the representation of objects on the conceptual plane, however rudimentary.

While silence can carry the ultimate truth, concepts are very useful for self-understanding. A creative, accurate and deep processing of concepts can pierce into understanding and bring us to the border between mind and beyond-mind.

> Words are as much a barrier, as a bridge, [the mind] shapes the language and the language shapes the mind. Both are tools, use them but don't misuse them. Words can bring you only up to their own limit; to go beyond, you must abandon them. Remain as the silent witness only (Maharaj, 1982, p.451).

While people on spiritual paths may talk about "no mind" and of going beyond the mind, they perceive ordinary mind as nothing more than a biocomputer. This is true, but – the mind can be overcome only if it is allowed its fullness. And in any case, the mind will come along with us even after spiritual enlightenment, so it is better to have a mind that is brilliant and expansive, so that we can better communicate our state and the way to reach it to others who follow behind us on the path. "With the lamp of word and discrimination one must go beyond word and discrimination and enter upon the path of realization" (*Lankavatara Sutra*).

Similarly, a musician can escape the structure of musical scales to improvise melodies only after mastering musical scales. Otherwise he produces only meaningless noise. Mental capacities that have been restrained invite rigidity and intolerance. Then mind becomes easily manipulated by populist slogans and simplistic messages which leverage the most superficial feelings.

On the Net there's little on-going, continuous narrative which can deepen a subject, while there is rapid consumption of information that doesn't value the full potential of words and concepts. Words, as the basic medium of individual consciousness, are the tool that connects us with our interiority. Images (whether static or in motion) and sounds are internalized, and together translate into inner words and concepts for understanding the inner and the outer.

Reading is the most creative among the ways to acquire information. Reading a book is an interactive process between our interior and its contents. The process can be enriching and soul-transforming. TV and videos come to consciousness through modalities and with a pace we have less control of, but reading allows us to determine our absorptive and reflective rhythms. The slowing down and pausing allows us to treasure the words and metabolize them. A book can carry us into the depths because its approach is gentle and respectful. Reading is an inner act, like its companion, writing.

In the beginning the Internet was mainly a textual medium. For many years low bandwidth limited information mainly to text and some pictures. The Internet was about reading and writing – often done offline, free from the Net's interruptions. That allowed introspection and reflection.

Indeed, speed matters. More than being merely a quantitative issue, speed changes the quality and modality of how we approach and use concepts and information. For instance, if we walk in a terrain we have a completely different perception of it than if we cross it by car.

Do We Know with our Brains?

The cognitive scientist Marvin Minsky (1988) wrote:

> If we could really sense the working of our minds, we wouldn't act so often in accord with motives we don't suspect. We wouldn't have such varied and conflicting theories for psychology. And when we're asked how people get their good ideas, we wouldn't be reduced to metaphors about "ruminating," and "digesting," "conceiving" and "giving birth" to concepts – as though our thoughts were anywhere but in the head. If we could see inside our minds, we'd surely have some more useful things to say (p. 63).

The prevailing idea is that mind and thoughts are exclusively the brain's. It wasn't always that way, and now even science has discovered that we have "brains" in our heart and in our belly, so the metaphors Minsky ridiculed have some truths in them. The nervous system in the heart interacts with the brain and can even induce autonomous decision-making processes. From *Science of the Heart*:

> After extensive research, one of the early pioneers in neurocardiology, Dr. J. Andrew Armour, introduced the concept of a functional "heart brain" in 1991. His work revealed that the heart has a complex intrinsic nervous system that is sufficiently sophisticated to qualify as a "little brain" in its own right. The heart's brain is an intricate network of several types of neurons, neurotransmitters, proteins and support cells like those found in the brain proper. Its elaborate circuitry enables it to act independently of the cranial brain – to learn, remember, and even feel and sense (Institute of HeartMath, 2001).

The magnetic field of the heart is more than 5,000 times greater than that of the brain, and can be detected several feet away. It is perhaps the neurophysiological counterpart of intuition and empathy. It's at least curious that what has been observed for so long on the intuitive level is not acknowledged until it's observed scientifically. The cognitive possibilities of the heart have already been expressed by many authors, including Aldous Huxley (1945):

> We can only love what we know, and we can never know completely what we do not love. Love is a mode of knowledge, and when the love is sufficiently intense, the knowledge becomes unitive knowledge and so takes on the quality of infallibility. Where there is no disinterested love (or, more briefly, no charity), there is only biased self-love, and consequently only a partial and distorted knowledge both of the self and of the world of things, lives, minds and spirit outside the self (p. 81).

If the heart is a cognitive organ, it's not the only one to keep company with the brain. Scientists have discovered a structure in the digestive tract composed of an array of 100 billion brain-type cells – more than in the spinal cord. Researchers believe that this abdominal brain could be responsible for the feelings of joy or sadness and could even store information related to physical reactions. Those discoveries are compatible with the ancient views of the belly as a repository of sensations and instinctual cognitive capacities.

Jesse J. Prinz, author of *Gut Reactions* (2008), posited that the neuronal net in the abdomen is the source of unconscious decisions which the brain later claims as its own. The brain in the gut was first documented in the nineteenth century by German neurologist Leopold Auerbach whose studies were not given serious consideration until recently. We see again that what science is just now prepared to approach has already been known for ages.

> I must refer again to the story of my friend, the Pueblo chief, who thought that all Americans were crazy because they were convinced that they thought in the head. He said: "But we think in the heart." That is *anahata*. Then there are primitive tribes which have their psychical localization in the abdomen (Jung, 1996, p. 34).

In this age we need all the centers – brain, heart and belly – to understand the complex challenges and act wisely on them. The brain alone is too limited to help us cope with the present crises with the environment, energy, ethics, and economics that are exacerbating each other. While the science of complexity has made significant steps toward a more holistic approach to science, it is unable to jump to a broader view of life that includes the spiritual as well. The much-quoted words of Einstein offer us guidance once more: "The significant problems that we face cannot be solved by the same level of thinking that created them." Perhaps we should be moving from the level of the mind to the wholeness of our soul.

Externalizing Thinking

Neil Postman (1988) said that one of the basic tenets of technology is that it can do our thinking for us. The Singularity project to download minds to the Net could challenge our identification with the mind. If it can be copied, reproduced and shared between people, will it still be considered as ours? Dissolving that identification offers us the opportunity to escape the cage of our thoughts and to approach a higher awareness and intelligence.

But the intention behind downloading our mind to the computer is not to disidentify from it, but to cling to the identification with it even after our physical death. U.G. Krishnamurti (1982), perceiving the nature of the mind and of thoughts, said that in fact we are all thinking and functioning in a "thought sphere," where the brain is merely an antenna for picking up thoughts. The brain, then, is seen as a receiver, rather than a thought-producing machine.

Thus the paternity of an idea or thought is no longer at issue, once a certain stage of awareness is reached. The ancient Hindu sacred scriptures, the Upanishads, don't bear the signature of any author. They were written in a state of absence of ego. There's no need to copyright ultimate understanding. The concept of the individual mind itself is being refuted by mystics of the Advaita tradition. Ramesh Balsekar (1992) said:

> You see, the basic point I'm making is, no brain can create a thought with the material of which it is. A thought can only come from outside. Then there can be a reaction at any moment, but the thought comes from outside. [Then when a student asked:] The concept of "outside," I find difficult. Outside what? [Ramesh answered:] That is the point. Really, there is no outside or inside. All there is, is Consciousness (p. 28).

And Yogananda (1952): "Thoughts are universally and not individually rooted; a truth cannot be created, but only perceived." To keep the structures of our mind intact as long as possible on the Net protects the mind from the journey toward the Absolute where it will no longer be at the center of the stage. Nevertheless our soul feels the overbearing presence of the mind, so outsourcing it to data centers ("the cloud") is an attractive means to free it from its limited capacities. But this is really another trick of the mind to guarantee its survival.

The desire to upload thoughts to a safer medium than the mortal biological body represents again the Cartesian dream of pure thought without connection to the body. Descartes talked about the "prison" of the body as an obstacle for scientific inquiry, a hindrance that has to be fixed to reach truth. The Fall, for Christianity and other monotheistic religions, was the fall to Earth, into matter, into the mortal body. Science and religion both strive to be free of the body in order to regain pure thinking and the purity of the soul.

Thus the body has rarely been welcomed as a source for the spiritual quest, much less for scientific inquiry. But the body, too, can open toward awareness and be a door toward our depth, in cooperation with the mind. In the spiritual inquiry of A. H. Almaas (2000):

> It is important to keep sensing your body – to stay in direct touch with its movements and sensations. This includes the numbness, the dullness, or the tensions you may feel. To ground your awareness in your bodily experience is important because your essential qualities are going to arise in the same place where you experience your feelings, emotions, and reactions. They are not going to appear above your head, they are going to arise within you. So your body is actually your entry into the mystery... So the inquiry has to begin by activating and enlivening the body (p. 294).

When we don't acknowledge the value of the body, it is considered something mechanical, something to ignore or replace with technology. If we understand that whatever is created by the mind cannot be the real thing, technology might even stimulate our search for something further. Or we could be entranced by the infinite forms that technology can continuously project like a fascinating psychedelic vision. The digital realm can amaze us forever, but basically it goes no farther than the mental level from which it was created.

CHAPTER 14

UPGRADING TO HEAVEN

Through technological achievements we try to compensate for our inner deficiencies. Unconsciously we even attempt to emulate advanced psychological and spiritual levels of human development, levels which can't be reached by the conceptual mind. Technology is the contemporary method for the will to infinity. Quoting Alan Watts:

> The sense of isolation and loneliness of the ego is one of deep insecurity, manifesting itself in a hunger to possess the infinite... This will take the form of trying to make the finite infinite through technology, by abolishing the limitations of space, time and pain. In terms of philosophy it involves giving the human ego the value of God... By the exercise of his brilliant reason he will abolish the painful finitude of being an ego. He will forget his loneliness in crowded urban life, in an orgy of superfluous communication and social agitation (pp. 101–3).

And in the '50s the amount of superfluous communication was just beginning! We want to render the finite infinite because we believe we are separate from the infinite and from the divine. We've been told that human beings can't reach the divine, at least in their earthly lifetime. Technology, then, promises redemption from limitation, imperfection and the original sin, fixing what has gone "wrong."

Ken Wilber (1980) wrote:

> Every individual *correctly* intuits that he is of one nature with Atman, but he *distorts* that intuition by applying it to his separate self. He feels his separate self is immortal, all-embracing, central to

the cosmos, all-significant. That is, he *substitutes* his ego for Atman. Then, instead of finding actual and timeless wholeness, he merely substitutes the wish to live forever; instead of being one with the cosmos, he substitutes the desire to possess the cosmos; instead of being one with God, he tries himself to play God (p. 120).

And Aurobindo: "Every finite being strives to express an infinite which is perceived as being its real truth" (Satprem, 1974). Through technological advancement we try to grasp the infinite with the mind, then download the mind's contents to the Net. Technology simulates the drive toward the spiritual plane, stepping beyond identification with the body – but prematurely, and in a withdrawn, schizoid way. It achieves the opposite result, however, of inhibiting the soul's evolution. We cannot go beyond the body by bypassing full engagement with our body.

The body, being body-mind, holds our mental conditioning as much as the mind does. There is nothing like pure mind. Every belief, emotion, and conditioning is as much in the body as in the mind. Freedom from the identification with and limitations of body and mind begins with becoming aware of and inquiring into both.

Creating Consciousness

For millions of years, as long as the world has been in existence, consciousness has been engaged in the play of form, of becoming the "dance" of a phenomenal universe, "lila." And then consciousness becomes tired of the game [chuckle] (Tolle, 2000, p. 109).

The universal Consciousness plays by hiding itself in myriad individual consciousnesses which believe they are separate from Consciousness. When Consciousness becomes tired of the game, the individual consciousnesses rejoin Consciousness. IT in its turn simulates the universal Consciousness functioning on a mental level. IT developers have designed the Net to attract billions of individual minds to it. The Net then acts as Consciousness itself, directing the myriad of individual consciousnesses, in the developers' own game of *lila*. Then the individual minds join the Net consciousness to the loss of their individual ones.

What technology unconsciously wants to achieve is a simulation of the spiritual conditions of a global Consciousness, the one that *already* pervades the universe. The longing to rejoin global Consciousness is felt by every human being. But when we identify with our individual ego-mind, we cannot be embraced by a deeper awareness that can lead us there. Nonetheless, unconsciously we perceive a faint echo of the existence of a universal Consciousness, so we try to create a conscious universe through technology. Being a pale reflection on the technological level, this does not threaten individual egos, which are still not ready to join into the one Consciousness. Actually, the simulation by technology keeps the ego-mind stuck in an unending game and in repetitive patterns that preserve its need to be at the center of attention and in control.

Mystics say that thoughts are not produced by the mind/brain, that the organ in fact picks up what's already available in the global thought-sphere. Wi-Fi, the "Internet of things," and augmented reality projects are in this regard a simulation of a global, pervasive, non-localized consciousness: a tight net of data and objects communicating intelligently with each other. With our tools we can receive information produced by these intelligent entities, and feel connected to the global thought-sphere.

"Reality mining" is the term coined by MIT Media Lab that sums up the various objects that can be transformed into data spots through tiny radio-connected sensor chips. The lead article in the July/August 2007 issue of *Technology Review*, "Second Earth," defined data spots as "everything worth monitoring, including bridges, ventilation systems, light fixtures, mousetraps, shipping pallets, battlefield equipment, even the human body" (Roush, 2007).

The appeal of wireless networks is not just avoiding messy cables or the convenience of being able to connect to the Net anywhere. To our psyches they seem like conscious, almost alive presences spreading everywhere, a net of infinite eyes and a pervasive awareness in which everything is interconnected. While science considers the brain as the place where thoughts are formed and consciousness is created, mystics like Nisargadatta Maharaj, who have explored the ocean of consciousness first-hand, say, "You are so accustomed to think of yourselves as bodies having consciousness that you just cannot imagine consciousness as having bodies" (1982, p. 327).

Since consciousness is universal I am not surprised that the seat of human consciousness is elusive to neuroscientists who look for it in the brain. Cloud computing and the massive data centers storing all possible kinds of data – including our personal data and maybe soon our lifelogging records and physiological parameters – which are accessible from anywhere, are simulating Consciousness.

The Stoic philosophers considered the world to be permeated by *spermatikoi logoi*: seminal reasons, inseminating verbs. Various mystic philosophies consider universal concepts and the universal mind as ubiquitous entities. As mystics see concepts and the universal mind pervading existence, technology again is simulating this as millions of people gather on the Net, bouncing their thoughts and concepts all over the planet.

The competition for first place in search engines reflects the spiritual state of awareness of universal concepts and global consciousness – transposed to the level of ego. But instead of knowing ourself as part of it, on the ego level we want to drive traffic to our conceptual arenas and be able to manipulate the global mind through our digital domination of it.

In creating virtual worlds we simulate Universal Consciousness, which multiplies itself in infinite individual consciousnesses. Ramesh Balsekar (1989) expressed it as:

> The matter of thoughts arising, or the mind conceptualizing, has been one of considerable confusion and misunderstanding. If Consciousness has always been free and unfettered, why did consciousness identify itself with each individual body and thereby cause its own limitation as personal consciousness or mind, and thus unnecessarily cause all this trouble about bondage and liberation in the first place?! There are two ways of looking at the question, and both perspectives dissolve it, so that an answer becomes superfluous. *If* Consciousness is originally and always quite unfettered, totally free, why should it *not* limit itself and thereby engage itself in the *lila* that this life is? This deliberate act to restricting itself into an individual consciousness is part of its freedom! Also, it is only through this division into subject and object relationship that Consciousness can perceive and cognize the phenomenal universe that it has "created" within itself. One sentient being becomes the subject and perceives the other sentient beings as objects, and this is the "mechanism" for Consciousness to cognize the manifestation (p. 69).

We simulate Consciousness by creating "conscious" technological entities from scratch, through artificial intelligence or by transferring our already conscious mind onto the Net. In developing technology, we project our consciousness on the external in our desire to render every entity intelligent and conscious – because we are not seeing that the universe is intrinsically conscious and has no need of our help.

The universe as a pervasive conscious entity is a condition described by mystics of every tradition. This consciousness has been called cosmic consciousness, conscious universe, universal mind. Erwin Laszlo, in an interview with *What is Enlightenment?* magazine, talked about the conscious universe in these terms:

> To me it's very obvious that consciousness is not simply an epiphenomenon, not a byproduct of the brain; it's something that's pervading the whole universe... Consciousness is not simply produced

The Digitally Divided Self

by a complex set of neurons. It's there, in the whole body, and in all of existence (Pitney, 2010).

Since we don't see our individual consciousness as connected to the infinite consciousness that pervades everything – as part of the same ocean – we think we are limited in our knowing capacities, so we want to extend it through external tools. We are infinite, but we can't approach the infinite with the ego. Nonetheless, even ego feels a pull toward the infinite and wants to experience the infinite at its level.

Technology as an Ego Maintainer

Ordinary mind in itself can't reach states beyond the ego. Thoughts drag us in every direction, often in conflict with each other, stirring in emotions as well. We manage an unstable center of consciousness which we call "I" by erecting mental structures. When this center is absent, we label it a psychotic state – but it's just a matter of degree. Every ego is a mess, masking its fragility with beliefs, self-images, and other sorts of deception in order to feel there is some substance to it.

Witnessing our thoughts detaches the identification with them and gives a center to the fragility of the ego-mind – which is a first step toward a spiritual evolution that can even attain enlightenment. The irony is that both spiritual enlightenment and the psychotic condition share the absence of any center to coordinate the psyche, and if we are unable to create a holding structure, the outcome of the whirling changes of the mind is mental pathology.

Both psychopathology and enlightenment lack the sort of structure which is present on the ego level - as a deluded organization or, in more mature souls as a mature individuality based on essential qualities - which provides a center of gravity to our psyche. Our inner capacity to observe our thoughts and feelings is an evolutionary step beyond mechanically identifying with the objects of our experience. Meditation is the best way to develop the inner observer.

Witnessing our experience reinforces a higher point of observation, while being completely identified with an experience is a pathological condition. This witnessing is different from the spiritual state of being so totally into an experience that the experience, the awareness of it, and the experiencing subject are inseparable. When we are taken over by external inputs we can hardly be aware of the observer, and our awareness itself is lost.

Yet in advanced stages of meditation, even the observing center can eventually be lost, along with any sense of identity.

We need to differentiate the condition of the diffusion of the observer, as defined in meditational practices, from the absence or weakness of the observer in some forms of psychopathology. In this latter case, it is the lack or distorted development of one of the ego functions, that of being a somewhat detached center of observation. This is not a state of boundless awareness, but of being so involved and identified with the particulars of experience that one cannot merely observe them. So it is a condition of total identification that usually indicates a regressive state, while the diffusion of the observer in spiritual experience is a state of total disidentification with any content of experience (Almaas, 1996, p. 517).

To function in the world we *need* to crystallize a personality which acts as a center for our psyche. Then through a spiritual path we can progress by melting the ego in the fire of awareness, till we no longer need a center. We flow with existence without resistance, our action arising out of pure awareness.

When we are scattered over the Net running after any inducement it presents, tracking many things at once, we are simulating the open, receptive, free, centerless and universally connected condition which comes with ultimate understanding. By continuously morphing our identities online we can get a fake glimpse of the boundless freedom of "not being" – a condition that arises when we become free of inner images and identifications. In the advanced stages of spiritual growth, the ego's structures melt and aren't needed any more, but a personality is still needed to function in the world and to maintain an "I" that is not subject to inner fragmentation. The dispersive stimuli of technology make the structuring of a solid personality difficult. This is especially so in kids whose relationships are mostly driven by online media.

The fragmented psyche and the weakening of the self have difficulty recognizing their own condition, since the inner witness is also weak. With the ever-expanding influx of information, the technological extensions of our mind and the information stream become the anchors of the ego. These provide a sort of sense of direction, and stimulate unceasing mental and emotional activity, so the ego is being kept busy and alive. The flow of information glues our identities together in a very fragile way. We identify with information fed to us, so its cessation means the disappearance of our identity. We are literally outsourcing our "I" to technology where IT companies can play with our identities.

The mind understands and creates reality by filling the gaps in our fragmented perception, so that our experience is perceived as stable and constant. The mind does this mostly unconsciously through thoughts, emotions, and sensations. The mind has these intrinsic ways to sustain the illusion of a solid ego, so it has no need for a stream of external information. Yet information technology has expanded the external stream to unprecedented levels, producing food for incessant mental activity.

Identifying with individual thoughts carry us further away from a witnessing attitude, inducing a further cascade of thoughts. This faster and faster stream of information keeps us unaware of gaps in the mental activity, so we have no opportunity to question our choices or the reality of the ego itself. In order to break the spell and become aware of the mind's activity, some meditation techniques suggest finding the empty space between two thoughts.

IT Beyond Me: Unlinking Ourselves through Technology

Through technology we externalize parts of our mind to the Net. On an evolutionary plane of the psyche, externalizing parts of ourself through technology could appear similar to the process of disidentification that occurs on the path toward self-knowledge. The more we deepen our self-knowledge, then the more we can let go of identification with inner self-images, beliefs, preferences, aversions, images of our body, and personality that we have built defensively since early childhood.

Several spiritual paths emphasize that the body and the mind are impermanent entities, so identifying with them makes it impossible to reach ultimate awareness. Our body is liable to continuous change and decline. Similarly, the mind is subject to continuous transformation: how quickly we change opinions, thoughts, feelings, inner states! We even create and dissolve our subpersonalities. While flexibility of mind is indeed positive, like being free of rigid opinions, most of the time our shifting views are being driven by external happening with little influence of our own presence.

Buddha found that we don't exist as the individual body-mind entity, which is a construction without substance. Today, the very existence of an "I" is being challenged both by spirituality and science, and neuroscience is claiming that there is no center of consciousness to coordinate the different parts of our psyche.

If we are not our body-mind, then what we are? This question can only be answered through inquiring into our subjective experience. Though every spiritual teacher has described a state beyond the body-mind, the path still has to be trod individually. While scientific knowledge can be transferred from one person to another without the recipient repeating every stage, spiritual knowledge requires a personal and experiential engagement. While scientist can capitalize on the progress of science and develop it further, a spiritual path has to be traversed for each of us from the beginning, in order to progressively lighten our load of identifications.

The more we inquire into ourself, the more we realize that what we thought to exist was actually a mental construct. This process of disidentification, though liberating, is not easy to undertake. The loss of our identifications can bring stages of mourning and confusion, because our (fake) supports are disappearing. Therefore, it is a process which demands Compassion – which is the main support for staying with the experience of pain – along with Strength, Will, and Perseverance.

The process of disidentification from the mental, bodily, emotional, or relational self-images takes place when we become aware of those aspects and can observe them without further interference from our conditioned patterns. It is important to understand how we have positioned ourself in relation to our identifications, and to feel them, inquiry into them, and then let them go. We can release an identification only when we have understood it wholly.

In using technology there's a progressive withdrawal from direct connection with the body/mind – which looks more like schizoid withdrawal than a conscious disidentification from those parts of our personality which have been clearly observed. The movement of withdrawing from the resource of attention dis-integrates us, instead of making us free. For instance, by sitting for a long time, we lose touch with our legs – which is hardly going beyond our identification with that part of our body and becoming a flying angel. Rather it deprives us of the conscious experience of a part of ourself which could be useful for our soul's evolution, as our legs are connected to grounding, to not straying from our practice, and to our capacity for standing on our own – attributes which are basic to any spiritual path.

The process of spiritual evolution starts from wherever we are, and draws on every human quality at our disposal. We fuel awareness with the qualities of Clarity, Peace, Will, Joy, Compassion, and Strength. When we project and externalize our memory skills to the computer, or our need for connection with people to social networks, or our drive for understanding to Google, we deprive our soul of exercising those inner qualities needed for its maturation.

Extending our functions through technology has the effect of anesthetizing parts of us, while overshadowing the corresponding inner function of the body or psyche. If we substitute a car for our legs, we won't notice the weakness in our legs that sets in. If we substitute our need for human connection with Facebook, we numb our need for genuine contact. Fast answers from Google inhibit a deeper inner connection with the subject of our search. Technologies bypass our awareness. As our extensions, they suppress our recognition of the corresponding inner function.

Here and Now

Being "here and now" is a state of spiritual attainment. The sage has no past and no future. His actions aren't influenced by past conditioning or by future plans. They arise according to the reality of the moment. Living in the here-and-now and living without identifying with a personality are interconnected. When we are without such identification, our reactions to life are devoid of the weight of our conditioning and happen with immediacy – the here-and-now. Our personality is mainly a product of the past, of previous impressions and experiences which solidified into a structure that divides our spaciousness and obstructs the fluidity of our nature. In the absence of those constraints, life presents itself with immensity and spontaneity. Numerous spiritual teachers have described this state and the various paths to reach it.

Is technology speeding up the process and bringing us to a condition of inner freedom by keeping us in a continuously streaming updated "now"? The most popular websites give priority to the latest news, blog posts, and updates on the social media. The "now" condition, with its lack of a solid identity, which occurs under the pressure of the media, is a simulation on the personality level of the transcendent state –but it is a mere echo of that state. It seems free of past and future burdens, involved only with what is happening in the moment. But to transcend a personality, we *need* one. The real here-and-now transcendent state arises as an intimate association of the observer, the observed object, and awareness. They are one with reality, flowing with reality without thoughts interfering. In this synchronization with reality, the mind no longer filters what should be from what is.

With the dissolving of identifications, since there is nobody left to want to change anything, the alignment with reality is total. Such states are not exclusive to enlightened people: everyone can catch a glimpse of them, if only briefly. Plunging into full involvement with information shows the need, limited to the mind's plane, to participate seamlessly in the flux of existence. But with information we are not transcending ourself, we are *forgetting* ourself.

Devotionally Disappearing into Technology

Among spiritual traditions, one of the paths toward truth is the way of devotion, in which the disciple melts his ego in the flames of love, trust, and devotion to the spiritual guide, who is a mirror for the whole of existence.

The way of devotion is not fashionable in this culture obsessed by individualism. We want to determine our lives without being guided by anything or anyone. To clarify here: the principles of individual freedom and self-determination present in our society are important social and historical achievements. Being able to determine our life as an individual is an evolutionary step compared to the compliance once owed to feudal lords, priests, kings, dictators, and ideologies.

But even in achieving our individuality, there remains the spiritual need of our soul to transcend ego and honor something higher. If this need is not satisfied through the spiritual search, it will settle on a different evolutionary level – devotion as the fan of a band or a sports team, or fealty to political or religious fundamentalism, or seeking highs from art, lovemaking, raves. These are, ultimately, all acts of love – though distortions of that love can engender conflict and war. When we devote ourself to something bigger, we transcend our small, narcissistic ego which always wants to be the center of attention. Dedication annihilates a part of ourself and at the same time it lifts us up to a higher state. McLuhan (1964) said:

> By continuously embracing technologies, we relate ourselves to them as servomechanisms. That is why we must, to use them at all, serve these objects, these extensions of ourselves, as gods or minor religions. An Indian is the servo-mechanism of his canoe, as the cowboy of his horse or the executive of his clock. Physiologically, man in the normal use of technology (or his variously extended body) is perpetually modified by it and in turn finds ever new ways of modifying his technology. Man becomes, as it were, the sex organs of the machine world, as the bee of the plant world, enabling it to fecundate and to evolve ever new forms (p. 46).

We give ourself to IT, we trust machines, and we nullify ourself in technology. We are religiously devoted to the objects of technology, which absorb most of the time of an increasing number of people. We become the sexual organs of the machine by feeding it with the power of our brain.

As devotees we are nourished by our technological objects of devotion which direct our choices and fill our minds, while desiccating our interiority. The guidance of our actions does not derive from our inner lives, but from the flow of information. While spiritual teachers help us empty our mind from conditionings, filling us with love and awareness, IT fills our minds, eclipsing our awareness and inner guidance.

We expect direction and grace from technology, and count on it to solve our problems. In our relationship with technology, we let go of ourself, allowing it to guide us – never doubting the value of its expansion. We might get cross with the designers of bad technology, but we never question the need for the development itself. Kevin Kelly (2010) in *What Technology Wants* said that "we have a moral obligation to increase the best of technology."

Devotion to technology then becomes a substitute for devotion to something grander – and on a plane that is more reassuring for the ego. Interacting with technology, the mind is not transcended. It enters into a self-supporting loop where only those parts of it needed for interacting with the tool are used. Therefore the capacities that support observation and transcendence of the mind are weakened – among them deep reflection, inward silence, concentrated and sustained attention, and connection with the body.

The Immortal Mind
Technologies have been associated with immortality for a long time. The printing press was valued as a tool for leaving our thoughts for future generations, making our mind immortal – while the contemporary version is downloading our mind to the computer. As Maggie Jackson (2008) reported, Thomas Edison himself worked for years to build a machine that could pick up signals from the dead.

Kurzweil is right in saying that we human beings have the potential to expand our possibilities beyond mortal life, but he sees this happening by merging with technology and downloading our mind to the Net. One of the differences between humans and animals is the conscious and widespread use of tools. Since the beginning, human culture and the nervous system have been shaped by the use of tools, including the media. For humans it is just "natural" to go beyond our limited natures through external tools and technology.

Intelligence, knowledge and the mind are, doubtless, the most advanced aspects of the human experience shy of spiritual enlightenment. So the efforts made by people like Kurzweil to preserve and enhance them are understandable. However, as much as Kurzweil's project seems revolutionary – even outrageous – the expansion he offers is still limited in comparison to actual human potential.

We can expand knowledge and the mind's contents, we can even link our nervous system with chips or merge it with the Net, but mind and knowledge are not *awareness*. Awareness can use, cooperate, and be enhanced by knowledge and intelligence, but it belongs to another level. Awareness belongs with spiritual work and can be expanded by inner tools more than outer ones.

Spiritual work in a way is even more unnatural than what Kurzweil is forecasting. Natural psycho-spiritual development brings us to different stages of cognitive and psychological maturity. Those forces can create, in the best of cases, a healthy, creative and rounded ego, a valuable attainment, indeed. But its limit is not the end of the line. Human potential is much more than that, being nothing less than merging with the Divine, *becoming* Love and Universal Awareness.

Other than rare instances of the soul being taken directly to ultimate Realization – some traditions would explain it as karma from previous lives, others as God's grace – for the rest of us, evolving our souls and psyches requires conscious effort. This work is highly unnatural since we need to abandon our revered ego – which will resist our attempts by every possible means.

Kurzweil's vision is a reflection on the technological level of the spiritual quest to go beyond identification with the body-mind, which is indeed fragile and subject to decay, as he has observed. But the quest driven by technology keeps us on the same plane of the mind, however expanded and sophisticated it can become through external supports and enhancements.

For a culture which gives the mind the superior role, immortality means preserving its information. But the essential qualities of the soul which are specifically human require the wholeness of our being and cannot be transferred to the Net. Our soul is already immortal – in the realm of awareness, but not in the contents of the mechanical mind. Osho (1993) reminded us that awareness and meditation are the only treasures we can hold on to.

> Remember, only that which you can take with you when you leave the body is important. That means, except meditation, nothing is important. Except awareness, nothing is important, because only awareness cannot be taken away by death. Everything else will be snatched away, because everything else comes from without. Only awareness wells up within. That cannot be taken away. And the shadows of awareness – compassion, love – they cannot be taken away. They are intrinsic parts of awareness. You will be taking with you only whatsoever awareness you have attained. That is your only real wealth (discourse of March 3, 1979).

Immortality was pursued way before the advent of IT and biotechnologies. Taoism approached immortality through Outer and Inner Alchemy. Outer Alchemy encompasses mostly practices to keep the physical body in its form indefinitely, thus giving more time for the person to advance spiritually. The goal of Taoist Inner Alchemy, rather more than preserving the body, is to move our awareness from the physical toward the subtle planes, so our awareness can be present even after physical death. Inner Alchemy emphasizes ethics and integrity, qualities which are basic to the path. The subtle and immortal *chi* energy is connected to meditation and noble human qualities.

Spiritual Powers through Technology

Every technology promises to recapture our lost needs and qualities and to fill our need for expansion of our soul. Technology is not satisfied with simulating the recovery of our human qualities: it wants to bring humans to a superhuman condition that emulates what are called *siddhis* in the Hindu tradition. These spiritual powers come to advanced practitioners as side effects of their spiritual progress and include that *siddhi* which allows instant relocation flying (Google Earth and other simulators) and one which creates worlds (virtual worlds like Second Life) and has the ability to manipulate matter (nanotechnologies).

On genuine spiritual paths *siddhis* may be obstacles rather than aids, because their dazzle distracts from the goal. Expanding our powers through technology seems a religiously unquestionable assumption. Technology, in the Judeo-Christian tradition, assumed the role of savior of the human condition following the Fall, and it has been deputized to create a new paradise on Earth.

As the attachment to individual spiritual powers blocks further spiritual evolution, on a collective plane attachment to powers offered by technology likewise blocks the awareness of what we are collectively losing in human qualities. Lured by the magical gadget, we cannot distance ourself for it enough to question its broader effect.

Another spiritual power accesses the Akashic records, which can be understood as a universal database which stores any kind of information. Edgar Cayce asked us to

> imagine having a computer system that keeps track of every event, thought, image, or desire that had ever transpired in the earth. Imagine, as well, that rather than simply a compilation of written data and words, this system contains countless videotape films and pictures, providing the viewer with an eyewitness account of all that had ever happened within any historical time frame. Finally, imagine that this enormous database not only keeps track of the infor-

mation from an objective perspective but also maintains the perspectives and emotions of every individual involved. As incredible as it may sound, this description gives a fairly accurate representation of the Akashic Records (Todeschi, 1998, p. 1).

Some mystics say that this knowledge can be accessed through advanced states of consciousness. From biologist Rupert Sheldrake's (1988) perspective, "the organizing fields of animal and human behaviour, of social and cultural systems, and of mental activity can all be regarded as morphic fields which contain an inherent memory" (p. 112). Akashic records and morphic fields function as universal memory banks.

Through its huge archives that record everything that happens on the Net – every bit of information, knowledge, visited site, interaction and click, and perhaps in the future, every byte of lifelogging of thoughts and feelings, Google is now mimicking the role of the Akashic records.

Are we Machines?

The fundamental metaphorical message of the computer, in short, is that we are machines – thinking machines, to be sure, but machines nonetheless (Postman, 1993, p. 111).

That we act like machines is another observation shared by neuroscientists and spiritual teachers, though from very different viewpoints.

You will be peaceful when all your ideas about awareness are dropped and you begin to function like a computer. You must be a machine, function automatically in this world, never questioning your actions before, or after they occur. (U.G. Krishnamurti, 1988, p. 30)

This statement, which at first can sound like encouragement to become moronic, in fact hides another message. Spiritual awakening occurs when we abandon every idea, every point of view, every judgment and all conditioning – when our mind works in alignment with reality as it is in the moment, not as a reaction based on structures built in the past. When our mind works without impressions from the past, without judgments, with no likes and dislikes – like a computer, as U.G. said – it carries no further implications with it. It produces no more thoughts, leaving it void of additional weight and patterns.

Every spiritual master, including Gurdjieff, has said that a not-yet-awakened person lives mechanically. The mechanicaless of the unawakened person is a relentless and mostly unconscious interpretation of reality based on previous conditioning. In contrast, the mechanical action of the awakened one flows without resisting reality and with no burden from the past.

Cognitive science and neurophysiology both challenge the existence of an individual personality that directs our show. Experimenters have observed that the brain has automatic reactions with no aware intention behind them. Experiments by John-Dylan Haynes of the Bernstein Center for Computational Neuroscience, Berlin, showed that "patterns of brain activity can reveal which choice a person is going to make long before he or she is aware of it." The team

> scanned the brains of volunteers who held a button in each hand and were told to push one of the buttons whenever they wanted to. The scientists could tell from the scans which hand participants were going to use as early as 10 seconds before the volunteers were aware that they made up their mind (Branan, 2008).

Such experiments seem to challenge the very notion of free will, demonstrating that the source of our actions is unconscious brain activity preceding "our" choices. The mind needs to feel in control, in charge of our decisions, thus taking the credit for our actions. Science is saying that we are deluded in thinking that we have power over our actions, and in believing we have an "I" that determines them. But similar statements convey a very different meaning when spoken by spiritual teachers. Nisargadatta Maharaj (1982) described his enlightened state, in which body and mind are guided by existence itself, no longer from an illusory personality.

> I appear to hear and see and talk and act, but to me it just happens, as to you digestion or perspiration happens. The body-mind machine looks after it, but leaves me out of it. Just as you do not need to worry about growing hair, so I need not worry about words and actions. They just happen and leave me unconcerned, for in my world nothing ever goes wrong (p. 18).

But the perspective that our mind and our actions happen without our control and participation is terrifying for a culture which identifies the highest qualities of a human being with the mind and the actions it produces.

Our mind, the source (and object) of our pride, is at the same time a burden for the soul, even without psychopathologies. The mind judges us, limits us, activates repetitive behaviors and often plays dirty tricks on us. It seems that we cannot really control our mind, that it is a foreign entity, it is not "us." And there's truth in that. Science has shown us how human beings are fundamentally mechanical, annihilating our pride and ego which leaves us in despair because there's nothing else science can see after the ego is destroyed. Spiritual teachings, while taking away the ego, give back much more. It's a better deal to trade the ego for an expanded awareness, even though the ego would never sign such a deal.

While the approach of science can lead to a nihilistic perspective which degrades our life as it advances, spirituality elevates us to the position of *sat-chit-ananda* (truth-consciousness-bliss).

The Will to Create Mental Worlds

Beginning at the neurophysiological level, we create reality. The process of vision – as well as our nervous system as a whole – creates, filters, and interprets reality. Then our mind acts as a further barrier to reality, creating structures and concepts which we call "ideas," "opinions," "principles," "truth," "objectivity," "good," "evil," and so forth.

Finding shelter in a mental world made of images, fantasies, and projections represents an unavoidable defense mechanism which was set in place during the construction of our egos, as a protection against unpleasant sensations. We compensated by creating a fantasy world made of hopes. When this fantasy world develops excessively and takes up an autonomous life, we speak of psychosis. But since the created world we live in is a communal experience, psychosis is really a question of degree.

Rationality itself, even if it can support the search for truth, often is instead a trick of the mind that further deceives us by allowing us to think we are capable of objectively seeing things as they are. Thus rationality and rationalizations can easily serve as self-defense against truth, while on the technological level rationality is the ideal instrument for creating artificial worlds. Technology, as the apotheosis of the rational, becomes a defense mechanism at a collective level, creating sophisticated digital tools to channel communication that supports a schizoid withdrawal.

Spiritual realization brings us back to reality, free from interpretative constructions, piercing the system of filters that obscure our full perception of reality. Awareness of the illusory reality created by the mind is what is called "spiritual enlightenment." So Nisargadatta Maharaj could say, "I used to create a world and populate it – now I don't do it any more" (p. 392).

It is true on both the neurophysiological and spiritual levels that our ordinary perception is not of the real. In the Eastern traditions, the world is considered *maya*, an appearance or illusion. Since our experience is always mediated by our senses, as well as by our nervous system which interprets reality, we might conclude that there is no objective reality, perhaps no reality at all.

There is apparent agreement among neuroscientists, technical creators of virtual worlds, and spiritual teachers. They all see that the world in an illusion. Since the times of Buddha and Plato, there have been philosophical, metaphysical, and spiritual investigations into our representations of the world. Our ideas, wants, beliefs and interpretation of reality are mostly devoid of substance, when investigated in the light of self-awareness.

Nonetheless, our human position, however subjective and illusory, open by becoming aware of the world of matter and forms. And living with full awareness of our body-mind nature will take us beyond matter, form, body, and mind. The evolution of human beings cannot be driven exclusively by the mind – in a disembodied "I think, therefore I am" mode, where human and technology intermingle – but through the involvement of mind, body, feelings and awareness. Affirming that the world is unreal because neuroscience say so is not backup by experience nor does give any hope beyond the acknowledgement of the illusion. We will know whether or not the mind re-creates reality if we know the mind's mechanisms from the inside – not as an intellectual exercise, but by using that observing capacity which can see the mind as it is.

Witnessing the mind has a very different quality from being compulsively entangled in its contents. Whether the content comes from external media or from our own elaborations doesn't matter. Saying intellectually that the world is a representation makes us withdraw both from the world and from our inner experience. Affirming that "it's all in the mind" has to come from a level beyond the mind and its illusionist tricks. Otherwise we end up living solely in our mind, out of touch with reality, our body, or higher awareness.

The goal of meditation is to be in touch with reality. Most people who ignore spiritual pursuits believe that a spiritual path is something alien to reality, a world devoid of matter, passions, and everything worldly. After all, according to Christian beliefs, human beings were created on the last day of creation and are different from and superior to nature and to the world of matter. According to this, we are temporarily borrowed by the earth, but are intended to be returned to the heavenly realms in an afterlife where we will live on as disembodied souls. In this line of thought the body has no role in returning to the spiritual realms. In fact, it is considered a hindrance.

This misunderstanding holds that spiritual work is something detached from reality, or is perhaps a spaced-out state. The opposite is true. Meditation and the path toward the truth are journeys toward reality which bring us in touch with our feelings, passions, sensations, and with our real nature. We can't pass beyond the worldly level before mastering it through our awareness. We can't go beyond passions if we don't become aware of them in our sensate experience. We also can't go beyond the mind if we don't observe and master its mechanisms from the inside.

The spiritual path is, in a way, scientific and very tangible. Rational thinking rejects spiritual work as "unreal" and not objective. Yet rational thinking is not rejected by the spiritual attitude – it can even support spiritual inquiry. Paradoxically, when rational thinking is pushed to its extremes, it develops virtual worlds that are further from what is real and true, misplacing representation for reality. Through meditation we recognize that we construct reality, and that the mind leads us astray.

But it will be difficult to be aware of the unreality of the mind's beliefs from the intellectual level or by living in a virtual environment. Technology, rationality, the media and representation are very important milestones in the human path, but more often than not they become psychological defenses against reality and its unpredictability. Nor are they the end of human development.

CHAPTER 15

BITING THE SNAKE

I n ancient tantric traditions, some practitioners would test the strength of their awareness with intoxicants or the bite of a poisonous snake to see if they could sustain the totality of consciousness. In the '60s, Richard Alpert (Ram Dass) gave a huge dose of LSD to his Indian guru. What a lesson to him that it had no effect. This is one tale of that fabled era, and whether true or not does not change the fact that when we are master of our mind, nothing can affect or change the awareness that is beyond the mechanical mind.

But for those of us who are neither enlightened gurus nor advanced tantric practitioners, any intoxicant is going to change our perception of the world. We usually only consider substances like alcohol, heroin, cocaine, ecstasy and marijuana as altering our perceptions. Yet a tantric practice for our information society might be to sustain self-awareness while we're connected to the Internet, where we tend to forget ourself in the flow of information. This would serve as a great exercise for self-understanding.

In the Indian metaphysical tradition, we are composed of seven different bodies. Physical, emotional, and mental are the first three, and the awareness body is the fourth. In our time, we are fully into the mental body, which impacts our soul in ever more powerful ways. While the third body is shaped by thoughts, the fourth is reinforced by consciousness, by awareness which can watch thoughts. The awareness body is developed through self-reflection – not in a "thought-crunching" way but by mindfully observing ourself in the wholeness of body, mind and feelings without trying to change anything. The fourth body is strengthened by an observing meditative attitude.

The awareness body is said to be harmed by intoxicants – to which I would add the information overload that makes it difficult to become still enough to observe thoughts, rather than be caught by – and identified with – them. By calling on our Will we can always stop and meditate – but even to activate such Will, we need a certain detachment from our thoughts. The Internet challenges our capacity to be with our full presence and not seduced by messages that want to stake their claim to a territory of our mind.

With part of our mental activity "outsourced" to technology, and our attention locked away, a specific meditation technique for the Net is needed. We can begin by observing the incoming mental stimuli. Then naming them for what they are and noticing how they provoke reactions. Feel the compulsion to click. Breathe, and... let them go. Then another stimulus... and let it go – like inhaling, exhaling.

The Internet is an accelerated journey toward the mind where the multiplying of mental stimulation will reach its limits – until we are dropped into an observing attitude that feels like the still eye of the hurricane. Technology could then even help us become more aware of our mechanical mind – but that's a double-edged sword. The more we feed the mind, the fewer inner resources are available to detach from its compulsive activity. So we need to willingly stop our mental racing and collect the needed inner resources to bring ourself back to our inner presence. Again and again and again.

Writing – especially not limited to 140 character tweets – enhances the connection with our presence. To write, we need to form an image of our narrative and link it to the intention behind our communication. In this way, blogging can be a tool for inquiry, as diaries have always been. Unfortunately, most of us usually write online, so the quiet space where insights arise is mostly gone.

Out of the Loop

Every activity on the Net could become an opportunity for self-remembering. When we are searching the Net, we can sense an energy – the excitement of discovery like a flame burning within us. When our search does not yield what we hoped, the feeling shifts to frustration because the ego wants results – and wants them fast. Remaining with the quest – instead of acting out the demand – could bring unexpected results both for our inner process and about the object of our search.

A couple of years ago there was an odd problem with my Internet provider, lasting more than a week. Maybe they were having trouble with their DNS servers, but the result was that about 20 percent of websites could not be accessed, apparently at random. I never knew whether a site would be reachable. Irritating – but also a great chance to let go. Is it *that* important? Do I really need that information? Right now? How attached am I to that content? What kind of anxiety is driving the need for that information? As a self-remembering exercise, Gurdjieff would unexpectedly shout "Stop!" to remind his students to be aware of themselves and drop their mechanical functioning. Not being able to reach a site could be used as a Gurdjieffian "Stop!"

Another good exercise for becoming aware of our information cravings is to stay in front of a screen – ready for action, but without clicking on anything. What's the feeling of being stuck in the sea of information with neither wind nor engine to move our boat? What do we experience when our mind is not fed with novelties?

We can consciously undertake exercises to provide a little space between information input and our involvement with it. When a new SMS or email arrives, what about first taking a few deep breaths instead of rushing to read it? We run after our messages as if they are likely to be urgent, or as if it they would evaporate or expire if we didn't grab them. Our information society creates peculiar beliefs which, with the light of inquiry, are revealed to be false – like most beliefs. Yet giving up the "new, more and fast" attitude is not easy.

The technique of inquiry can bring more clarity to any issue in our life. It can take the form of an inner monologue, or it can answer certain specific questions. We can explore the benefit we get from our continuous involvement with information: What kind of feelings do I get from it? Am I soothed? Excited? What do I get from staying in the information loop? Are there other ways for me to arrive at the same feelings? What am I *really* looking for? Such inquiries can be done as a repeated question – better with a partner who asks it over and over for a pre-determined period of time, perhaps fifteen minutes.

This inquiry method, used in Almaas' Diamond Heart school, can reach successively deeper layers. Approaching the buried motivations of our habits can reveal that they substitute for other kinds of needs. Or they may be seen as psychological defenses that hide other kinds of feelings. If we approach self-inquiry in an open and non-judgmental way, the journey they take us on can be unpredictable and rich in insights. Inquiry can accomplish miracles.

Screen Media vs. Meditation

Scientists who study brain-wave activity found that the longer one watches television, the more likely the brain will slip into "alpha" level: a slow, steady brain-wave pattern in which the mind is in its most receptive mode. It is a non-cognitive mode: i.e., information can be placed into the mind directly, without viewer participation. When watching television, people are receiving images into their brains without thinking about them (Mander, 1991, p.82).

Alpha brain waves are present regardless of the content we are watching, for the medium itself causes changes in brain activity. Alpha waves are electromagnetic frequencies of about 10 Hz produced by the electrical activity of the brain. Alpha frequencies are associated with meditation and clear, relaxed states. Most experienced meditators can go to delta, with frequencies around 2 Hz, in which the flow of thoughts is much reduced.

The presence of delta waves is normally associated with deep, dreamless sleep, but delta waves during meditation are not an unconscious state like sleep. There they accompany clear awareness of our inner state. Though meditation and staring at a screen both induce alpha waves, they are actually different states by virtue of what is being observed – internal vs. external – and whether there is a identification. A similarity that meditation and screen viewing share is the receptivity of the mind, along with keen observation. In front of a screen we observe words, pictures and videos – at least that is how we experience the flow of pixels. In meditation we observe whatever emerges in our thoughts and sensations, without judgment, without identification, without being carried away.

The alpha brain frequency from looking at a screen seduces us with a feeling of relaxation. But without that being integrated with attentive and aware observation, it changes into restlessness and stress – often unrecognized until it becomes full-blown. Jerry Mander again:

> So television viewing, if it can be compared to a drug experience, seems to have many of the characteristics of Valium and other tranquilizers. But that is only half of the story. Actually, if television is a drug, it is not really Valium; it is *speed* (p. 66).

And the remote control becomes our action tool in searching for something "better." I surmise that stress accrues from following only external events without presence, conscious attention, and awareness.

Meditation, without judgment of the content that comes into awareness, requires an openness that has no goals. Computer use involves even more goal-orientation than does watching TV, since we actively direct the action through the mouse, touch screen, or keyboard. The interactive nature of the Internet most probably activates also higher brain frequencies that are associated with alertness, action, and anxiety. Being more passive, TV engenders a more relaxed state. Yet, with faster bandwidth, videos are more common on the internet, which turns our mouse or touch-screen into a hyper remote control.

The Digitally Divided Self

Before meditation/screen viewing. There is usually some resistance to begin meditating, so sitting down to it requires an act of will. Our mind is creative in finding innumerable excuses that are germane to our life in order to avoid or postpone meditation. That's understandable, since the mind must give up center stage. Instead, in meditation it will be witnessed, its cascading thoughts ignored rather than attended to. Conversely, starting to watch a screen is very easy. We know that anything that moves in front of our eyes triggers instinctual reflexes which are hard to resist. Any TV set which is on, any smartphone or computer screen is enticing. Our act of Will is to resist being pulled away from our intention.

At the beginning of meditation/screen viewing. At the beginning of a meditation session there is still resistance and, more often than not, there are frustrating moments when we experience difficulties in simply staying with What Is and observing it. We are allured by various streams of thought – among them, one I think every meditator has had: "I want to stop meditating right now."

In contrast, as we begin viewing a TV screen, we usually relax instantly and are gratified. Thoughts slow down. We seem to feel at peace, though in starting up the Internet there is a little restlessness at the beginning as we open sites and applications to claim our stake in virtual territory. Then we feel at home and in control of our environment, soothed in a merging state which can easily slip into a negatively merged state if we are frustrated by loss of data, delays, unanswered messages, or – heaven forfend – a virus.

During meditation/screen viewing. During meditation, after a while things usually get better. The improved state arises after anywhere from a few minutes to more than an hour of sitting. After the initial difficulties, the stream of thoughts is less perturbed. We can concentrate better on the simple observation of thoughts and sensations, while feeling present, relaxed, and brightly aware. We are capable of subtle discrimination among various inner states.

Thoughts, emotions and sensations become clearer as we don't identify with them, letting them simply arise and pass away. Inner knots and issues can melt in the fire of the observing awareness, releasing worry and anxiety. Sometimes we can find a solution to some problem, or realize that the problem wasn't actually there – that we had created it ourself. The muscles around the eyes relax and there's a sense of space and alertness.

By contrast, after a while in front of a TV, both dullness and an undischarged frustration start to emerge. Then we push the remote control buttons compulsively – even in our lethargy – and are dissatisfied with whatever we find. When we have been on the computer for a long time, the muscles around our eyes contract. Our mind often enters an information bulimia that is stressful, as we chase more information and stimulation for the mind. "Enough" never arrives. New information gives birth to yet more information.

Information reaches puberty immediately, multiplying itself in early pregnancies that lack the maturity to attend to its offspring, abandoning them to chase after more information. At this stage, faster brain frequencies are likely to take over, bringing restlessness and difficulty slowing down and concentrating. We swallow anything set in front of us without chewing – like information-hungry beasts.

With protracted TV viewing, the mental state is more a hypoactivity that hinders our ability to analyze, process, and act on mental inputs. Hyper- and hypoactivity both hinder clarity. Without introspection and aware attention, our mind can easily slip either into frenzy or passivity. Mental agitation and dullness also arise at times in meditation practice – as obstacles to our progress in developing awareness.

After meditation/screen viewing. After meditation our mind feels fresh and light. The sense of presence is amplified, as well as attention and our ability to understand reality, without the heavy baggage of conditioning. We address practical activities without a compulsive quality. Impulses in our mind are more synchronized with our actions.

Conversely, the pace of a running mind is much faster than the biological or practical capacity to attend to every thought consciously. Before we have given space to a thought or impulse, another is crowding it out. Like a car sliding in mud or ice, the more we floor the accelerator, the more the sliding and frustration. Our mind feels engorged, while in our depth we feel empty.

Meditation

For thousands of years meditation has been benefiting people – in daily life and in spiritual advancement. In the last few decades, science has corroborated the value of meditation with hundreds of scientific studies, supported by the Dalai Lama's passion for scientific understanding of meditative states.

The April 2010 issue of *Consciousness and Cognition* presented the results of a study about meditation and cognition. It had always been assumed that extensive training was essential, yet an experiment showed that even short exercises in meditation improved cognition. Though this is desired by many people, the perception that rigid discipline is required deters them. Not so, it turns out. Only four days of training for just twenty minutes led to significantly higher performance in cognitive tests. "It goes to show that the mind is, in fact, easily changeable and highly influenced, especially by meditation" (Zeidan, 2010).

A study published in *Psychological Science* found that meditation increased attention span and discriminating awareness, and that the benefit persisted for months after training, especially for those who continued their practice (MacLean, 2010).

The anterior cingulate cortex is the part of the brain involved in rational cognitive and emotional functions, like reward anticipation, decision-making, emotional awareness and empathy. A recent study found that just a few hours of meditation based on traditional Chinese medicine increased activity of the anterior cingulate cortex, improved self-regulation and fractional anisotropy, an index indicating the integrity and efficiency of white matter, which is important in self-regulation and overall mental balance (Tang, 2010).

Several other studies on meditation associated it with increased cortical thickness and growth of the areas dedicated to attention, even reversing neuronal processes related to aging.

The tools of technology are more "natural" for our minds than meditation. Technology amplifies the natural tendency of the mind to be center stage and continuously stimulated. Introspection, meditation, and the emptiness of the mind are the most unnatural experiences for the ego. The ordinary evolution of the soul creates at best a healthy ego. To go beyond this stage requires a lot of "unnatural" work. What is more unnatural than to disidentify from the personality's chatter in our mind?

Internet technology has a distinctive way of feeding our attachment to mental material. Its structure of links is a metaphor for the functioning of the mind, which jumps from one branch to another – something we soon observe in meditation. But when we are following links on the Net, we are not practicing meditation, so we have more difficulty focusing internally and letting go of the mind's directives.

Our spiritual journey carries us toward reality, not toward illusory projections. Meditation means being in touch with the reality beyond symbolic representations. Meditation practices point us toward awareness of the mind's addiction to thoughts. Over and over, we come back to concentrating on something neutral, like the breath. During meditation, we can be carried off by any sort of thought, and it can take some time before we are aware of having been hijacked away from the object of concentration. Becoming aware of being sidetracked is somehow the essence of meditation, so labeling the habits of mind as we notice them arising (Planning,

Longing, Anger, Planning, Spaciness, Longing) supports our concentration.

Through meditation we can even replace the longing for the latest event happening on the screen with the wondrous variety of inner events and insights.

IT is basically Counter-Meditative

We can succeed in gaining control over automatic reflexes by using meditation to take our awareness beyond the mechanical cravings of the mind. That there is something "beyond the mind" puzzles most people, since our culture considers the mind the peak of evolution. Not so for mystics. The mind and its contents are not the ultimate playground of awareness, for awareness can observe our mind's contents.

For those of us who are not experienced meditators, how can we avoid being caught in automatic mechanisms – like the orienting response which points us in every direction? There are two ways to cope with the impact of the orienting response. We can go *beyond* the mechanical mind and thoughts through meditation, or we slip *under* the mind, reacting in predictable ways. In the former, we observe the mind and its reactions. In the latter, we are removed from inner observation – along with depth, critical analysis, and interpretation. In other words, we make ourself dumber, giving bits of fragmented attention to endless external stimuli which keep the mind, and the ego, occupied.

The fight-or-flight and the orienting responses, as well as other instinctual mechanisms, are believed by scientists to be unavoidable – wired into our nervous system's sensitivity to external stimuli. In *Destructive Emotions: A Scientific Dialogue with the Dalai Lama* (2004), a book about meditation and neuroscience, Daniel Goleman describes the startle reflex, one of the most primitive responses in the human repertoire, that involves a cascade of very quick muscle spasms in reaction to loud, surprising sounds and sudden, jarring images.

Five facial muscles suddenly contract, especially around the eyes. Nobody is expected to bypass this reaction which, like all reflexes, occurs in the brain stem – the most primitive, reptilian part of the brain. As far as brain science has determined, even for police marksmen who are used to firing guns, the mechanism cannot be modified by intention, since it lies beyond the range of voluntary regulation.

Paul Ekman, head of the Human Interaction Laboratory at the University of California at San Francisco, tested the startle reflex on Lama Oser, a European Buddhist who has practiced in long, intensive, solitary meditation retreats. While he engaged in various meditation practices, his startle reaction almost disappeared. Moreover, the "one-pointedness" meditation produced even a decrease in his heart rate and blood pressure, instead of the usual rise (Goleman, 2004).

If meditation works on a hard-wired reflex, we can work at not activating the instinctual orienting response to movements on a screen, thus freeing ourself from the mechanical reactions triggered by screen media. Since the efficacy of meditation in becoming aware of and overcoming our mental conditioning has been tried by millions of people around the world over the ages, it's a technology that has definitely passed beyond beta testing. Meditation then can support us in deciding when and how to direct our attention. We can become masters of our attention again. (My apologies to advertisers and the thousands of sites competing for our attention.)

Another Maya Layer through Technology

Maya, the illusory world created by the mind, is divine play called *lila*. But the world of maya does not need to be rejected. We can, instead, enter the illusion with awareness. Being aware of what is true allows us to return to the illusory world, which can then be seen as one of the many manifestations of reality. Ramakrishna (1963) pointed out the two views of maya: "It is through *lila* that you should open your path up to *nitya* [the eternal; the true]. And so it is from *nitya* that you must come back to *lila*, who is then no more unreal, but an expression of *nitya* for your senses." And Nisargadatta instructs: "Let the dream unroll itself to its very end. You cannot help it. But you can look at the dream as a dream, refuse it the stamp of reality" (Maharaj, 1982, p. 258).

With virtual worlds, such as Second Life, a further maya layer has developed, which overlays the illusory view of reality held by the ordinary mind. With virtual worlds the artifice and the unreality of such environments becomes evident, but at the same time, it makes evident that our reactions and emotions are basically the same both in ordinary life and in online worlds – which perhaps should be called Maya 2.0.

When online we use some parts of our psyche more than others – particularly the rational-technical, information-hungry, attention-limited, detached-from-the-body cognitive parts. Nevertheless, our interactions still reflect our mental structures and the shape of our ego personality. The basic core of the conditioning which creates our sense of identity is not freed by digital interaction, even though we may be less inhibited by virtue of anonymity and the feeling that we can redefine ourself according to the situation. Our automatic reactions are not transformed by online interaction.

Our online experience, however, offers us the opportunity to question the reality of our mind as part of the dream. This is not a nihilistic view – as in "all is unreal, my mind included" – but in a more constructive "the mind is no more real than the products it builds through technology, but I can contact a dimension more anchored in reality and truth." Swami Nityananda said, "To consider Maya, a deeper Maya is needed" (1962). A deeper illusion might then open the way for reality.

If we turn our attention 180 degrees from the screen to our own inner life, we have the opportunity to not forget ourself in the medium – so we would be in a position to question the reality of both maya layers. In Eastern traditions there are tales describing incidents which caused immediate awareness of the real. The nun Chiyono studied long, but unsuccessfully, in search of enlightenment. As she walked along, she admired the reflection of the full moon in the pail of water she was carrying. Suddenly the bamboo straps broke and the pail fell apart. The moon's reflection disappeared as the water gushed out.

Osho commented:

> Suddenly, the water rushed out and there was no moon. So she must have looked up – and the real moon was there. Suddenly she became awakened to this fact, that everything was a reflection, an illusion, because it was seen through the mind. As the pail broke, the mind inside also broke (1999, Card 05: Ultimate Accident).

Today many new technologies present us with incidents that reveal the illusion of the reflected moon – things like our hard drive crashing with no backup, or the unavailability of an Internet connection in our time of need.

The Net has its own tendency toward the truth. We are likely, in a couple of decades, to be able to share thoughts electronically. Imagine advanced neurotechnological tools, like fMRI machines that are integrated into our gadgets, which broadcast our inner states. It might start discreetly as a way to interact with the Net with no pointing device or touch screen. (As I write in 2011, such projects are in development.) This could expand to reading our thoughts. Certainly it could be fun reading the thoughts of the person next to us or of a politician. But after a while this will become as boring as the continuous flow of messages through social networks. We will then see thoughts for what they are – bubbles arising in Consciousness, forms of *lila* dancing through time.

APPENDIX

THE PEOPLE OF CONTEMPORARY IT
AND WHAT DRIVES THEM

M any people have contributed to the development of contemporary IT: mathematicians, philosophers, entrepreneurs, politicians, programmers. Since it's impossible to list all who have planted the theoretical seeds and developed practical solutions, I'll mention some who in my opinion are representative. Far from being accurate biographies, I have chosen to explore a bit of their personal stories in relation to their intellectual accomplishments.

Charles Babbage

Charles Babbage (1791–1871) was a mathematician, philosopher and mechanical engineer credited with having theorized the programmable computer. His "difference engine" and "analytical engine" already employed the basic concepts of computers. His more advanced projects could not be completed during his life, but the London Science Museum has since built them to acknowledge this father of IT.

Babbage also developed theories for the rational organization of labor and the division of work that set the stage for modern specialization – and, as well, for the transformation of humans into servomechanisms of technology.

In his *Ninth Bridgewater Treatise*, "On the Power, Wisdom and Goodness of God, as Manifested in the Creation" (Babbage, 1837), he compared God to a divine legislator with the power of creating species at the right times. In his vision, God looked like the master programmer of Creation – whom Babbage tried to follow through understanding the mechanical procedures of life. According to Babbage we could even expand God's plans.

> The advancement of man in the knowledge of the structure of the
> works of the Creator, might furnish continually increasing proofs of its

authenticity; and that thus by the due employment of our faculties, we might not merely redeem revelation from the ravages of time, but give to it a degree of force strengthening with every accession to our knowledge (Babbage, 1837, quoted in Noble, 1997, p. 72).

Babbage is reported as having "a dislike of untidiness," which seems a characteristic among people of Apollonian nature who prize rationality. In keeping with this, Babbage campaigned against street music and boys playing on the streets, perhaps because they didn't fit into his orderly world.

Eliminating "noise" from signals is one of the main engineering and cybernetic goals – which is an interesting parallel. The attitude of the digital mind brings forth an over-discrimination that is always splitting – good from bad, signal from noise, if-then-else.

Ada Lovelace

Ada King, countess of Lovelace (1815–52), was a brilliant English mathematician. She is often referred to as the first programmer in history. She wrote programs for Babbage's analytical engine, and foresaw the scope of algorithms to process data beyond numerical calculations, which no one had yet conceived. The programming language *Ada* was named in her honor.

Ada Lovelace was the daughter of the romantic poet Lord Byron. He and his social entourage were disappointed with his child's gender, and he soon separated from both her mother and England. Byron died when Ada was 9. Her mother arranged the girl's life so as to avoid contact with either her father or his attitude toward life. She considered Lord Byron insane and, worrying that her daughter might share it, educated Ada in mathematics from a very early age, even through prolonged health problems constrained the girl to bed rest. Ada Lovelace died at 36 from uterine cancer and requested to be buried next to Lord Byron. She finally joined the father she never really knew.

John von Neumann

John von Neumann (1903–57) was a European-born American mathematician who developed the theoretical bases of many of the contemporary models of computer science, quantum mechanics, game theory and artificial life. The von Neumann architecture describes the structure of nearly every computer.

John von Neumann became one of the most important figures of the Manhattan Project that developed the atomic bombs dropped on Hiroshima and Nagasaki. He also collaborated in the development of the hydrogen bomb. He was strongly militaristic and fascinated by the power of atomic technology. He advocated for the use of nuclear weapons in a pre-emptive attack on the former Soviet Union. He proposed some of the first geoengineering projects. One was to raise global temperatures by spreading colorant on polar ice, so that the world would have produced larger harvests. He also suggested detonating nuclear weapons in the Atlantic to "improve" the African climate.

A man whose vision was on the scale of Armageddon could not miss reflecting on what life is. He found points of contact between life and machines, worked on cellular automata as self-reproducing mechanisms, and became the father of A-Life or Artificial-Life.

After planning to annihilate the whole world with an apocalyptic nuclear war, John von Neumann seemed equipped to act like God in recreating life and the material world through A-Life and geoengineering projects.

Norbert Wiener

American mathematician Norbert Wiener (1894–1964) was deeply affected by the Nazi persecution of Jews. During World War II he analyzed data about enemy aircraft (position, speed, and so on) to develop anti-aircraft artillery. Through the analysis of the feedbacks between enemy aircraft and the anti-aircraft artillery, he expanded communication theory.

His concept of information feedback loops is fundamental to cybernetics. Harkin (2009) called Wiener's ideas the glue which holds together Cyburbia – our life on the Net. "Wiener began to see feedback loops everywhere... Wiener drew the conclusion that messages between humans, animals and machines were now of the same fundamental nature" (pp. 23, 26). Event-driven programming languages used for most Internet programming look like they are built on Wiener's ideas.

The analysis, control and feedback of messages was important to survival during wartime, when silence of the feedback system meant big trouble. We today have inherited an approach which was created for military purposes. Now we behave as if we are suffering from post-traumatic stress disorder – compulsively caught up in the loop, anxiously looking for updates on news, email, Twitter or Facebook pages.

After the war Wiener became concerned about the ethical implications of science. Having seen his work used for military purposes, he became pessimistic about the use of science and refused to work on nuclear weapons projects, unlike von Neumann. He wrote about the developments of automation and computers which could turn people into slaves of machines, trapped in their mechanical operations.

Wiener explored the similarities between human and mechanical communication. What he did not see was that even though the mind can act in a mechanical way, we are not just the mind. One of the reasons why humans want to be part of a mechanical loop is the feeling of liberation that comes with outsourcing our mind to something which takes away the burden of having a mind. After all, the mind is as much a burden as a joy. And there might be in our soul the hint of a state where the mind is no longer the master. "Cloud computing," through which software, our data and online lives are being stored on giant computer processing services, goes in the direction of outsourcing the mind to something "bigger", mistaking the cloud of IT companies for heavenly clouds.

Alan Turing

Alan Turing (1912–54), English mathematician and cryptoanalyst, had enormous influence on computer science. During the Second World War his cryptoanalysis was fundamental in breaking the German ciphers, contributing to the defeat of Nazism. His Turing machine incorporated important advances in the formalization of algorithms and computability. He conceived the Turing Test which defined a "thinking machine" as one that fooled a person into believing he was having a conversation through a keyboard with a human being in a remote location.

In his era, homosexuality in England was subject to criminal prosecution. In 1952, after admitting to having sex with a young man, Turing was given the choice between incarceration or a treatment with female hormones ("to reduce the libido"). How absurd that after helping save his country from Nazism, it treated him as a criminal. In 1954, Turing died of poisoning. In 2009, British Prime Minister Gordon Brown apologized on behalf of the British government for the way he was treated.

Jaron Lanier, in "One Half a Manifesto," commented on the tragic death of Turing in these terms:

> Turing died in an apparent suicide brought on by his having developed breasts as a result of enduring a hormonal regimen intended to reverse his homosexuality. It was during this tragic final period of his life that he argued passionately for machine sentience, and I have wondered whether he was engaging in a highly original new form of psychological escape and denial; running away from sexuality and mortality by becoming a computer.

I think the denial is deeper than the sexuality issue: it has to do with the denial of anything but the "pure" Cartesian mind – including the body and its sensuousness. With two pillars of contemporary IT, Ada Lovelace and Alan Turing, we see how a denial of sexual identity, the sensuous, and the non-rational world shaped their lives. Lovelace's gender was rejected by her father, while her mother pushed her toward a purely rational life. The law repressed Alan Turing's homosexuality, as he likely did himself.

The mind is regarded as the most important human feature, and the identification with it is so deep that we want to reproduce it in machines, becoming creators in our turn. The Turing Test allows us to ascertain the "intelligence" of a machine.

Joseph Weizenbaum in 1964 created Eliza, an interactive program that simulated a Rogerian psychotherapist. Weizenbaum himself was surprised and concerned to see that users were taking Eliza's words seriously. While the mind can be simulated by software, a successful Turing Test tells us tells us nothing about what's going on *inside*. However, it does underscore how much the mind can be fooled, and how we can actually behave mechanistically.

Al Gore

Al Gore, born in 1948, served as vice president of the United States during the Clinton presidency. A politician of rare farsightedness, his commitment to telecommunications dates back to the 1970s. His father, a senator as well, had promoted the American highway system, and the son became one of the greatest promoters of the information superhighway, later known as the Internet.

As a senator, Al Gore promoted the High Performance Computing and Communication Act of 1991, known as "The Gore Bill." This helped create the National Information Infrastructure (NII) which, together with software developments he supported funding for, like the first Web browser Mosaic, expanded the Internet from the use of academics to what it is today.

Al Gore saw how the previous development of highways triggered economic growth and the development of real estate. He regarded the Internet as a way of making information accessible to everybody, reducing the gap in education and health, thereby enhancing democracy and participation.

Gore regarded the influence of TV as the factor which emptied public debate, creating an "Assault on Reason" (as he titled one of his books). He recognized that the power of TV images overwhelms reason with fear. The Internet, with easy access for everyone to participate in dialogue, is in his view a way of reversing TV's threat to democracy.

He started Current TV, the Internet channel aimed at quality video content. While it is a great endeavor, in my opinion it has missed seeing the medium as the message. On the Internet, the passive mode of video combines with the infinite distractions on the Net.

Steward Brand

Prior to hippies arriving on the scene, computers and the Internet were developed by Apollonian attitudes of order, rationality, tidiness and control. Mathematicians and engineers laid the theoretical bricks of IT and the early Internet was developed by the military. At a certain point, however, the IT world saw players like Steward Brand, Kevin Kelly, Jaron Lanier, Howard Rheingold, and Steve Jobs come on the stage from a different background. The 1960s culture – chaotic, psychedelic, environment-friendly, anti-authoritarian, and communal – had breached the IT world.

Steward Brand, born in 1938, remains an icon of the Californian hippie culture. He was involved in many creative projects – the Merry Pranksters, experiments with LSD, and seminal magazines like the *Whole Earth Catalog*. Brand also created The Well ("Whole Earth 'Lectronic Link"), one of the first online communities and a forum for intelligent discussions.

Brand applied the counterculture attitude – regaining power for the individual and small communities, which had been propagated through his *Whole Earth Catalog's* tools – for communal living and for the empowerment of The Little Guy. In the *Whole Earth Catalog*, tools were reviewed by people and information shared among readers in a sort of offline forum. Rural communities became "virtual communities," as Howard Rheingold, deep observer of the social aspects of the Net, titled his book about the emerging phenomenon, and the original anti-technological and anti-corporate attitude of some hippies transformed into Internet start-ups and Nasdaq IPOs.

The idea was that technology, given back to individuals, could change the world for the better. After all, electric guitars, the earlier solar panels, the manufacture of LSD and many tools for communal living caused an explosion of creativity and self-sufficiency. Hippies abandoned living in rural communities for less physically-taxing virtual communities, stopped tripping on LSD and started to get high on fractal animations, video games, software programming and virtual reality environments.

Above all, they believed that the exchange of information through electronic messages between members of virtual communities would change and expand the consciousness of people, and greatly empower them socially and politically.

In those years of massive spread of the Internet, there were numerous references to the Jesuit mystic and scientist Teilhard de Chardin who foresaw an "Omega Point" as the final outcome of evolution of both matter and spirit. The Omega Point would be arrived at by the development of the noösphere, the place which emerges out of the interaction of human minds. McLuhan himself had strong Christian beliefs and was influenced by the ideas of Teilhard. He talked about the computer and the "electric world" in Pentecostal terms, with technology bypassing languages to allow the creation of a cosmic consciousness.

Kevin Kelly

Kevin Kelly, born in 1952, has popularized technological culture since the 1970s through the *Whole Earth Catalog* and its successor the *Whole Earth Review*, then as the executive editor of *Wired* magazine, the voice of the digital culture. With Stewart Brand, he started The Well.

Kelly is the author of books on technology. *Out of Control: The New Biology of Machines, Social Systems, and the Economic World* (1994) is probably the best-known. One of the major themes of the book is that biology and technology will merge, evolving by themselves according to principles he defined as "The Nine Laws of God." A devout Christian, at 27 he had a mystical experience in Jerusalem after sleeping on the spot where Jesus was supposed to have been crucified. He lived the next six months as if they were the last ones of his life. It seems he has the same strong faith in God that he has in the evolution of technology.

Renewing Babbage's vision of God as the divine programmer, "Kelly claimed to have discovered that 'the universe is a computer,' and that the idea of computer networks would soon help to explain life, the universe and everything" (Harkin, 2009, p. 84).

Kelly has strongly advocated technology as a way of expanding human freedom, choices and our free will (again, a basic theme of Christianity). In "Expansion of Free Will," he wrote: "Technology wants choices. The internet, to a greater degree than any technology before it, offers choices and options... The technium continues to expand free will as it unrolls into the future. What technology wants is more freedom, expanded free will" (Kelly, June 2009).

According to Kelly our human potential can be developed through the expansion of technological options – to which I agree, if we mean that technology can (partly) support the *expression* of our talents. The unleashing of our full potential comes from being in touch with our inner qualities – without which technology is not of much help.

238   *The Digitally Divided Self*

Bill Gates

Bill Gates, born in 1955, is well-known for being Mr. Microsoft. The company he started with Paul Allen accompanied the PC revolution of the last few decades. The richest man in the world, in recent years he has dedicated much of his time and wealth to philanthropic endeavors through his foundation.

His was a typical nerd, into computer programming at an early age. "There was something neat about the machine" (Gates, 1996), something orderly. He redeemed himself in my eyes – for I have been incensed by of the bugs in Microsoft's software – when he said that poor countries need a cure for malaria more than computers.

Steve Jobs

Steve Jobs, co-founder of Apple with Steve Wozniak, was born in 1955 while his mother was a single college graduate. Unable to support her baby, she put him up for adoption. It mattered to her that his adopting parents were college graduates. However, when the couple she had arranged with learned the baby was a boy, they reneged.

The next couple willing to adopt him did not have degrees. So she continued to nurture him for a few months until the adopting parents committed to seeing him graduate – though, ultimately, he dropped out anyway. In line with the counterculture of the '70s, he explored LSD and went to India for a spiritual retreat. (He identifies himself as a Buddhist.) In 1978, repeating his own history, he fathered a girl who was raised on welfare while he denied paternity on the grounds of being sterile.

Continuing to move with the times, he became one of the most innovative and often controversial entrepreneurs in IT. Apple gave new meaning to personal computing, introducing visual cues and user-friendly interfaces.

In 1998, the Dalai Lama gave permission for Apple to use his image with the words, "Think different." China at the time was not an attractive market for Apple products. But business is business even for Buddhist ex-hippies. Under Jobs, in 2009, Apple blocked a number of applications related to the Dalai Lama from Chinese iPhones. Apple spokeswoman Trudy Muller responded, "We continue to comply with local laws... not all apps are available in every country." And recently Apple admitted that child labor was used in factories in China that produce their hardware.

However, his life with Apple was not a straight road. In 1985, he was fired by the board of directors. He then founded NeXT computers, later bought by The Graphics Group which turned it into Pixar, the most prolific computer graphics company which produced *Toy Story*, *Finding Nemo*, and *Ratatouille*. In 1996, Apple bought NeXT, bringing Jobs back to his original company as CEO. In 2004, he was diagnosed with a rare, operable form of pancreatic cancer. Five years later a liver transplant allowed him to continue his creative mission.

In many parts of the world, adopted children are considered "nobody's children." Perhaps a scanty identity drove him to India in search of his soul, but then he chose to construct a more socially acceptable one. Through prestige and money he built a well-defined "I" – iPod, iMac, iPhone, iPad. Many anecdotes about his management style describe Jobs as having one of the biggest egos in the IT world.

A pattern that emerges from the overview of his life is a repeated dropping out and returning the stage. Rejected by mother, potential parents, the very company he started; rejecting his education and his daughter; to nearly being rejected by life through major health problems.

Even making a home has been hard. Legal and bureaucratic problems surrounded a historic mansion he purchased in 1984 in Woodside, California. After living in it unfurnished for years, he planned to demolish it to build a new house, but a local preservation group stopped him. He also spent years renovating an apartment on the top floors of a New York City building, but never moved in. He seems in perpetual search of both inner and outer homes, bouncing back from every difficulty with new tools and renewed skills to lay before the world.

Withdrawing into the Mind

As with Ada Lovelace, regarded as the first programmer, someone rejected at birth grew into an icon in IT. Steve Job's story is typical of the Type Five personality in the Enneagram (even though elements of the histrionic Type Seven are definitely there), a pattern shared by many people in the IT world. This psychospiritual system identifies nine styles of personality. Probably of Sufi origin, the Enneagram was brought to the West by George Gurdjieff around 1900, then spread in the 1970s as Oscar Ichazo and psychiatrist Claudio Naranjo elaborated the core qualities of the nine types. It was later popularized by Don Riso and Russ Hudson, as well as by Helen Palmer. A. H. Almaas elaborated the spiritual dimension in the 1990s.

Early insecurity about survival can shape a schizoid personality, to which Enneatype Five is the closest. Rationality and orderliness are valuable defense mechanisms against the threat of being separated from life, assembling everything into its proper place.

Type Fives escape into their mental world for safe haven. They want to be accepted for their capabilities, often disappearing from the scene to stay with their own minds and develop skills. These give them confidence to re-enter as talented (thus, accepted) persons with innovative ideas to display.

They are most successful by creating a niche which no one else occupies – which gives them an acknowledged place in the world. Apple's technology is proprietary, guaranteeing Jobs his unique place and highlighting the tendency of Five personalities to horde – whether in keeping their emotions and possessions to themselves, or proprietary information. As with Ada Lovelace, someone rejected at birth grew into an icon in IT. Ada Lovelace had been rejected by the father because of her gender and Jobs has been put up for adoption.

The schizoid Type Five personality seems more widespread than others in the modern, technology-dependent world.

Bibliography

Aardema, Frederick, O'Connor, Kieron, Côté, Sophie and Taillon, Annie, "Cyberpsychology, Behavior, and Social Networking," August 2010, vol. 13, no. 4, pp. 429–35: doi:10.1089/cyber.2009.0164: <www.liebertonline.com/doi/abs/10.1089/cyber.2009.0164>

Aguirre, Anthony. "The Enemy of Insight?" from "The Edge Annual Question 2010", 2010, www.edge.org/q2010/q10_10.html

Aldhous, Peter, "Psychologist finds Wikipedians Grumpy and Closed-Minded," *New Scientist*, 3 Jan 2009: <www.newscientist.com/article/dn16349-psychologist-finds-wikipedians-grumpy-and-closedminded.html>

Alliance for Childhood, *Fool's Gold: A Critical Look at Computers in Childhood*, Codd Park: Alliance for Childhood, 2000.

Almaas, A. H., *Essence: The Diamond Approach to Inner Realization*, York Beach: Samuel Weiser, 1986.
—*Elements of the Real in Man*, Berkeley: Diamond Books, 1987.
—*The Pearl Beyond Price*, Berkeley: Diamond Books, 1988.
—*Being and the Meaning of Life*, Berkeley: Diamond Books, 1990.
—*The Point of Existence*, Berkeley: Diamond Books, 1996.
—*Spacecruiser Inquiry*, Boston: Shambhala, 2002.
—"Tools for the Maturation of the Soul: Interview with Almaas," *Innernet*, 14 Feb 2008: <www.innernet.it/tools-for-the-maturation-of-the-soul-interview-with-almaas/>
—"Loving the Truth for its Own Sake: Interview with Almaas," *Innernet*, 21 Aug 2009: <www.innernet.it/loving-the-truth-for-its-own-sake-an-interview-with-almaas/>

Anderson, Chris, "The End of Theory: The Data Deluge Makes the Scientific Method Obsolete," *Wired*, June 2008: <www.wired.com/science/discoveries/magazine/16-07/pb_theory>

Assagioli, Roberto, *Psicosintesi*, Roma: Mediterranee, 1971.

Babbage, Charles, *The Ninth Bridgewater Treatise: a Fragment [1837]. Second edn.*, London: Pickering, 1989.

Balsekar, Ramesh, *A Duet of One*, Los Angeles: Advaita Press, 1989.
—*Consciousness Speaks*, Redondo Beach, CA: Advaita Press, 1992.

Barlett, C., Harris, R. and Bruey, C., "The Effect of the Amount of Blood in a Violent Video Game on Aggression, Hostility, and Arousal," *Journal of Experimental Social Psychology*, vol. 44, no. 3, 539–46, May 2008.

Barlow, John Perry, *A Declaration of the Independence of Cyberspace*, 8 Feb 1996. <homes.eff.org/~barlow/Declaration-Final.html>

Bateson, Gregory, *Steps to an Ecology of Mind*, San Francisco: Chandler Press, 1972.

Berman, Marc G., Jonides, John and Kaplan, Stephen, "The Cognitive Benefits of Interacting With Nature," *Psychological Science*, 2008: <pss.sagepub.com/content/19/12/1207>

Berninger, Virginia W., Abbott, Robert D., Augsburger, Amy and Garcia, Noelia, "Comparison of Pen and Keyboard Transcription Modes in Children with and Without Learning Disabilities," *Learning Disability Quarterly*, vol. 32, no. 3, Summer 2009.

Block, Gerald, "Out of this World," *Standpoint*, August 2008: <standpointmag.com/node/315/full>

Branan, Nicole, "Unconscious Decisions: As We Mull a Choice, Our Subconscious Decides for Us," *Scientific American*, August 2008: <www.scientificamerican.com/article.cfm?id=unconscious-decisions>

Bright, Susie, *Sexual Reality*, San Francisco: Cleis Press, 1992. <www.susiebright.com>

Brook, James and Boal, Iain. A., eds., *Resisting the Virtual Life: The Culture and Politics of Information*, San Francisco: City Lights, 1995.

Brooks, Michael, "Unknown Internet 2:

Could the Net Become Self-Aware?" *New Scientist*, 30 Apr 2009: <www.newscientist.com/article/mg20227062.100-could-the-net-become-selfaware.html>

Carr, Nicholas, "Is Google Making Us Stupid?" *Atlantic*, July/August 2008: <www.theatlantic.com/magazine/archive/2008/07/is-google-making-us-stupid/6868/>

— *The Shallows: What the Internet is doing to our Brains*, New York: W.W. Norton & Company, 2010.

CBS 60 minutes. "J. Craig Venter: Designing Life". 21 Nov 2010. <www.cbsnews.com/video/watch/?id=7076435n>

Chandler, D. L., "Rethinking Artificial Intelligence," *MITnews*, 7 Dec 2009: <web.mit.edu/newsoffice/2009/ai-overview-1207.html

Chitrabhanu, Gurudev Shree, *Twelve Facets of Reality, The Jain Path to Freedom*, New York: Dodd, Mead & Co., 1980.

Church, Dawson, *The Genie in Your Genes*, Santa Rosa, CA: Energy Psychology Press, 2007.

Cioran, E. M., *Précis de Décomposition*, Paris: Gallimard, 1949.

Clotfelter, Charles T., Ladd, Helen F. and Vigdor, Jacob L., "Scaling the Digital Divide: Home Computer Technology and Student Achievement," Duke University, July 29, 2008.

Csikszentmihalyi, Mihaly, *Flow: The Psychology of Optimal Experience*, New York: Harper Perennial, 1991.

Damasio, Antonio, *Descartes' Error: Emotion, Reason, and the Human Brain*, New York: Harper Perennial, 1995.

Davitt Maughan, Patricia. "Assessing Information Literacy among Undergraduates: A Discussion of the Literature and the University of California-Berkeley Assessment Experience". *American Library Association*. Jan 2001.

Dawkins, Richard. *The Selfish Gene*, New York City: Oxford University Press, 1976

De Berardis, Domenico, D'Albenzio, Alessandro, Gambi, Francesco, Sepede, Gianna, Valchera, Alessandro, Conti, Chiara M., Fulcheri, Mario, Cavuto, Marilde, Ortolani, Carla, Salerno, Rosa Maria, Serroni, Nicola and Ferro, Filippo Maria, "Alexithymia and its Relationships with Dissociative Experiences and Internet Addiction in a Nonclinical Sample," *CyberPsychology & Behavior*, 10 February 2009, 12(1): 67–9, doi:10.1089/cpb.2008.0108: <www.liebertonline.com/doi/abs/10.1089/cpb.2008.0108>

Debord, Guy. *Society of the Spectacle*. 1967. <www.marxists.org/reference/archive/debord/society.htm>

de Decker, Kris, "Faster Internet is Impossible," *Low-Tech Magazine*, 7 Feb 2008: <www.lowtechmagazine.com/2008/02/faster-internet.html>

— "The Monster Footprint of Digital Technology," *Low-Tech Magazine*, 16 Jun 2009: <www.lowtechmagazine.com/2009/06/embodied-energy-of-digital-technology. html>

Deida, David, *The Way Of The Superior Man: A Spiritual Guide to Mastering the Challenges of Woman, Work, and Sexual Desire*, Brazos, Texas: Plexus, 2006

Derbyshire, David, "Social Websites Harm Children's Brains: Chilling Warning to Parents from Top Neuroscientist," *MailOnline*, 24 Feb 2009: <www.dailymail.co.uk/news/article-1153583/Social-websites-harm-childrens-brains-Chilling-warning-parents-neuroscientist.html>

Dery, Mark, ed., *Flame Wars: The Discourse of Cyberculture*, Durham, NC: Duke University Press, 1994.

— *Escape Velocity: Cyberculture at the End of the Century*, New York: Grove Press, 1996.

Descartes, René, *Discourse on the Method (The Philosophical Writings of Descartes)*, Cambridge: Cambridge University Press, 1985.

Digital Nation, Interview with Clifford Nass, *Digital Nation*, 1 Dec 2009: www.pbs.org/wgbh/pages/frontline/digitalnation/interviews/nass.html>

Dirac, Leo, "Really New in Labs this Time: SMS Text Messaging for Chat," *Gmail Blog*, 10 Dec 2008: <gmailblog. blogspot.com/2008/12/really-new-in-labs-this-time-sms-text.html>

Divan, Hozefa A., Kheifets, Leeka, Obel, Carsten and Olsen, Jørn, "Prenatal and Postnatal Exposure to Cell Phone Use and Behavioral Problems in Children," *Epidemiology*, July 2008, vol. 19, no. 4, pp. 523–9, doi: 10.1097/EDE.0b013e318175dd47.

Economist, "Great Minds Think (Too Much) Alike," July 2008: <www.economist.com/node/11745514?story_id=11745514>

Edelman, Ben, "Google Toolbar Tracks Browsing Even After Users Choose 'Disable'," January 26, 2010 (1): <www.benedelman.org/news/012610-1.html>

— "Facebook Leaks Usernames, User IDs, and Personal Details to Advertisers," May 20, 2010 (2): <www.benedelman. org/news/052010-1.html>

— "Hard-Coding Bias in Google "Algorithmic" Search Results," November 15, 2010 (3): <www.benedelman.org/hardcoding/>

Ellul, Jacques, *The Technological Society*, New York: Knopf Publishing, 1964.

Engels, F. The Origin of the Family, Private Property and the State. Middlesex: Penguin. 1985.

Gates, Bill, *The Road Ahead*, New York: Penguin, 1996.

Gentile, D. A., "Pathological Video Game Use Among Youth 8 to 18: A National Study," *Psychological Science*, vol. 20, pp. 594–602, 2009: <www.drdouglas.org/page_resources_articles_2009gtext.html>

Goleman, Daniel, *Destructive Emotions: A Scientific Dialogue with the Dalai Lama*, New York: Bantam, 2004.

Greenfield, Susan. House of Lords. 12 Feb 2009. <www.publications.parliament.uk/pa/ld200809/ldhansrd/text/90212-0010.htm>

Hafner, Katie, "Texting May Be Taking a Toll," *New York Times*, 25 May 2009: <www.nytimes.com/2009/05/26/health/26teen.htm>

Harkin, James, *Lost in Cyburbia: How Life on the Net Has Created a Life of Its Own*, Toronto: Knopf Canada, 2009.

Herrigel, Eugen, *Zen in the Art of Archery*, New York: Pantheon Books, 1953.

Hillman, James and Ventura, Michael, *We've Had a Hundred Years of Psychotherapy: And the World's Getting Worse*, San Francisco: Harper Collins, 1993.

Hoffman, Stefanie, "Montana City Asks Job Applicants to Fork Over Social Networking Passwords," *CRN*, June 19, 2009: <www.crn.com/blogs-op-ed/the-channel-wire/218100385>

Holmes, Bob, "The Not-so-Selfish Gene," *New Scientist*, 7 March 2009.

Hu, Mu, "Will Online Chat Help Alleviate Mood Loneliness?" *Cyberpsychology, Behavior, and Social Networking*, 28 Feb 2009: <www.liebertonline.com/doi/abs/10.1089/cpb.2008.0134>

Huxley, Aldous, *Brave New World*, New York: Harper & Row, 1932.
— *The Perennial Philosophy*, New York: Harper & Row, 1945.

Institute for Social Research, "Empathy: College Students Don't have as Much as They Used to," University of Michigan News Service, 27 May 2010: <www.ns.umich.edu/htdocs/releases/story.php?id=7724>

Institute of HeartMath, "Science of The Heart: Exploring the Role of the Heart in Human Performance," Boulder Creek: Institute of HeartMath, 2001: <www.heartmath.org/templates/ihm/downloads/pdf/research/e-book/science-of-the-heart.pdf>

Jackson, Maggie, *Distracted: The Erosion of Attention and the Coming Dark Age*, New York: Prometheus Books, 2008.

Jackson, T., Dawson, R. and Wilson, D., "Case Study: Evaluating the Effect of Email Interruptions within the Workplace," In: *Conference on Empirical Assessment in Software Engineering*, Keele University, EASE 2002, Keele, UK, April 2002, pp. 3–7.

Jung, Carl Gustav, *The Psychology of Kundalini Yoga*, New Jersey: Princeton University Press, 1996.

Junghyun, Kim, LaRoseand, Robert and Peng, Wei, "Loneliness as the Cause and the Effect of Problematic Internet Use: The Relationship between Internet Use and Psychological Well-Being," *CyberPsychology & Behavior*, Aug 2009, vol. 12, no. 4, pp. 451–5, doi:10.1089/cpb.2008.0327: <www.liebertonline.com/doi/abs/10.1089/cpb.2008.0327>

Kakabadse, Andrew P., Nada K., Bailey, Susan and Myers, Andrew, *Techno Addicts*, Cambridge: Sigel Press, 2009.

Kaki, M., "Welcome to Cyberia: An Economic Primer," Minutes of the Lead Pencil Club, ed. Bill Henderson, New York: Pusicart Press, 1996.

Kasparov, Garry, "The Chess Master and the Computer," *New York Review of Books*, Feb 2010: <www.nybooks.com/articles/archives/2010/feb/11/the-chess-master-and-the-computer/>

Kelleci, Meral and Inal, Sevil, "Cyberpsychology, Behavior, and Social Networking: Psychiatric Symptoms in Adolescents with Internet Use: Comparison Without Internet Use," doi:10.1089/cpb.2009.0026: <www.liebertonline.com/doi/pdf/10.1089/cyber.2009.0026>

Kelly, Kevin, *Out of Control: The Rise of Neo-Biological Civilization*, Reading, MA: Addison-Wesley, 1994.
— "Technophilia," *Technium*, 8 Jun 2009: <www.kk.org/thetechnium/archives/2009/06/technophilia.php>
— "Why Technology Can't Fulfill," *Technium*, 26 Jun 2009: <www.kk.org/thetechnium/archives/2009/06/why_technology.php>
— "Expansion of Free Will," *Technium*, 13 Aug 2009: <www.kk.org/thetechnium/archives/2009/08/expansion_of_fr.php>
— *What Technology Wants*, New York: Viking, 2010.

Kirsh SJ, Mounts JR, Olczak PV. "Violent media consumption and the recognition of dynamic facial expressions," *Journal of Interpersonal Violence*, May 2006;21(5):571-84. <www.ncbi.nlm.nih.gov/pubmed/16574633>

Ko Chih-Hung; Yen Ju-Yu, Liua Shu-Chun, Huanga Chi-Fen and Yen Cheng-Fang, "The Associations Between Aggressive Behaviors and Internet Addiction and Online Activities in Adolescents," *Journal of*

Adolescent Health, vol. 44, no. 6, pp. 598–605, June 2009: <www.jahonline.org/article/S1054-139X%2808%2900676-9/abstract>

Ko Chih-Hung; Liu Gin-Chung; Hsiao Sigmund; Yen Ju-Yu; Yang Ming-Jen; Lin Wei-Chen, "Brain Activities Associated with Gaming Urge of Online Gaming Addiction," *Journal of Psychiatric Research*, vol. 43, no. 7, pp. 739–47, April 2009.

Krishnamurti, U. G., *The Mystique of Enlightenment*, Post Betim, Volant, Goa: Dinesh Vaghela, 1982: www.well.com/user/jct/mystiq.htm

—*Mind is a Myth*, Post Betim, Volant, Goa: Dinesh Publications, 1988.

Kruger, Justin, Epley, Nicholas, Parker, Jason and Ng, Zhi-Wen, "Egocentrism over E-mail: Can We Communicate as Well as We Think?," *Journal of Personality and Social Psychology*, December 2005, vol. 89, no. 6, pp. 925–36: <psycnet.apa.org/?&fa=main.doiLanding&doi=10.1037/0022-3514.89.6.925>

Kurzweil, Ray, *The Singularity Is Near: When Humans Transcend Biology*, New York: Viking Adult, 2005.

—in Hamilton, Craig, "Chasing Immortality: The Technology of Eternal Life," interview with Ray Kurzweil for *EnlightenNext*, Sep–Nov 2005: <www.enlightennext.org/magazine/j30/kurzweil.asp?page=3>

Kurzweil, Ray and Grossman, Terry, *Fantastic Voyage: Live Long Enough to Live Forever*, New York: Rodale, 2004.

Kushner, David, "When Man & Machine Merge," *Rolling Stone*, 19 Feb 2009. <www.rollingstone.com/news/story/25939914/when_man__machine_merge>

Laing, R. D., *The Divided Self*, London: Tavistock Publications, 1959.

Lakoff, George, interviewed by Iain A. Boal in "The Conduit Metaphor," *Resisting the Virtual Life: The Culture and Politics of Information*, Brook, J. and Boal, I. A., eds., San Francisco: City Lights, 1995.

Lanier, Jaron, "One Half a Manifesto," *Edge*: <www.edge.org/3rd_culture/lanier/lanier_p1.html>

Laski, Margharita, *Ecstasy in Secular and Religious Experience*, Los Angeles: J. P. Tarcher, 1990.

Lavin, Timothy. *How the Recession Changes Us*. The Atlantic. Jan/Feb 2001. <www.theatlantic.com/magazine/archive/2011/01/how-the-recession-changed-us/8347/>

Lenhart, Amanda, Purcell, Kristen, Smith, Aaron and Zickuhr, Kethryn, "Social Media and Mobile Internet Use Among Teens and Young Adults," *Pew Internet*, Feb 2010: <www.pewinternet.org/Reports/2010/Social-Media-and-Young-Adults.aspx>

Levine, Laura E., Waite, Bradley M. and Bowman, Laura L.,"Electronic Media Use, Reading, and Academic Distractibility in College Youth," *CyberPsychology & Behavior*, August 2007, vol. 10, no. 4, pp. 560–6, doi:10.1089/cpb.2007.9990:<www.liebertonline.com/doi/abs/10.1089/cpb.2007.9990>

Levine, Peter A., *Waking the Tiger: Healing Trauma, The Innate Capacity to Transform Overwhelming Experiences*, Berkeley: North Atlantic Books, 1997.

Levy, Pierre, *Collective Intelligence: Mankind's Emerging World in Cyberspace*, New York: Plenum Press, 1997.

Lipton, Bruce, *The Biology of Belief: Unleashing the Power of Consciousness, Matter and Miracles*, Santa Rosa, CA: Elite Books, 2005.

Lowen, Alexander, *Bioenergetics*, New York: Coward, McCann & Geoghegan, 1975.

—*Joy: Surrender to the Body*, New York: Macmillan, 1995.

MacLean, Katherine A., Ferrer, Emilio, Aichele, Stephen R., Bridwell, David A., Zanesco, Anthony P., Jacobs, Tonya L., King, Brandon G., Rosenberg, Erika L., Sahdra, Baljinder K., Shaver, Phillip R., Wallace, B. Alan, Mangun, George R. and Saron, Clifford D., "Intensive Meditation Training Improves Perceptual Discrimination and Sustained Attention," *Psychological Science*, 11 May 2010: <pss.sagepub.com/content/early/2010/05/11/0956797610371339.full>

Magatti, Mauro, *Libertà Immaginaria: Le Illusioni del Capitalismo Tecno-Nichilista*, Milano: Feltrinelli, 2009. Quotations are author's translation

Maharaj, Nisargadatta, *I Am That*, Durham: Acorn Press, 1982.

—*Prior to Consciousness: Talks with Sri Nisargadatta Maharaj*, Durham: Acorn Press,1985.

Mander, Jerry, *Four Arguments for the Elimination of Television*, New York: William Morrow, 1978.

—*In the Absence of the Sacred*, San Francisco: Sierra Club, 1991.

Mapes, Diane, "Bury Me With My Cell Phone," *Msnbc.com*, December 16, 2008: <www.msnbc.msn.com/id/28182292>

Martini, Carlo Maria, "Lectio Divina e Pastorale: A Cura di Salvatore A. Panimolle, Ascolto della Parola e Preghiera, La 'Lectio Divina' ," Città del Vaticano: Libreria Editrice Vaticana, 1987.

McLuhan, Marshall, *Understanding Media: The Extensions of Man*, New York: McGraw Hill, 1964.

—*Understanding Me*, Cambridge, MA: MIT Press, 2005.

McLuhan, Marshall and Powers, Bruce R., *The Global Village*, New York: Oxford University Press, 1989.

Mehdizadeh, Soraya, "Self-Presentation 2.0: Narcissism and Self-Esteem on Facebook," *Cyberpsychology, Behavior, and Social Networking*, 16 Feb 2010: <www.liebertonline.com/doi/abs/10.1089/cpb.2009.0257>

Meister, Eckhart, *La Via del Distacco*, Milano: Mondadori, 1995.

Minsky, Marvin, *The Society of Mind*, New York: Simon & Schuster, 1988.

Moravec, Hans, *Robot: Mere Machine to Transcendent Mind*, New York: Oxford University Press, 1999.

Morin, Edgar, *La Méthode 3: La Connaissance de la Connaissance*, Paris: Editions du Seuil, 1986.

Morozov, Evgeny, "Texting Toward Utopia: Does the Internet Spread Democracy?" *Boston Review*, March/April 2009: <boston-review.net/BR34.2/morozov.php>
— "Wrong Kind of Buzz Around Google Buzz," *Foreign Policy*, 18 Aug 2010: <neteffect.foreignpolicy.com/posts/2010/02/11/wrong_kind_of_buzz_around_google_buzz>

Mostrous, Alexi and David Brown, "Microsoft Seeks Patent for Office 'Spy' Software," *Sunday Times*, January 16, 2008: <technology.timesonline.co.uk/tol/news/tech_and_web/article3193480.ece>

Mumford, Lewis, *Technics and Civilization*, New York: Harcourt, Brace and Co., 1934.
— *The Myth of the Machine*, New York: Harcourt, Brace & World, 1966.

Nityananda, *Voice of the self*, Madras: P. Ramanath Pai, 1962.

Noble, David F., *The Religion of Technology: The Divinity of Man and the Spirit of Invention*, New York: Alfred A. Knopf, 1997.

Osho, *Meditation: The Art of Ecstasy*, Cologne: Rebel Publishing House, 1976.
— *The Search: Talks on the Ten Bulls of Zen*. Cologne: Rebel Publishing House, 1977.
— *The Heartbeat of the Absolute*, Cologne: Rebel Publishing House, 1980.
— *Theologia Mystica*, Cologne: Rebel Publishing House, 1983.
— *The Dhammapada: The Way of the Buddha, Series 2*, Cologne: Rebel Publishing House, 1990.
— *The Book of Wisdom: Discourses on Atisha's Seven Points of Mind Training*, Cologne: Rebel Publishing House, 1993.
— *Osho Transformation Tarot* [Cards]. New York: St. Martin's Press, 1999.
— *The Psychology of the Esoteric*, Cologne: Rebel Publishing House, 2008.

Page, Angie S., Ashley R., Cooper, Pippa Griew, Russell Jago. "Children's Screen Viewing is Related to Psychological Difficulties Irrespective of Physical Activity". *Pediatrics*, Vol. 126 No. 5. November 2010, pp. e1011-e1017 (doi:10.1542/peds.2010-1154) <pediatrics.aappublications.org/cgi/content/abstract/126/5/e1011>

Pagnoni G., Cekic, M. and Guo, Y., 2008, "Thinking about Not-Thinking: Neural Correlates of Conceptual Processing During Zen Meditation," PLoS ONE 3(9): e3083, doi:10.1371/journal.pone.0003083. 3 set 2008.

Parker, A. and Dagnall, N., "Effects of Bilateral Eye Movements on Gist-Based False Recognition in the DRM Paradigm," *Brain and Cognition*, vol. 63, pp. 221–5, Apr 2007: <dx.doi.org/10.1016/j.bandc.2006.08.005>

Pearce, Joseph Chilton, "Gathering Sparks," interview by *Parabola* magazine, selected by David Appelbaum and Joseph Kulin, New York: Parabola Books, 2001.
— *The Biology of Transcendence*, Rochester: Inner Traditions, 2002.

Perlow, Jon, "New in Labs: Stop Sending Mail You Later Regret," *Gmail Blog*, 6 Oct 2008: <gmailblog.blogspot.com/2008/ 10/new-in-labs-stop-sending-mail-you-later.html>

Pirandello, Luigi, *One, No One, and One Hundred Thousand*, Translated and introduction by William Weaver. New York: Marsilio Publishers, 1992.

Pitney, Joel, "The Conscious Universe," *EnlightenNext*, 5 Apr 2010: <magazine.enlightennext.org/2010/04/05/enlightennext-mp3-dr-ervin-laszlow/>

Postman, Neil, *Amusing Ourselves to Death: Public Discourse in the Age of Show Business*, New York: Viking Press, 1985.
— *Technopoly: The Surrender of Culture to Technology*, New York: Vintage Books, 1993.

Prinz, Jesse J., *Gut Reactions*, Oxford: Oxford University Press, 2008.

Ramakrishna, Shri, *L'Enseignement de Ramakrishna*, 1963.

Ram Tzu, *No Way for the Spiritually 'Advanced'*, Redondo Beach: Advaita Press, 1990.

Research Digest Blog, "Improve Your Memory: Wiggle Your Eyes Back and Forth," *British Psychological Society at the Research Digest Blog*, 26 Mar 2007: <bps-research-digest.blogspot.com/2007/03/improve-your-memory-wiggle-your-eyes.html>

Rideout, V. and Hamel, E., *The Media Family: Electronic Media in the Lives of Infants, Toddlers, Preschoolers, and Their Parents*, Menlo Park, CA: Henry J. Kaiser Foundation, May 2006.

Risen, James and Lichtblau, Eric, "E-Mail Surveillance Renews Concerns in Congress," *New York Times*, 16 Jun 2009:

<www.nytimes.com/2009/06/17/us/17nsa.h tm?_r=2>

Riso, Don Richard, *Personality Types, Using the Enneagram for Self-Discovery*, New York: Houghton Mifflin, 1996.

Rheingold, Howard, *The Virtual Community: Homesteading on the Electronic Frontier*, Reading, MA: Addison-Wesley, 1993.

Rose, Alexander, "Are We Losing Our Memory?" *The Long Now Blog*, 22 Mar 2009: <blog.longnow.org/2009/03/22/are-we-losing-our-memory/>

Roush, Wade, "Second Earth," *Technology Review*, Jul/Aug 2007.

Rowlands, Ian, Nicholas, David, Huntington, Paul, Gunter, Barrie, Withey, Richard, Dobrowolski, Tom, Tenopir, Carol, Williams, Pete, Fieldhouse, Maggie and Jamali, Hamid, "Behaviour of the Researcher of the Future," University College London Centre for Publishing for the British Library, January 16, 2008: <www.bl.uk/news/2008/pressrelease20080116.html>

Russell, Peter, *The Global Brain Awakens*, Maui, HI: Global Brain, 1995.

Salganik, Matthew J., Dodds, Peter Sheridan and Watts, Duncan J., "Experimental Study of Inequality and Unpredictability in an Artificial Cultural Market," *Science*, vol. 311, p. 854, 10 Feb 2006: <www.sciencemag.org/cgi/content/abstract/311/5762/854>

Sanders, Barry, A is for Ox: The Collapse of Literacy and the Rise of Violence in an Electronic Age, New York: Vintage Books, 1995.

Satprem, *Sri Aurobindo, or the Adventure of Consciousness*, New York: Harper & Row, 1974.

Schwartz, Barry, *The Paradox of Choice: Why More Is Less*, New York: Harper Perennial, 2004.

Sheldrake, Rupert, *The Presence of the Past: Morphic Resonance and the Habits of Nature*, New York: Times Books, 1988.

Siegel, Lee, *Against the Machine*, New York: Spiegel & Grau, 2008.

Slouka, Mark, *War of the Worlds*, New York: Basic Books, 1995.

Small, Gary and Vorgan, Gigi. *iBrain: Surviving the Technological Alteration of the Modern Mind*, New York: William Morrow, 2008.

Smith, Aaron, "The Internet and Civic Engagement," *PewInternet*, September 1, 2009: <www.pewinternet.org/Press-Releases/2009/The-Internet-and-Civic-Engagement.aspx>

Steiner, Rudolf, *The Evolution of Consciousness*, Sussex: Rudolf Steiner Press, 1991.

Stepanikova, Irena, Nieb, Norman H. and Hec, Xiaobin, "Time on the Internet at Home, Loneliness, and Life Satisfaction: Evidence from Panel Time-Diary Data," *Computers in Human Behavior*, vol. 26, no. 3, May 2010.

Stepp Sessions, Laura, *Unhooked: How Young Women Pursue Sex, Delay Love, and Lose at Both*, New York: Riverhead Books, 2007.

Stone, Allucquère Rosanne, *The War of Desire and Technology at the Close of the Mechanical Age*, Cambridge, MA: MIT Press, 1996.

Talbott, Steve, *The Future Does Not Compute: Transcending the Machines in Our Midst*, Sebastopol, CA: O'Reilly & Associates, 1995.

— "Are Our Brains Changing?" *Netfuture: Technology and Human Responsibility*, 30 Jul 1997: <www.netfuture.org/1997/Jul3097_54.html>

— "Multitasking Ourselves to Death," *Netfuture: Technology and Human Responsibility*, 30 Jul 1998: <www.netfuture.org/1998/Jul3098_75.html#2d>

— "Twilight of the Double Helix," *Netfuture: Technology and Human Responsibility*, 12 Mar 2009: <www.netfuture.org/ 2009/Mar1209_175.html>

Tang, Yi-Yuan, Lu, Qilin, Genge, Xiujuan, Stein, Elliot A., Yang, Yihong and Posner, Michael I., "Short-Term Meditation Induces White Matter Changes in the Anterior Cingulate," *Proc Natl Acad Sci USA*, August 16, 2010: <www.pnas.org/content/early/2010/08/10/1011043107.abstract>

Technorati, "State of the Blogosphere," 2008: <technorati.com/blogging/feature/state-of-the-blogosphere-2008/>.

Thomas, L. E. and Lleras, A., "Moving Eyes and Moving Thought: On the Spatial Compatibility between Eye Movements and Cognition," *Psychonomic Bulletin & Review*, vol. 14, pp. 663–8, 2007.

Thompson, Clive, "Your Outboard Brain Knows All," *Wired*, November 25, 2007: <www.wired.com/techbiz/people/magazine/15-10/st_thompson>

Todeschi, Kevin J., *Edgar Cayce on the Akashic Records*, Virginia Beach: A. R. E. Press, 1998.

Trungpa, Chogyam, *The Heart of the Buddha*, Boston: Shambhala, 1991.

— *Great Eastern Sun*, Boston: Shambhala, 1999.

Turkle, Sherry, *The Second Self: Computers and the Human Spirit*, New York: Simon and Schuster, 1984.

— *Life on the Screen: Identity in the Age of the Internet*, New York: Simon & Schuster, 1995.

— Interview by *Digital Nation*, 2 Feb 2010: <www.pbs.org/wgbh/pages/frontline/digitalnation/interviews/turkle.html>

Twenge, J. M., Konrath, S., Foster, J. D., Keith Campbell, W. and Bushman, B. J., "Egos Inflating Over Time: A Cross-Temporal Meta-Analysis of the Narcissistic Personality Inventory," *Journal of Personality*, 2008, vol. 76, no. 4, 875–902, DOI: 10.1111/j.1467-6494.2008.00507.x

Umiltà MA, Escola L, Intskirveli I, Grammont F, Rochat M, Caruana F, Jezzini A, Gallese V,. Rizzolatti G.,"When Pliers Become Fingers in the Monkey Motor System," *Proc Natl Acad Sci USA* (2008) 105: 2209–13.

University of California, San Diego. "How Much Information? 2009 Report on American Consumers". Dec 2009. <hmi.ucsd.edu/howmuchinfo_research_report_consum.php>

Walker, Danna L., "The Longest Day: Could a Class of College Students Survive Without iPods, Cellphones, Computers and TV from One Sunrise to the Next?," *Washington Post*, August 5, 2007: <www.washingtonpost.com/wp-dyn/content/article/2007/08/01/AR2007080101720.html>

Wallace, B. Alan, *The Taboo of Subjectivity*, New York: Oxford University Press, 2000.
– *The Attention Revolution*, Boston: Wisdom Publications, 2006.

Watts, Alan, *The Supreme Identity*, New York: Pantheon Books, 1950.

Webb, Richard, "Online Shopping and the Harry Potter Effect," *New Scientist*, 22 Dec 2008: <www.newscientist.com/article/mg20026873.300-online-shopping-and-the-harry-potter-effect.html>

Weiner, Norbert, *The Human Use of Human Beings*, Boston: Houghton Mifflin, 1950.

Weizenbaum, Joseph, *Computer Power and Human Reason*, San Francisco, CA: W. H. Freeman, 1976.

Venter, Craig, "How to Make a New Life Form," *Guardian*, May 20, 2010: <www.guardian.co.uk/science/video/2010/may/20/craig-venter-new-life-form>

Vigdor, Jacob L. and Ladd, Helen F., "Scaling the Digital Divide: Home Computer Technology and Student Achievement," National Bureau of Economic Research Working Paper No. 16078, June 2010: <www.nber.org/papers/w16078>

Wilber, Ken, *The Atman Project*, Wheaton, IL: Theosophical Publishing, 1980.

Wintour, Patrick, "Facebook and Bebo Risk 'Infantilising' the Human Mind," *Guardian*, 24 Feb 2009: <www.guardian.co.uk/uk/2009/feb/24/social-networking-site-changing-childrens-brains>

Yogananda, Paramahansa, *Autobiography of a Yogi*, Los Angeles: Self-Realization Fellowship, 1952.

Zeidan, F., Johnson, S. K., Diamond, B. J., David, Z. and Goolkasian, P., "Mindfulness Meditation Improves Cognition: Evidence of Brief Mental Training," *Consciousness and Cognition*, Jun 2010: <www.ncbi.nlm.nih.gov/pubmed/20363650>

Zimmerman, F., *Children's Media Use and Sleep Problems: Issues and Unanswered Questions*, Menlo Park, CA: Henry J. Kaiser Foundation, June 2008.

Index

The Digitally Divided Self

CPSIA information can be obtained at www.ICGtesting.com
Printed in the USA
LVOW12s1947140514

385785LV00027B/1201/P

9 788897 233008